Indian and American Foreign Policies:
From Confrontation to Co-operation

Indian and American Foreign Policies:

From Confrontation to Co-operation

Prof. P.M. Kamath

KALPAZ

First Published, 2021

Published by

Kalpaz Publications
C-30, Satyawati Nagar,
Delhi – 110052
Ph.: 011-47034999, 9811692060
www.kalpazpublications.com
E-mail: kalpaz@hotmail.com

Printed at: Gyan Press, Delhi.

Cataloging in Publication Data—DK
Courtesy: D.K. Agencies (P) Ltd. <docinfo@dkagencies.com>

Kamath, P. M., author.
Indian and American foreign policies : from confrontation to co-operation / Prof. P.M. Kamath.
pages cm
ISBN 9789353243180 (HB)
ISBN 9789353243197 (PB)

1. India—Foreign relations. 2. United States—Foreign relations. 3. India—Foreign relations—United States. 4. United States—Foreign relations—India. I. Title.

LCC DS449.K36 2021 | DDC 327.54 23

Foreword

The end of the Second World War heralded the beginning of a new World Order that was steered by the leader of the democratic block, America, on the one hand and its leadership fiercely contested by the Soviet Union, leader of the then Communist bloc. This race for supremacy posed a serious question before many of the emerging nation-states as to which block to choose to be in. But there were countries which decided to be equidistant from both camps, the capitalist block led by the US and the Communist block led by the Soviet Union. India was the main architect of this third block, popularly called the Non-aligned Movement (NAM). Many questions about India's decision about remaining non-aligned are being raised in retrospect. Among the scholars and academicians who attempted to answer these questions even at that time in history Prof. P.M. Kamath was one of the pioneers.

The author in the very first chapter of this book has forcefully argued that in the given situation when the newly Independent India's priority was development and poverty alleviation, the best decision was to remain away from both the blocks which were essentially a contest to safeguard the respective national interests of these two powers rather than making the world a peaceful and prosperous place to live.

What began as a fool proof strategy for India in the fifties to concentrate on development without getting into the West versus East contest did not remain relevant to follow as a policy three decades later. In the eighties the regional balance underwent a metamorphosis as Pakistan became part of the American military alliance like SEATO while the Soviet Union began unfolding its strategic outreach in Asia, engaging with the emerging situation in Afghanistan and expanding its footprints in India's neighbourhood. After the 1962 experience with China, 1965 aggression by Pakistan and the 1971 Bangladesh liberation

India's tilt towards Moscow was more evident even as New Delhi continued to adhere to Non-alignment in principle. The author has provided a detailed analysis of the events that tested India's resolve, laid the roadmap for policy recalibrations and forced the policy makers to take cognisance of the changing dynamics of the international relations.

The book includes the author's views on the emergence of economic power centres like Japan and (West) Germany and the salience of multipolarity as a new tool of power struggle obliterating the military force as a deciding factor in the power struggle. The policy of non-alignment continued but with innumerable challenges.

The most striking challenge was the making and unmaking of the foreign policy. While both the US and India had their own respective world view, both had a compulsion to go back to their drawing boards to reframe foreign policy. The US had put in place a robust administrative system while India continued with the British model that it inherited. The residual problems of the tragic Partition of India and the creation of Pakistan on the Western and Eastern sides of India, posed a new set of problems to tackle.

The first Prime Minister of Independent India Pandit Jawaharlal Nehru preferred to have a Gandhian view of politics and India's relations with neighbours. The 1962 conflict with China came as a rude shock to Nehru. The need for an independent foreign policy department with experts on Defense, security and strategy was felt more than ever before. But it was the third Prime Minister and his daughter, Indira Gandhi who changed the course of India's Foreign Policy.

The book succinctly takes the reader through the boisterous history of those times when India showcased the hard power aspect of foreign policy. The change over from idealism to pragmatism was evident in the Liberation of Bangladesh and annulling Partition, albeit partially. More importantly, the grit and determination to face the intimidation of America during the 1971 War laid the foundation of a new relationship between India and the US.

The book takes the reader through the four years of Ronald Reagan in the White House during which time three apex leaders of the Soviet Union died in office. India was witness to the three Summits (Geneva in 1985, Reykjavik in 1986 and Washington, DC Summit in December 1987) and the inking of Intermediate Range Nuclear Forces (INF)

Treaty agreeing to withdraw and destroy completely one category of nuclear weapons, which US had placed in Europe. Reagan had also given a positive turn to US relations with India by inviting Mrs Gandhi in July 1982 where she cleared India's position as neither pro-Moscow or against the US but as pro-India. Rajiv Gandhi visited the US in 1985, as another young leader, he played a role in facilitating Moscow's agreeing to withdraw of troops from Afghanistan.

Inclusion of articles like "Assessing India's Fifty years: A foreign policy perspective" gives an overview of India's journey in the geopolitical landscape and also pinpoints the pitfalls that the policy makers encountered and managed to avoid also, at times. The wars that were thrust upon India, the Khalistan imbroglio and the Sri Lankan turmoil that ultimately cost the life of two prime ministers and the ghastly terror attacks on the two democracies, India and the US, brought the two countries together on a number of global issues.

With the passage of time, some of the issues that the two countries had to surmount have been thoroughly analysed by the author especially as they were happening. It is a great experience to read the timely articles in retrospect and draw conclusions from them. The importance of the articles are even more pronounced as the times have changed, style of leadership in the two countries are different, geopolitical dynamics have transformed and new realities are evident. But the challenges remain more or less the same. Democracies have to interact and cooperate even more intensely, at times setting aside personal preferences and national predilections. The book will serve as a ready reckoner to any student of geopolitics and international relations as well as to the practitioners of foreign policy.

Dr. Seshadri Chari
Director (International Affairs),
Institute for National Security Studies (INSS),
Director, Forum for Strategic & Security Studies (FSSS),
Secretary-General, Forum for Integrated National Security (FINS),
Director, Chronicle Society of India for Education &
Academic Research (CSIEAR)

Preface

I had specialised in foreign/National Security Policy and Policy making in India and the US. These were the subjects, I was assigned to teach in Bombay University, Dept. of Civics and Politics (BUDCP). Over the years—stretching for two decades, in addition to teaching them in the class rooms, I was invited to deliver public lectures as well to comment on the foreign policy crises at different occasions. I was a public speaker in demand.

Preparing for public lectures made me get into a more analytical mode than merely being a descriptive narrator. These qualities drew commendation and encouragement from the then visiting Fulbright Professor in the BUDCP, Prof. C. Edwin Gilmour from Grinnell, IOWA. A feature of Indian mindset is: If an American is a specialist on India in his own country, in India he was competent to speak on the US, as well in addition to his specialisation. I was selected in UDCP to specialise on the US, but during my visit to the US, Americans preferred me to speak on India rather than on my area of specialisation! Hence Gilmour was teaching India in the US but in India he visited to teach on America! Thus, he was often a co-speaker in many of my speaking events in India or sometimes, he will be in audience. Whenever a question was raised to be answered by him on the US, he then redirected them to me stating 'when Prof Kamath is there, let him answer'!

Second person who was to become a great admirer of me and my presentations was Dr Ramu Pandit; the then Secretary General of the Indian Merchants Chamber, Bombay. He was instrumental in promoting my lectures in different forums mainly on the US! I dedicate this work to the memories of late Dr C. Edwin Gilmour of Grinnell, IOWA and late Dr Ramu Pandit, Secretary General, IMC, Bombay.

I am grateful to the family of publishers Mr Amit Garg. Having published many books by me, he literally got attracted by my writings, as he began to say: If it's P M Kamath, we will publish whatever he gives us. (But I have never given him any sub-standard work; always maintained high standard in all my publications). I also owe my grateful thanks to Mrs Anita Shetty, Research Assistant in VPM. Many friends have helped me to proof read and felicitate publication of this volume. Despite all that, in case if any errors are left in the book, I alone is to be held responsible for the lapses.

1-6-2021

P.M. Kamath

Mumbai

Contents

Introduction

Soon after I joined as a post-graduate teacher in the Bombay University (BU) Department of Civics and Politics (UDCP) in June 1972 as Lecturer in American government and Politics, the then Head of the Department (HoD), Dr Aloo J. Dastur informed me that though University level teachers are recruited to specialize in a particular area- in my case American Studies, I need also to take one more area for individual specialization. She was then teaching International Relations (IR) and West Asia. She suggested that I take over one of two areas. I had an aversion to the entire area and its politics called West Asia by we Indians and Middle East, by the US and the rest in Europe. Hence, I opted to teach IR. Gradually, I also took other papers then listed as Foreign Policy, Diplomacy and International organizations.

Another characteristic of my academic behaviour was: I was ever willing to explore studying and teaching newer subjects. This was evident not only in the UDCP but while I was teaching in the South Indian Education Society's briefly called SIES College of Arts and Science in Sion, Mumbai. During eight years of my tenure in SIES, I had really a broad foundation in not only papers like Political Science and India and South East Asia, Indian Constitution and Indian Constitutional History and British Constitution and British Constitutional History. I remember, I had offered voluntarily and willingly to teach a paper called Public Administration, when the then my senior colleague, Mr. Raghavendra R. Hebsur was to go to the US as a Fulbright Research Fellow. I had taught World History in Inter Arts; after a year or two, BU authorities raised objection for a teacher of Political Science teaching History, I gave it up! The similar trend continued after I joined the UDCP. Obviously, my experience in the SIES, helped me considerably to acquire a very broad perspective on all issues rather than merely discussing in classes issues merely based on prescribed text books.

India then, newly entering in the arena of International Relations, designated its relations with other nations in the world in a broad framework as "Non-alignment". This was in the context of the then major powers in the World which were divided in two blocs. The West led by the then Super Power No. 1 the United States (US) while the then Soviet Union (SU) led the other bloc, called East. The two blocs-West and the East were not water-tight as in the Western bloc, there were Japan or Pakistan from East were part of the US bloc. On the other hand, Cuba was from the West was in the Eastern bloc.

Pandit Nehru, Indian Prime Minister (PM) then was one of the architects of the Non-alignment. Others were like Gamal Abdel Nasser Hussein of Egypt, Sukarno of Indonesia and Marshall Josip Broz Tito of Yugoslavia. Looking purely from the perspective of India, it was a master stroke on Nehru's part in the beginning as at the early stage of India's operations in International Relations, foreign policy was a new subject for Indians. India needed to concentrate on her economic development rather than play politics of East or West. It was similar to the concept of "Isolationism" popularised by the founding father of the US, George Washington. He refused to take sides between the warring nations of Europe from where majority of the settlers in the US had initially come, and settled into a British Colony.

Non-Alignment: Beginning & Later

Thus, the first article in this collection: **"Relevance of Non-alignment in Cold War"** *(Deccan Herald (Bangalore)*, 21 May 1980), is on the renewal of Cold War in the 1980s, with the Soviet Union militarily intervening in Afghanistan-then a non-aligned country. Non-alignment in the 1980s was not what it was in the 1950s. The entrance of Pakistan into American military alliances like SEATO, and getting military aid from the US in the pretext of fighting against communism, pushed India towards the Soviet Union.

After October 1962, border war between India and China, latter cultivated friendship with Pakistan on the theory that enemy of enemy is a friend of China. Seeking to balance power, India leaned towards the Soviet Union. This was despite Nehru's belief that traditional theory of 'balance of power' is not relevant to newly independent India! This tilt towards the Soviet Union was nowhere so clearly visible as during the 1971 War between India and Pakistan over the birth of Bangladesh in erstwhile East Pakistan. The US and China supported

Pakistan and the Soviet Union backed India. However, the Soviet Union was willing to back India only with a legal basis after India signed a Peace and Friendship Treaty, 1971 with the Soviet Union.

"India in International Affairs: Twin Challenges of 80s" *(The Radical Humanist*, October 1980) discusses India's relations with the Super Powers and challenges it faced in the 1980s. Reemergence of the Cold War in the 1980s is foreseen with a difference. During the period of *detente,* the US had accepted a parity of power between itself and the Soviet Union. Another feature that emerged then was a determined effort by China to be a Super Power. However, Carter's National Security Adviser (NSA), Zbigniew Brzezinski characterized it as 2 1/2 Super Powers!

India which was then domestically passing through a phase of political instability perceived these changes differently. While the PM then under fading Janata Party rule, Charan Singh called the Soviet military intervention in December 1979, beyond its sphere of influence in Afghanistan, perceived it, as a military threat to India and called upon the Soviet Union to withdraw its troops. But Mrs. Gandhi returning to power in early January in 1980 did not break with 'special relationship' she had established with the Soviet Union; though while in opposition she had called Russian presence in Afghanistan as a threat to India!

"Challenge before the Non-aligned" (*The Free Press Journal*, 9 February 1987) raises a pertinent question during the period of second Cold War that began in the 1980s. Nehru the founder of India's Non-alignment policy wanted to retain India's right to "follow an independent policy from the power politics of groups aligned one against another".

But in the 1980s author perceived emergence of multi-polarity with growing at least economic power, if not military power, of Japan and Germany. Hence, emergence of multipolarity which posed problems of unity within non-aligned movement, because of growing regional groupings like-ASEAN, OAS, OAU and Organisation of Islamic Co-operation. Yet, non-aligned nations pursued unity on broad principles; hence, the author lists several challenges within the non-aligned group!

Process of Making of Foreign Policy: Indian & American

Moving from issues in Indian Foreign Policy, I move to process of making it in India and the US: After World War II in the US when not only a National Security Council (NSC) was created, but it also went through an evolutionary process towards emergence's of National Security Adviser (NSA) as a dominant official in President's White House in making of foreign policy. The article **"National Security Adviser in the US: Exit of Richard Allen"** *(The Mahratta,* March 1982) brings out clearly the power struggle between NSA and the Secretary of State, during the Ronald Reagan's presidency between Richard Allen and the Secretary of State, Alexander Haig, Jr.

"The Sikh Extremists in the US: Need for Effective Lobbying" *(The Radical Humanist,* September 1985) highlights great lacunae in Indian Foreign Policy-making, particularly in relation to the US, because US Foreign Policy to that matter even any (domestic) policy as well. There is a greater centralization in foreign policy making in a parliamentary system as in India, in contrast to the US where the process of Foreign Policy is divided amongst different institutions and agencies. In the 1980s, India was treated as nation to be contained as it was in the Soviet camp (from the US perspective) but (non-aligned) to Indians.

India did not involve any of its resources in lobbying in the US which is essential for achieving an orientation to an American policy; that was evident in when a handful of Sikh-extremists belonging to the so-called 'Khalistani Movement' used to agitate before Indian Embassy in Washington DC and certain Congressmen from constituencies where these agitators came from extended support to their cause. But Indian diplomats of the time were not attending the meetings of the Senate or the House Committee to put before them Indian perspective. The idea of need for India to appear before the various committees and their sub-committees in foreign policy-making and take advantage of presenting Indian point of view was completely outside their perceptions!

"Foreign Policy, Formulation: Need for Open Discussion" (*Parlance,* May 1989) is based on my public lecture organized by Parlance as a part of the then PM, Rajiv Gandhi's drive to celebrate forty years of Indian Independence (1947-1987). Nehru was the architect of Indian Foreign Policy as for long he in addition to being the PM, also held the portfolio of External Affairs. He was both an idealist and realist. In 1954 as a realist he projected the emergence of India as the fourth major power, next to the US, Soviet Union and China occupying first three slots. But his idealistic streak emerging from idealism in his pursuance non-violence and non-interference, considering them as main policy principles made him to lose sight of Chinese perfidy that became evident in October 1962 border conflict.

The same realistic streak was evident in Indira Gandhi's use of power to liberate Bangladesh in 1971 but she did not remember the dictum: In International Relations there are neither permanent friends nor permanent enemies; there are only permanent interests. That led her to make India over-dependent then on the Soviet Union when more than 70 percent of weapons India procured from it. I can look back, with pride that I was the first one to advocate parliamentary government also to have a committee system on Foreign Policy and Defence. I had also initiated detailed discussion on India having a National Security Council (NSC) wherein I also spoke having a Policy Planning Council within the structure of NSC.

What's the role of secrecy in foreign policy-making? **"For your Eyes only"** *(The Illustrated Weekly,* 22-28 April 1990) analyses it. Executive head is always reluctant to share information with Legislative branch on the ground that they have not developed any mechanism to safeguard any State secrets. But when Legislature insists that some information be shared by the President, for instances in the US, presidents have claimed Executive Privilege to deny it.

In India too, if a member of the Parliament asks for information, despite PM or Minister for Foreign Affairs stating that information is of delicate nature and that might be leaked to Indian adversaries; if it happens in reality, then members can be accused of being unconcerned of national security or not concerned with safeguards of the nation's interests!

"Need for developing foreign Policy expertise" *(FPJ*, 18 August, 1990) discusses a crucial missing need in Foreign Policy making in early period of independence. Since British had not trained Indian Civil Services (ICS) men in foreign policy-making, as it was controlled by British themselves. Nehru depended on inherited men from ICS, soon after he took control of India's external relations. Foreign policy needs far more information in comparison to domestic affairs. However, nation also needs to have many well informed citizens to take interest in foreign affairs. Foreign Relations have become an important field of knowledge necessary to be developed as many as seven nations have nuclear weapons overtly; and at least another 20 or more have the nuclear know-how. They can destroy the world with one wrong step. Similarly nations have become extremely inter-dependent.

Even otherwise, India as a democracy needs to have knowledgeable people to explain foreign policy of their State. Increasingly wall between domestic affairs and foreign affairs is also crumbling and one becomes an extension of other. For Indian democracy as an emerging major power, growing need is to guide nation's policy.

"Turmoil and Triumph" is a review of foreign policy making and substantial issues addressed by the Reagan Presidency *(Span,* August 1994). Reagan believed that Foreign Policy comes from the Oval office and with the help of a fine Secretary of State. Reagan had initial 18 months spent in resolving internal turf war between his National Security Adviser Richard Allen and Secretary of State-Alexander Haig. Reagan tried to buy restoration of peace in the process of foreign policy making first by changing his NSA and later, bringing in a new Secretary of State, when he appointed George P, Shultz to the office.

During the first four years of Reagan in office, he saw three Soviet leaders Brezhnev, Andropov and Chernenko die in office. It was only when a young leader Mikhail Gorbachev took office in March 1985, two nations held 3 Summit meetings in Geneva in 1985, Reykjavik in 1986 and Washington, DC Summit in December 1987 when INF (Intermediate range nuclear forces) Treaty was signed. It was agreed to withdraw and destroy completely one category of nuclear weapons, which US had placed in Europe, were completely withdrawn.

Reagan had also given a positive turn to US relations with India by inviting Mrs Gandhi in July 1982 where she cleared India's position as neither pro-Moscow or against the US but as pro-India. Rajiv Gandhi visited the US in 1985, as another young leader, he played a role in facilitating Moscow's agreeing to withdraw of troops from Afghanistan.

"A Pledge for Peace" (*One India One People*, April 1998) make a case for India to streamline its foreign and national security policy making by institutionalizing policy making process, which since

Nehru's time has been ad hoc. Under Mrs. Gandhi too, it has been so: as former FM under her (1967-70), Dinesh Singh said: Foreign policy making was "one of carrying on, merely responding to situations!"; since adoption of NSC system was advocated by this scholar and a few others in the 1990s largely to co-ordinate military, domestic, economic inputs in making of National Security/Foreign policy, as India enters into the 21st century with better armed to make effective policy for the nation.

"Not the PM's job" (*Mid-day*, 3 April 1998) makes a case for PM, Vajpayee not holding on to an additional portfolio, MEA as FM on several grounds. PM is the ultimate co-ordinator of policies of the government, and if he is saddled with a Ministry, he will not be able to act as an arbitrator between the various ministries as he is also FM. In any conflict between various ministries author makes his case by giving concrete cases of his time.

Author states in his article on **"Assessing India's Fifty years: A foreign policy perspective"** (*OIOP*, August 1998) Keeping India's territorial integrity intact is the greatest achievements of India in the first fifty years since independence. Pakistan got disintegrated as many others in the period after the end of the Cold War in 1991. However, many crises of Nehru's time, like Kashmir, Tibet, unsettled India-China borders have remained sore points of the fifty years legacy. But we cannot ignore important achievements like nuclear tests of 1974 and 1998; or developing Indian space programme, its growing naval power and science mission to Antarctica. While every PM either had vocally stated or nourished the unstated ambition to make India a great power, it had to wait until India could place one major political party to move in that direction into power in the 21st century.

"Shaping foreign policy" (*OIOP*, July 2002) takes on a newer aspect like the role played by PIOs and *NRIs* in foreign policy formulation. There are over 20 million persons of Indian origin who went voluntarily to different countries abroad, and those who were involuntarily taken to newer lands conquered by western colonisers in the past. But after independence, they may have moved to different countries in the world wherever they could make a living. These are called NRIs (Non-Resident Indians). In 2002 there were 1.5 million (today in 2020 number has shot up to nearly one billion Indians in the US alone. They play an important role in a country made a country of their residence by immigrants. After 1991 their role has increased considerably. After India conducted May 1998 nuclear tests, Indian-Americans called practically every American law maker in the political system to influence the US decision-making. However, government/s should also know it NRIs and PIOs can play a negative role as well.

September 11 usually identified as 9/11 in the chronicles written on international terrorism changed the perceptions of Americans and rest of the world that no longer the US mainland had remained invincible to international terrorists. In the background of the first ever, international terrorist attacks on the US economic assets—world trade centre in New York and military prowess—Pentagon were directly hit by terrorists flying into the US territories on 9/11/2001.

Turning to foreign policy making process in the Federal government under the UPA I (2004-2009) the damaging role of Foreign Minister, Natwar Singh, has been discussed in the next piece, **"Time to replace Natwar With one with having clean image"**, (*FPJ*, 4 November 2005). To begin with, he blamed NDA government for conducting nuclear tests in 1998 "though you cannot put it back in the tube..." though PM Manmohan Singh had said that nuclear weapons will stay as a part of India's strategic policy.

Natwar Singh was also accused of accepting kickbacks from Saddam Hussein in the UN sponsored oil for food programme. BJP led-NDA government-had with hard bargaining forced Musharraf to commit Pakistan in January 2004 not to permit Pak controlled territory to be used to promote terrorism against India. But after the UPA government as the FM, he permitted Pakistan to dilute its earlier commitments on terrorism by his accepting Pakistan's formulation on India and Pakistan jointly fighting terrorism!

"Foreign Policy must match with national goals" (*FPJ*, 5 April 2008) highlights perennial problems of cacophony in public expression as to what is India's foreign policy on a given issue and lack of co-ordination in the formulation of nation's foreign policies. A few national security experts like this author and K Subramanyan had for years advocated an organised security/foreign policy formulation through National Security Council (NSC). However, under the pressure from status quoist Indian Administrative Service (IAS) officers, as they feared they might lose control over the policy making if a larger body is created with participation of not only foreign service but also men from military establishment!

"Is India a major Power?" (*OIOP*, March 2012) discusses the concept of major power; pyramidic structure of power, its components and the conditions amongst the nations at the time of writing the article. "Major Power" is a concept based on hierarchy of powerful states in the world by taking into consideration-tangible and intangible elements of power. Though Nehru projected in 1954 that India will be a fourth major power, next to the US, Soviet Union, China. But internationally it is the US under Ronald Reagan presidency in the 1980s that termed India as a major regional power and also emerging major global power. So far, in India's search for the major power status, China has been a major hindrance. Hence, India needs to decouple India's rise as a major power in competition and in comparison with China. Even in that direction, author finds lack of will-power as the major obstacle on India's path to progress towards its emergence as a globally major power.

"Should Pravasis be given political Rights?" (*FPJ*, 30 January 2014) philosophically consider most of Indians as Pravasis wherever, they are resident might have come from another city/state as in Mumbai or Delhi, a majority are non-originals of place of their work and residence. That apart, beyond India as a nation, more than 20 million of them are Videshi Pravasis. We make a distinction among them. Some are recent migrant to a foreign country called NRI. But many Indians were involuntarily taken by colonial masters to foreign countries-wherever they have colonies. In the Indian context they are called PIOs-(Persons of Indian Origin). During the BJP led NDA rule under Vajpayee, NRIs and PIOs demanded the right to vote in Indian elections! Then why not right to hold office? Since India does not have the concept of multiple citizenship, hence, only one Indian citizenship. Hence, voting and holding office wherever resident enough if they are given right to buy home's, properties and make their travel easy as of now without right to vote.

Elections of 2014 propelled Narendra Modi into Indian governing system as the Prime Minister with Sushma Swaraj as the Foreign Minister. Next piece in the foreign policy making section, **"Foreign Policy: Entirely Modi-Centric"** (*FPJ*, 10 December 2014, comments on who dominates the process of foreign policy and issues relating to its co-ordination. While process apparently was dominated by PM, Modi, FMs too have contributed to shaping foreign policy. Rightly, PM began his foreign policy by focusing on India's extended neighbhours-South Asia and South East Asia. Foreign Policy co-ordination remained with PMO though in 1998 the then PM Vajpayee had created for an organised foreign policy mechanism called NSC. It will strengthen, nation's foreign policy by ensuring inputs from all departments are brought into effective policy-making.

"Foreign Policy: Centre-State ties count" (*FPJ*, 20 December 2014) discusses issues peculiar to foreign policy formulation in a Federal State. In India while Federal Government has exclusive powers over foreign and national security affairs, in reality it has to consult, States and carry states along with its proposed policy options, even if state is ruled by the same political party at the State and Federal level as well. When they differ state/s can force a decision not in the best interest of the nation's relations with others. Thus, it is illustrated with experiences of the UPA government on the issue of PM Manmohan Singh attending Commonwealth Heads of Government Meeting in November 2013 as in Tamil Nadu main Dravidian Parties-DMK & AIADMK through a legislative Assembly resolution asked PM not to attend it to protest against Sri Lankan Army's Violation of Human Rights in their war against LTTE. Was it a right decision in the national interest?

"Vital role of India abroad" (*FPJ*, 1 January 2015) states that it has been policy of first PM, Nehru to ask all people settled abroad, whether as NRI or PIOS to assimilate with the people of countries where they live—whether in Africa, South-east Asia or anywhere abroad and not to look at India to help them. His logic was: charges of outsiders exploiting their former natives could be minimized. Yet Mrs. Gandhi rushed her minister to UK, when there were radical attacks in London or Sri Lanka to help to ease pressure on people of Indian origin. After him, all PMs followed Nehruvian guidelines; it was for the first time under Vajpyee consideration was extended to the PIOS with a positive outlook by celebrating *Pravasi Din* or Diaspora Day since 2003. This has helped India to get foreign exchange more than China from overseas Chinese.

American Foreign Policy

"American Foreign Policy Today" (*Freedom First,* May 1980) analysis four pillars of American Foreign policy. First, to maintain its neighborhood as an exclusive 'sphere of influence' based on Monroe Doctrine; second, globally maintenance of Balance of Power, third to be World's powerful nation economically and militarily and finally anti-communism-described by Fulbright as a "powerful prejudice".

These objectives of US foreign policy led to the Cold War between the US and the Soviet Union. While Cold War had its highest point, in the 1962 Cuban Missile Crisis, it also created an understanding between both sides, particularly, the US that it cannot confront its rival on all issues. The phase saw a period of *detente* indicating a limited issue-based understanding and not opposing the rival on every policy in international affairs.

American efforts however, continued to remain number one Super power in the world and that comes clearly in the discussion on **"American Foreign Policy since Kennedy: A historical perspective"** (*The Mahratta*,16 January 1982). Kennedy was an essentially cold-warrior; policy of containment of the previous regime was pursued with vigour, particularly in Europe. In his inaugural address, he had said: "Let every nation whether it wishes us well or ill, that we shall pay any price, bear any burden, meet any hardship, support any friend, oppose any foe to assure the survival and success of liberty". Obviously Kennedy policy as well as earlier Presidents were based on "containment" with a change from massive Retaliation to "flexible Response". Historically how this approach progressed under Johnson, Nixon, Carter and Reagan is essentially the content of this article.

Moving to the US policies, **"Games the Republicans play"** (*The Independent*, 19 October 1992), vividly brings out how US politicians, while in power particularly then numerically a minority, Republicans use foreign policy issues to win their re-elections. There are two Presidents in the post-World War period of American history, who turned out to be one-term Presidents as they lost their efforts to win a second term. In this Republicans, author contends, have excelled. Carter lost his re-election in 1980 against Ronald Reagan. Since, Reagan's campaign stealthily got Carter's talking points on impending Rescue Mission in October to get release of the hostages taken by Iran. William Casey who was a spy master did try to influence Iranian leaders on not releasing hostages till election results.

"Caution: Superpower looking for trouble" *(The Sunday Observer,* 2-8 May, 1999) focuses on the US foreign policy as clearly laid down by President, Bill Clinton in 1993. He had said "During the Cold war our foreign policy largely focused on relations among nations. Today our foreign policies must also focus on relations within nations, on a nation's form of governance, on its economic structure and on its *ethnic tolerance"* (emphasis added). Under this doctrine, US with nominal collaboration of the NATO, went to destabilise the Federal Republic of Yugoslavia without any sanction of the UN.

On the other hand, two permanent members of the UN—Russia and China—vehemently opposed the use of military power. It was a brazen use of force to secure compliance of Yugoslavia to terms of an agreement worked out by it with the consent of Kosovo Liberation Army (KLA). Author asks: why did the US collaborate with KLA which was declared as a terrorist group earlier and the NATO Summit in April 1999 for the first time agreed to fight against international terrorism. The brazen use of force in pursuance of the then doctrine of Clinton might put all multi-ethnic societies including India under the possible use of force by the US.

"Politics of US debt to United Nations" *{The Weekend Observer,* 27 November 1999) brings out a vital feature of the UN. It is not a supra-national body which functions independently but it is and infra-national organisation established by the sovereign nations. Hence, member-nations contribute to its up keep. The US as the nation that took initiative to setup the UN, and offered it space in New York, also is the highest contributor to its working. But in the 1990s it began using its contribution to the UN despite the rule that those who do not pay for two years, lose their right to vote in the various bodies. Hence, to retain its voting rights, though the House of Representatives had approved $926 million as a part of their total dues of $1.52 billion; but Republican controlled Congress agreed to release only $351 million minimum needed to retain its voting rights but rest it tied to certain conditions to see that it works to its dictates. How the US often bypasses the UN particularly after the end of the Soviet Union, has been brought out in the piece.

India-US Relations: From Confrontation to Co-operation

Moving to certain vital issues in the field of Indian foreign policy which were ignored by Pandit Nehru, the first PM of India. Though he recognised Israel, even before the US under Truman extended it, limited it to consular levels. I took up upgrading of India's diplomatic relations with Israel.

"Time to reassess ties with Israel" *(Business & Political Observer,* 12 April 1991) took up an important issue of Indian Foreign Policy in the early 1990s. Nehru did not establish full diplomatic relations with Israel on three grounds: (i) India's dependence on Arab/Islamic countries for energy (ii) to neutralize these countries blindly supporting Pakistan on Kashmir issue and (iii) his personal equation of friendship with the then Egyptian leader, Nasser who was co-founder of Non-Alignment Movement. Subsequently, PMs either followed Nehruvian lead or were not able to be innovative. But in the post-Cold War era, even Arab nations were moving in the direction of establishing diplomatic relations with Israel and India must not be left behind in the Defence and Security area. India stood to benefit from full diplomatic relations. The call is for political parties to look beyond their electoral gains.

"Opening ties with Israel" *(Business & Political Observer,* 25 December 1991) takes note of change in the approach of some non-aligned countries towards Israel after the demise of the Soviet Union. This was evident in change in their attitude towards a 1975 UN resolution (No 3379) equating Zionism with racism. In the post-Cold War period, Israel made with the backing of the US, efforts to rescind that resolution. Change in the approach was reflected in the UN Resolution to rescind the previous one was co-sponsored by Hungary and Czechoslovakia-two former countries of the Soviet bloc. The resolution was supported by III countries of the total UN membership of 166.

India too voted in favour of the resolution now; author reminds Indian foreign policy makers, Lord Palmerstone's old dictum that nations neither have permanent friends nor permanent enemies; they have only permanent interests. It was under the changed international scene of having no assured support of the Soviet Union; particularly its veto support in the UN; that emphasized the need to move to cultivate issue-based support to manage our relations with the nations who were hitherto in the Western side. India need not give up its support to Palestinian cause, on the other hand I pointed out: with regular diplomatic ties with Israel, it might "result in Israel becoming more open to Indian advice, perhaps even on the question of Palestine"

"Hard cheese, big bully" *(Mid-Day,* 14 May 1992) deals with the theme of developing India-US co-operation rather than the US acting as a bully. The US however, in the 1990s chose to opt for the latter option, when it pressurized Russia (successor state to the Soviet Union) not to sell latest technology to India under the 1991 treaty signed before the Soviet Union disintegrated. US informed Russia and India it will "impose sanctions, if deal went ahead".

With the demise of the Soviet Union, India lost its strong prop in International relations. Surviving Super Power, the US mounted pressure on India to mould Indian foreign policy to reflect its policy preferences. These developments are caught in **"Shortsighted American diplomacy"** (*OBP*, 20 May 1992). Thus, India was pressurized not to sell rice to Cuba, solitary communist state in the Western Hemisphere. These were in addition to making India to sign NPT; US Trade representative had suspended duty free treatment to the India pharmaceuticals and chemicals as "a minor first step".

Ostensibly, the US continued these steps of mounting pressure on India to move closer to the US. Way back in 1985, the then US Under Secretary Defence, Fred Ikle had projected: "India could be a power that contributes world stability as the US will see it, and to want to shape it in 1995 and the year 2025. A power with which we could work together.... to enhance our long-term national security aims." Author states with logical arguments: "In the changed world the US can only contribute to maintain world Peace and security with the co-operation of country like India, and not by bullying."

In the similar vein, in the next article on **"US-India Relations in the Post-Cold War Era"** (*Freedom First*, April-June 1993) author discusses, how two nations with the end of the Cold War, found albeit slowly a growing bond between the two nations of being pluralistic and vibrating democracies. But this did not emerge in 1991 soon after the demise of the Soviet Union. Since 1971, however, the US and China, as partners in international balance of power had played collective role to limit India. Hence, the Soviet equation became, which I defined as the "consideration by the US as to how its relations with another country help, or hinders her global policy of containment and confrontation of the Soviet Union".

Between 1971 and 1991 for twenty years we may say that globally US operated with a triangular balance of power-US and China checkmating the Soviet Union. While in South Asia it was a Pentagonal balance of power-US-China-Pakistan balancing power of Soviet Union and India, on the other side. With the Soviet demise in 1991, militarily US became sole superpower in a Unipolar world. In retrospect, Indira Gandhi, Rajiv Gandhi and P. V. Narasimha Rao were largely because of domestic constraints, were unable to catch up with the changes taking place in the world.

"No cause for complacency" (*OBP,* 21 July 1999) reflects on the US role in finding a solution to Pakistan's then General Musharraf who had commenced his Kargil intrusion to change the boundaries in the terrains of Kashmir. During the Kargil War, India restricted fight against intruding Pakistan's regular forces only from Indian side without crossing the international boundaries. This was appreciated by Bill Clinton, the then US President who had invited the then Pak PM, Nawaz Sharif to ask him to withdraw Pak troops. Pak began to give alibis, stating that those who fight are all freedom fighters; when that too didn't work, Pak said that while LOC is well-defined in the maps, are not defined on line; when that too didn't work Pak said: entire Kashmir issue to be discussed. In between threat of nuclear conflict between two newly nuclear armed nations was put forward to scare international community. Message of the article is: Appreciate the US supporting India but don't be carried away by its tilt till all facts became crystal clear.

"US President's visit to India Political Gains" (*FPJ*, 5 April 2000) recounts political gains which according to the then US Ambassador to India, Frank Wisner marks the "Possibility, of new age in Indo-US "ties". It brought a dramatic change in the US approach to thorny issues faced by India then like Kashmir, on which Clinton had made clear to Pak military rulers that there cannot be a military solution to the problem; asked Pakistan to respect LOC and stop terror. Both the nations agreed to work together on CTBT. What the US gained was access to Indian markets, investments. There was a realisation that US cannot put all her security eggs in Chinese basket!

"India-US Relations" (*The Observer of Business and Politics,* 18 May 2000) saw two important trends in US perceptions of India's security concerns after Bill Clinton's March 2000 visit to India. First there, was recognition that the international terrorism is supported by Pakistan, second, India is a multi-ethnic society and has a right to live like that. Third, India is a vibrating democracy. There was a new and welcome awareness on the part of Bill Clinton on the nature of Kashmir problem as earlier he had created an uncertainty in the minds of Indian policy makers by comparing in UN situation in Kashmir with Bosnia; and writing to Kashmiri lobbyist, Ghulam Nabi Fai expressing his willingness to work with him to establish peace in Kashmir! Author shows convincingly that these policy perceptions were already shared by his predecessors, George T W Bush. Hence, my conclusion in 2000 was prophetic on the then ensuing elections of November 2000:

If Democrat, Al Gore is elected he has promised to continue Clinton's policies. If Bush Jr. is elected, he will be, atleast on South Asia, moving ahead from where his father had left."

The article entitled **"India-US politico-military relations since September 11"** (*FPJ*, 15 October 2002) discusses the changes perceived in "India's relations with the US". As I predicted earlier, under George Bush US politically moved closer to India since, economic and military relations ultimately depend upon closer political understanding. However, US need to fine tune its relations with India by making first Pakistan accept that it cannot co-operate with the US in fighting terrorism in the West while promoting it in East; second India should in its changed nuclear status, in promoting non-proliferation and third US in its pursuit of uni-polar world, should take care to see it does not drive India to co-operate with Russia and China in promotion of multi-polar world.

Next article **"Major issues crucial for India's foreign policy"** (*FPJ*, 15 November 2003) was penned in the background of impending general elections in 2004; significantly for the first time, a government was completing its five-years term since 1996. Four areas of issues have been identified: First leaning towards the US with equally closer nations with France and EU; second closer relations with the entire neighbourhood-West Asia as well as the East; third, strategic partnership with the US with China as the main security threat and finally leaning towards Indian religionists nations, avoidance of the concept of clash of civilizations in Indian foreign policy.

The article discuss issues in the arena of promoting better relations with the US; while observing that occasionally the US condemned terror attacks from across the borders as done by George Bush, he was selective while mentioning it in the UN General Assembly terror attacks after 9/11; like in Bali, Mombasa, Casablanca, Riyadh, Jakarta and Jerusalem, but completely left out Parliament attack in India! Hence, I have argued that while leaning towards the US, we also need to maintain close relations with France and the EU. I have also made a suggestion that we need to also cultivate closer relations with South East Asian nations as these perceive a security threat from China while none see such a threat from India. India also needs to promote an Association of Indian Religionists to counter Organisation of Islamic Cooperation (OIC). There is also need to maintain cultural and economic relations with Taiwan.

Next article, **"Growth of a multi-dimensional India-US relationship"** (*FPJ*, 16 March 2004), finds since in 21st century India's relations with the US, though have downs are not creating a chasm between the two but ups have been too easy to climb! In the developing relations highest purpose was to create a strategic relationship. What influenced Clinton to step in to resolve Kargil crisis between Pakistan (perpetrator) and India (victim) then two nuclear armed neighbours was India's adherence to a tenet on nuclear behaviour amongst the nuclear weapons states. They do not violate their territorial boundaries whether accepted or disputed between the two neighbours. While Musharraf used the threat of escalating crisis into a nuclear conflict, Vajpayee limited India's efforts to throw out Pakistani army then fighting as freedom fighters! Indian markets were of considerable importance to the US for its investment and trade. Similarly under WTO agreement, Higher education in India was opened up for the US-collaboration.

"If CPM forces election on voters will Manmohan emerge stronger?" (*FPJ*, 10 September 2007), takes the readers to the period when under the UPA I, Manmohan Singh-Sonia Gandhi led Government depended on CPI (M)'s external support. Under the pressure of the Marxists, PM was wavering on domestic as well as foreign policy issues. PM had gained from George W. Bush administration a Civil Nuclear Deal (CND) which was aimed to bring out India from nuclear *apartheid* position in which US itself had taken lead initially to place India in that position. PM Singh, first said that implementation of CND is "non-negotiable". But later he showed his willingness to talk to opponents of the CND. The article advocate a firm stand on the part of the government to implement a CND.

India-China Relations: from Playing Second Fiddle to Assertion of National Interests

"Too much of a good thing" *(Mid-Day,* 8 June 1992) moves to discuss growing arrogant behaviour on the part of China that was evident during the first ever visit to China by an Indian President, R Venkataraman who returned on 24 May 1992. During his presence in China, it conducted a mega tonne underground nuclear explosion. This has been the method of China to show its prowess as it attacked India's friend in South-east Asia, Vietnam in 1979 when the then Indian Foreign Minister, Vajpayee was in China. Indian governments since 1962 border war have extended silent approval for all its anti-Indian acts and utterances. Thus, it dismissed border dispute as a historical legacy but used to publicly take up activities of Dalai Lama in India. For China Kashmir is also a historical legacy but while seeking recognition of Tibet as an autonomous part of China! In reality thus, nothing substantial came out of RV visit to China.

"Caution a Watchword" (*OBP*, 20 July 1992) continued efforts to ask Government of India not to get into celebrations mode as R. V.'s visit to China was described by the Chinese President Yang Shangkun as "a big success" others termed it as "land mark," opening a "new chapter" etc.

But the reality is: During RV's presence not only megaton nuclear weapon was exploded by China, this came at a time when US has been pressurizing India to sign the NPT though Pakistan and China were also there as non-signatories of the NPT. But pressure was mounted mainly on India. The article discusses short-term gains for India from its silence on Chinese double standards, as it gained concretely by India siding with China on the issue of the US pressure on both to improve their human rights record permitting the US to "pose as protector of human rights!".

China continues to be main threat to Indian security. P. V. Narasimha Rao, who had become in 1991, first ever PM outside Nehru-Gandhi family PM, had been, on his first visit to China, as PM. On his return he was anxious to renew spirit of Panchsheel!

My next article in this book on: **"Let's not be emotional about Panchsheel"** *(The Sunday Observer* 17-23 July 1994) was written after my return from attending a huge two day all-India Conference[2] organized by the IDSA on "Panchsheel and Global Diplomacy". P. V. Narasimha Rao justified his initiative by referring to a world "riven by ethnic, religious and communal conflicts.....antagonisms based on narrowly conceived rational interests......" Obviously then India as a democracy and China as the communist country facing American pressure on national record of protecting human rights and use of trade relations to mount pressure on them to improve the record.

Next article, **"India needs a Taiwan Policy"** *(Blitz,* 31 January 1998) states that Taiwan has lived as an independent country for the last 49 years, which was a permanent member of the UNSC until it was expelled in 1971, when the US normalised its relations with mainland China. But the US maintains its close economic, cultural and scientific relations with Taiwan. US is Taiwan's largest trading partner.

Taiwan has plenty of US dollars to invest in India as it aims to diversify its investments. India should overcome its shyness to maintain economic relations with it. On the other hand if mainland China can accept Taiwanese investments, India while accepting 'One China, but two systems' must be bold in accepting Taiwan's investments, as well.

Being a frequent visitor to the US, I had observed how Chinese toys made in China, for American major toy-makers, being very sub-standard often harmful for children's health. **"Push the sale of Indian toys in US market"** (*FPJ*, 10 October 2007) made a strong case for Indian government to take initiative to sell Indian toys and games which were much better in quality and durability. There is a suttle message to government to resist the inside pressure of "friends of China" in India!

"India needs to stand up to China" (*OIOP*, February 2013) notes the changes in the perceptions and policies brought in by newly appointed FM, Salman Khurshid by replacing S M Krishna. Khurshid said on 10 December 2012 that India "will have to accept the new reality of China's presence in areas that we consider an exclusive area for India and its friends, like South Asia". There was no evidence of China reciprocally accepting India's legitimate interests in South East Asia. On the other hand India was once again accepting publicly China's hegemony in the entire Asia. India seemed to go back to days of deference to China. Thus, while China was openly advising India to keep off the South China Sea, India didn't express similar concerns on China's activities in PoK. India need to stand up to big bully in Asia so that small bullies will also heed to India's concerns.

"Decisive Leadership and Geopolitics at its Best" (*The Leadership Review*, June 2016) analysis PM Modi's first two years' performance in the field of foreign policy with references to China. Modi as a candidate campaigning for the BJP had made it clear in Arunachal Pradesh in 2013 that China need to give up its "mindset of expansion" and work with India to avail fruits of "development and prosperity" for both nations. As far as its claim on Arunachal Pradesh goes Modi said: "No power on earth can snatch away Arunachal Pradesh from India". Xi Jinping was his guest in September 2014. Around the same time, President Mukherjee was in Vietnam to deepen India's bilateral security and economic relations. Modi's use of Geopolitics came out best by signing a deal in developing Chabahar Port in Iran to gain independent access to Afghanistan without going through Pakistan.

"Explaining India-China Doklam stand-off and thereafter" *(RKPN, India* connecting world, online, 26 March 2018) sees again repetition of past behaviour by China towards India when India was bending backward to cultivate friendship with it -a policy pursued by all governments since October 1962 border war. But Indian policy towards China was in the process of change under the Modi era was clear to Xi Jinping as during his first visit to Ahmedabad/ New Delhi. PLA intruded in Ladakh. Modi had clearly informed Xi that close economic relations cannot go on if such military intrusions continue to occur. After eight days, PLA withdrew; Xi expressed his sadness over the tensions between PLA and Indian Army while returning to China. In this background immediate provocation for China under Xi to again raise the issue of its claim over *Doklam-trijunction* area involving India, Bhutan and China, is India & Bhutan's refusal to participate Xi's personally promoted OBOR programme connecting roads to link nearly sixty countries in Asia, Africa and Europe with a GDP of $3 trillion. The article analysis events of 73 days by when China agreed to restore status quo ante.

India and her Neighbours

"Avoid past mistakes in Sri Lanka" (*OBP*, 11 May 2000) make a few valid suggestions to the then ruling NDA I government. At the outset, it says: Reject Dr Swami's suggestion of asking Sri Lankan government to seek to confederate with India, as Island State is not viable, on the other hand, India in strongest words, try to reassure Sri Lankan government that Indian commitment to its territorial integrity and ensure opposition party-the Congress concerns be taken into consideration and work to withdraw troops sent there by late PM Rajiv Gandhi and secure legitimate claim of political autonomy to majority Tamil areas.

Continuing commenting on the Sri Lankan developments, **"No Grand Designs"** (*Mid-Day*, 13 May 2000) deals with Sri Lankan ethnic crisis that finally led India under Rajiv Gandhi to send Indian troops to island states. It was a wrong step as until then India was playing a role of a honest broker. By agreeing to send troops, India took upon itself Sri Lankan job of maintaining peace; and getting regional autonomy to fighting Tamils. India failed in both the missions. 'IPKF' stood for Sri Lankan Tamils, Innocent People Killing Force. Successor to Jayavardhane, Premadasa, new president who got elected by promising to force India to withdraw IPKF! He even collaborated with LTTE by providing arms to them to fight against Indian troops! While LTTE has been eliminated by Sri Lankan forces, regional autonomy still eluded the moderate Tamils!

"What can India learn from Musharraf's domestic reforms?" (*FPJ*, 12 February 2002), is an extremely interesting piece as reforms introduced by Musharraf to present himself as a reformist and liberal Muslim. He did this as author notes, at the behest of the US authorities. Musharraf asked all Madrasas and Mosques to be registered; no mosques can be built without prior clearance of the government. They needed to teach modern secular scientific subjects. India needs to follow these in our interest to prevent Madrasas from leading and turning terrorists to fight against Indian government! Even in 2002 number of them on the India-Pakistan borders were in a staggering figures. On Kutch district alone there were 323 Madrasas; similarly large number of them exists on borders of Nepal, Rajasthan and Bihar. These are breeding grounds for creating radical Muslim clerics.

Turning to Pakistan, **"Peace lies in the corridors of learning"** (*The Indian Express*, 6 January 2004) proposes establishment Gandhi Peace Fellowships for the SAARC nations mainly beginning with Pakistan. I had expressed hope in early 2004 that idea will cater up the minds of policymakers. It has precedent in a bigger way, how the US created Fulbright fellowships mostly favouring then closed societies in the Soviet Union-its ideological rival bloc. But my regret today is that nothing of the kind has happened.

The above idea was further expanded in my next piece **"Institute Gandhi Fellowships to promote peace in South Asia"** (*FPJ*, 10 January 2004) when I put the idea before Pakistanis during my visit to Islamabad, I discovered even then more then 20 percent of Pakistani's had relatives in India and were yearning to visit them. People to people contacts at all levels of-College, school-teachers, scientist's and students could help.

But Pakistani adventures like Kargil (1999), attack on Parliament (2001) and 26/11 (2008) question the credibility of such proposals. Even Pakistan can come out with their own programme say Jinnah Fellowships for Indians to study how Jinnah shaped Pakistan. But history must be written and interpreted without any ideological distortions.

"India-Afghanistan Relations: The US and Pakistan as Conditioner" (*FPRC* Journal No 7, 2012) looks at Afghanistan since India's independence from British imperial rule and creation of Pakistan on our north-west borders, which has become a neighbour's neighbour-in terms of Chanakya, a friend. As on today, India's immediate neighbours-Pakistan and China-as an enemy of enemy has emerged as a close all weather friends of each other. The US as the global Super Power has been present in Afghanistan since October 2001. The article examines Pentagonal relations in the India's north west region.

Turning to Pakistan after Nawaz Sharif of (PMC-N) was elected for third time in May 2013, **"A new step for Pakistan, a new hope for India"** (*OIOP*, July 2013) hopes that he will be allowed to complete his term by all powerful Pak Army. It was an unique development for Pakistan's democracy: for the first time an elected government (led by PPP's) Yusuf Gilani was able to complete its term and hand over smoothly political power to another elected government! Yet author advises then ruling UPA II government to be cautious in trying to improve relations with Pakistan as the then PM, Manmohan Singh had expressed his desire to visit Pakistan to improve India's relations!

Issues in Indian Foreign Policy

"India Vision" (*Mid-Day*, 12 August 1997) comments on vision expressed by K R Narayanan few days before assuming office as President of India. He had said that "India could emerge in the 21st century as a major power in the World". I have agreed with it. But unfortunately in the last decade of the 20th Century, there is no indication to support such an idealistic projection of power on the 3 grounds: First end of the Cold War, second, collapse of Indian Economy by early 1990s and the lack of political stability, because of fragmentation of political parties. Though Nehru too had expressed his hope on India emerging as the Fourth major power, his successors in power had reduced India into a fourth-grade power.

Next article: **"Don't 'rogue states' need moral leadership?"** (*FPJ*, 21 August 1998) refers to conditions in the nation after Vajpayee conducted nuclear tests. After the tests, he was asked by the Congress not to take all credit for conducting nuclear tests; PM Vajpayee began to attribute all credit to "scientists". Congress party was hurt as after Indira Gandhi conducted nuclear test in 1974, according to R. Venkatraman the then Defence Minister that he had inspected in

1983 testing pits in Pokhran under Mrs Gandhi; Mulayam Singh Defence Minister under UF government led by Deve Gowda and I K Gujral had also made similar efforts. P. V Narasimha, before remitting office in 1996, too had made efforts for the same. While all these efforts failed, what Vajpayee provided to the scientists, political will and leadership to conduct nuclear tests without worrying about the economic consequences. Since India, prior to her nuclear tests, was under pressure to sign CTBT, NPT. India, author says should offer to sign non-comprehensive test-ban treaty and NPT in return for US support for seating India as a permanent member of the United Nations Security Council.

Next article "**Erect statues in other states too**", (*FPJ*, 24 Feb 2010) was written in response to criticism/legal challenge to the idea of erection of Shivaji statue in the Arabian Sea. Public criticism, based on scarcity of resources was motivated. However, I have brought out its usefulness in promoting national security and national and international tourism, which has been totally ignored by general public critical of the government proposals. In the arena of national security after the 26/11, base area of statue can be used for watch and observation; it is the first line of defence in protecting vast coastal area in the East, West and South. Every State on the West Coast and the East Coast, beginning from Gujarat and ending on the eastern side at West Bengal-all states have their own rich history depicting valour in defence. When all states establish such statues the string of pearls can act as the first line of national defence against sea-based International Terrorism.

"**Is an Idea man irrelevant for a man of action**? (*FPJ*, 15 July 2010), discusses the unending questions on the role of 'men of Ideas'. Provocation to write this article originated in when the then Minister for Highways Kamal Nath dismissed men of ideas as "arm chair advisers" with reference to Montek Singh Ahluwalia, then a member of the Planning Commission. If he had stated 'that the "Planning Commission" as irrelevant in democracy, that would have been a state of mind regarding an institution created by Pandit Nehru by an executive order. I have made an effort to convince readers by giving a few personal illustrations to highlight importance of men of ideas' as much as 'men of actions'.

"**Nehru's foreign Policy, flawed and all**", (*FPJ*, 26 November 2014) discusses tremendous responsibilities carried by Pandit Nehru in shaping foreign policy of an independent India since August 1947. He was even prior to India's independence the convener of the Congress party foreign policy cell since 1927. While being the architect of India's Foreign Policy, however, he erred in three major areas: Kashmir war 1947-48, in taking it to the UN, second looking at China as a friend despite contrary facts and third not going nuclear despite China exploding atomic bomb prior to NPT of 1968 despite having know how.

US Goes to War Against Iraq

"America putting maximum pressure on UN to authorise use of force against Iraq" (*FPJ*, 9 November 2002) takes readers to then developing issue of George W. Bush pitching to get rid of Saddam Hussein from ruling Iraq by suddenly switching his earlier focus on Osama bin Laden to capture him he had soon after 9/11 invaded Afghanistan. A serious study of the article makes a student of foreign policy and International relations to ponder: how much an elected US President searches for important issues to be used in foreign affairs to win next elections; for George W. Bush it was November 2004.

"Should India contribute to the stabilisation force in Iraq?" (*FPJ*, 8 July 2003) shows very clearly that for the US invasion is inexpensive in terms of lives lost but ruling a foreign country is extremely difficult. That is true of Afghanistan which the US invaded in 2001 and Iraq in 2003. Article discusses India's gains if it agrees to send stabilisation forces to Iraq and against Indian participation could have brought certain advantages like getting some subcontracts to rebuild Iraqi cities or participate under American tutelage in oil exploration. But a stronger case was made against Indian sending her troops to serve in Iraq under the US command. The Indian experience in IPKF was enough against any Indian participation under the US command. Hence, it is recommended that even at this stage (post-Iraqi surrender) to the US to take over as it was done in case of Kosovo.

"Next article, "**Iraq war: intelligence failure or intelligence cover?**" (*FPJ* 23 July 2003) examines another aspect of accusation denied by Iraq but used by the US was that Iraq was developing WMD. After Saddam Hussein was toppled on 29 April 2003 UN appointed weapons inspectors could not get any trace of WMD. When the issue of intelligence failure was raised by the White House, then CIA Director George Tenet owned up publicly responsibility for misinterpreting question of Iraq getting uranium from an African country Niger. A contrasting parallel was: John F. Kennedy ordering Cuban invasion in 1962 on the advice of the then CIA Director Allen Dulles, who was fired by President when Bay of Pigs turned a great fiasco! Circumstantial evidence made it clear that invasion was planned to gain a second term in 2004 Presidential elections.

Continuing analysis of Iraqi issue, the next article, "**French stand on Iraq misunderstood by US**" (*FPJ*, 7 October 2003) examines and presents an appreciative approach to American journalist writing in NYT that accused "France is becoming" American enemy and looks at France always maintaining its independent approach in its foreign policy despite its being in NATO and the EU. This is borne out by the fact in May 1998, soon after India conducted nuclear tests it supported India when the entire West led by the US was against India!

Way back in 1962, during the Cuban Missile Crisis, President Kennedy sent former Secretary of State, Dean Acheson to meet the then French President, De Gaulle, who didn't even agree to see satellite photographs of location of missiles in Cuba on the ground since the US has already decided to impose a naval quarantine of Cuba and Acheson had come only to inform it, France had nothing to do with it! What France always said was that US should not land itself in a quagmire in Iraq as it was in Vietnam.

1

NON-ALIGNMENT: BEGINNING & LATER

Relevance of non-alignment in Cold War

The decade of the 80s has begun with the re-emergence of the Cold War. The Soviet military intervention in Afganistan marked the beginning.

Cold War was a situation of intense conflict and confrontation between the two Super Powers, short of an outbreak into an open war is now renewed by the roles of the participants of the dramas of the 50s reversed. In the 50s the U.S with her military superiority vis-a-vis the Sovet Union was calling the tune while the Soviet Union was merely responding. Today the Soviet Union is calling the tune with its definite military superiority over the U.S and the U.S is mostly reacting to it.

The Super Power Cold War confrontation took place in the 50s and the 60s in Europe, Latin America and South-East Asia. Most of the Super Power military intervention were then within their respective spheres of influence. In the 80s soviet Union has chosen a non-aligned country to reinduct Cold War in international politics. Cold War of the 80s is also being played next to our own doors. The first victim of it has been Afganistan traditionally a friendly country of ours. The Soviet power threatens to come closer to India's north-western borders. Can our non-alignment survive in the wake of the Soviet, expansionism in South Asia? Is non-alignment relevant in the re-emerging Cold War internationl environment? Are there any obstacles in the way of practisting a policy of genuine non-alignment by India in 80s?

Nehru's statement

Non-alignment was the child of Cold War. Its Cold War parentage is clear from what Mr. Nehru said in 1947: "India will follow an independent policy keeping away from the power politics of groups aligned one against another." Non-alignment then essentially meant refusal by a nation to mortgage to one or the other Super Powers its freedom of action in international affairs by permanently aligning through membership of multilateral or bilateral military pacts. It did not mean neutrality or isolationist attitude on the part of a country. But it is retention of a degree of freedom to decide its response to each international crisis, depending upon its relevance to its national intereests.

However, the qualities of Indian non-alignment gradually got diluted and contaminated by changing international environment. The first and the most crucial blow to Indian practice of non-alignment came from Pakistan's abandonment of non-alignment in favour of alignment with the US in 1953. Pakistan exploited American anti-Communist phobia to develop a military machine with the US military aid ostensibly given to meet any Communist threat either from the Soviet Union or Communist China. But in reality it was aimed at the non-aligned India.

After the Chinese aggression of October, 1962 China also sought and secured the friendship of Pakistan- an Americanally, while globally the US and China were antagonists, in India their interest gradually began to converge.

In the 60s, India faced national security threat from two belligerents, Pakistan and China. In the diplomatic front Pakistan kept alive the Kashmir issue in the UN. Thus there was the need for a diplomatic and geopolitical ally for India, who could, on behalf of India, exercise the veto in the UN, and geopolitical pressure on China-and the Soviet Union filled the bill. Since the Soviet Union wanted a foothold in South Asia to counteract the growing American influence in Pakistan, India's growth and dependence was its aim. The Soviet Union did not feel any special attraction for India, though India was potentially much stronger than Pakistan. This is clear from the Soviet attitude towards the Indo-Pakistan war of 1965.

Soviet role

In the 60s, Pakistan was experimenting with a queer possibility of a aligning with the US. USSR and China simultaneously with the sole purpose of grabbing Kashmir. While cultivating friendship with India, the Soviets were also not averse to extend military aid to Pakistan with the purpose of weaning her away from the US. One must also recall that in the 1965 conflict the Soviet Union did not play the role of a friend of India, but that of a mediator between the two.

The Tashkent Conference was more aimed at isolating China in international politics than solving India's security problems.

But India's non-alignment began to tilt towards the Soviet Union with growing spirit of *detente* in major-power relations in the 1970s, especially the US and China. For India, it was clear that in the event of another Chinese aggression, the US assistance would not be available and only the Soviet Union with its growing schism with China can act as a geopolitical factor in relation to India's security. This was clearly demonstrated by the way the world powers ranged during the Bangladesh war of 1971.

The practice of non-alignment by India in the 70s-during the period of detente-brings out an important reality: The possibility of Cold War rivalry providing an additional sense of security to the non-aligned nations was no longer there. The help of one Super Power was not necessarily available without a price when the other power was not involved on the opposite side. This meant when a non-aligned nation like India, was threatened by a nation like Pakistan, with its alignment with a super power the support of the Soviet Union could come only through some kind of bilateral treaty arrangement this in fact, had come into operation during the detente a third category semi-aligned (bilaterally) in addition to aligned (multilaterally) and non-aligned.

Thus, when India was faced with the dilemma between choosing to have continued presence of 10 million in India or help people of Bangladesh to liberate their country so as to facilitate return of the refugees, the international circumstances ultimately forced India to accept the second course. But when Pakistan was supported by the US and China, India could not meet the challenge by itself in the diplomatic world. The Soviet Union was unwilling to extend the support to India unless this country agreed to sign a peace, friendship and mutual assistance treaty, the offer of which Mrs. Gandhi was resisting at least for three years.

It was only after India signed the Peace Treaty of 1971, that the Soviet Union firmly stood by India in the diplomatic world. This trend is also borne out by the fact that the Soviet Union gave a green signal to the Vietnamese occupation of Kampuchea, only after Vietnam signed a peace and friendship treaty in 1978. It is also interesting in the retrospect to know that while the Indo-Pak War of 1948 surprised India, the war of 1965 ended in a military stalemate, and the war of 1971 gave a decisive military victory to India. Though this was due to the military muscle and strategy of India, the significance of the Soviet diplomatic support as a contributory factor to India's military victory cannot be under estimated. But the military victory has been at the cost of our non-alignment since 1971 India became a semi-aligned nation.

Today within the non-aligned movement there are several semi-aligned nations. In fact the movement itself is chaired by Cuba- a semi-aligned nation. As a matter of fact the definition on non-alignment has been diluted to permit the membership in the movement for the nations which have a bilateral treaty with military overtones with one or the other Super Power- like Cuba, Vietnam, Iraq or India.

Significance

What can be done to make non-alignment more relevant to the present international scene with the Cold War assuming a new facet? In the renewed Cold War situation non-alignment has become as relevant as it was in the 50s. Non-alignment gains significance when it is valued by the significance when it is valued by the Super Power. While alignment contributes to increase tensions in international politics, when more countries embrace non-alignment, it contributes to reduce tensions. It is only non-aligned countries which can genuinely act as mediators and defuse Super Power conflicts and confrontations.

The Semi-aligned nations like India or Cuba or Egypt cannot play that role. There is developing pressure on semi-aligned nations to embrace complete alignment.

This idea has been stressed by Cuba at the Havana Conference of Non-aligned nations last year. President Castro forcefully tried to convince the conference delegates that the socialistic-bloc was a natural. This position is pregnant with long-term implications to the non-aligned implication to the non-aligned movement.

Firstly, the leader of socialist bloc- the Soviet Union is militarily already a dominant power vis-a-vis the US. Secondly. President Brezhnev has already enunciated a doctrine of limited sovereignty of the Socialist bloc nations. Do the non-aligned nations want to surrender their hard won freedom and independency by perpetuating their semi-aligned status? while it may not be difficult for communist led countries like Cuba or Vietnam, the democratic nations within the non-aligned movement cannot afford such a risk. Thirdly, persistent advocacy of the Castro line might lead to a division of non-aligned movement into non-aligned movement into non-aligned (pro-west) and non-aligned (pro-Soviet). This has been the aim of the Super Powers, since the weakened non-aligned movement will enlarge their respective sphere of influence and increase their influence in international politics.

Peace treaty

Hence, India as a founder nation of the non-aligned movement, should take the initiative to direct the movement back to the 50s, when none of the members of the movement was semi-aligned. This necessitates that India should renounce its semi-aligned status, in the wake of the reemergence of Cold War. In the ultimate analysis, India has to confine to the dust bins of history the Indo-Soviet Peace and Friendship Treaty of 1971.

In practical terms it may not be possible or desirable immediately because China continues to be a security threat to India, and to that extent we still need the support of the Soviet Union. But India can make a moderate beginning in that direction by openly advocating immediate and unconditional withdrawal of the Soviet troops from Afghanistan. After all even Iraq, with its pro-Soviet image and a bilateral treaty of peace and friendship with the Soviet, has been able to do China that in the event of any Sino- Soviet conflict India will not *ipso facto* toe the Soviet line.

India can and has to take this calculated risk. It is now facilitated by the disappearance of Pakistan as a security threat to India. Since the 1971 war, Pakistan has been reduced to one-fifth of India and its joining the non-aligned movement it has to be considered as a friend of this country.

The fragile non-alignment of Pakistan was threatened by the possibility of its accepting military aid from the US in the wake of the Soviet intervention in Afghanistan. But Gen. Zia's decision to reject

American military aid as "peanut" compared to the security threat faced by his country enable India to follow a policy or genuine non-alignment without tilts.

India sense, Pakistan's quitting the non-aligned movement introduced a tilt towards the Soviet Union in India's practice of non-alignment and now its coming back to the non-aligned fold should lead India to correct the tilt. What is needed is the ability to take bold decisions, breaking away from the past, so as to radically adapt non-alignment to the changing international environment.

Deccan Herald (Bangalore), 21 May 1980

India in International Affairs: Twin Challenges of 80's

Indian foreign policy has entered the most crucial stage. The strengths and weaknesses in our foreign policy in the 1980 and later would largely determine whether or not India would continue to live in future as a free, independent, sovereign and democratic power in the community of nations. I propose to discuss India's recent policies in international affairs with special emphasis on our relations with the Super Powers and then to deal with the challenges we face in formulating our policies towards them.

A nation's foreign policy is to some extent pre-determined by the prevailing international scene. The international scene is the setting in which India, like other nations, has to act. India has no control over the other actors or over the setting. Broadly the international scene in the post-World War II period has alternated between two patterns—Cold War and *detente.*

Since World War II, the international scene has been dominated by the two super-powers— the U.S.A. and the U.S.S.R. Since the seventies China has been making determined efforts to become a super power, but it has not yet become one. What was said as of item is that bipolarity of the 50s and 60s as observed by Zbigniew Brzezinski is being replaced by 2½ Super-Powers.

The international scene today is one of Cold War. Whether it is intense or mild, opinions may differ. *Detente,* formally established by 1972, after a long period of Cold War, is practically over now. The Cold War has reemerged with the Soviet military intervention in

Afghanistan. There is plenty of evidence for the reemergence of Cold War in Super Power relations. The American President has raised the defence expenditure by over 5 percent; for the fiscal year 1981 the military budget stands at over $ 146 billion, and there is a demand for more. Already certain restrictions on the covert operations of the CIA imposed in the aftermath of the Watergate have been withdrawn. American clamour for strong Presidential leadership in foreign affairs is a convincing proof of Cold War tensions.

But the Cold War of the 80s is different from the Cold War of the 50s and 60s. In the 50s and 60s the Soviet Union merely reacted to the moves of the U.S. The U.S. had definite superiority in military, economic and technological fields. However, the American experience in Vietnam led her to accept military parity with the Soviet Union, which had become the basis for the *detente.* During the period of *detente,* the Soviet Union set out to achieve military superiority *vis-a-vis* the U.S. In the 70s the Soviet Union also launched a series of military conflicts in the Afro-Asian region beginning with Angola in 1975 to test the American will. In all these conflicts the U.S. merely reacted to Soviet initiatives. And now at the beginning of the 80s the U.S. has been reduced to a position of military inferiority *vis-a-vis* the Soviet Union. To move from inferiority to parity; from parity to superiority, has been a great military achievement of the Soviet Union, since 1945. The military intervention in Afghanistan, the first ever outside its own sphere of influence, is an indication of its military confidence.

The American military weakness is also borne out by the fact of her unwritten alliance with Communist China. The Chinese border dispute with the Soviets has led the Soviet Union to amass more than 600,000 troops (1/4 of their entire military) on the Chinese borders. In the balance of power game it is an effort by 1½ powers—the U.S. and China—to balance the Soviet power. The American weakness has been compounded by its prolonged crisis with Islamic fundamentalism in Teheran over the American hostages. American weakness in international relations can be shown from a comparison of *The Mayaguez* incident of 1975 and the Embassy hostages in 1980. When the US ship *Mayaguez* was captured by Cambodia with its crew of 39, President Ford ordered military action to regain the ship. But in the embassy hostages issue, then almost eight months old, the US has not been able to gain freedom to the hostages. The US has severed diplomatic relations with Iran and made an unsuccessful bid to rescue the hostages through commando action. Now let me hasten to add that I do not advocate US military action to secure the release of hostages nor do I believe that Ford's action was necessarily a sound one. I intend only to show the weakened willpower of the U.S. in international relations.

The American response to Soviet intervention has been one of loud protest, without any visible effect on the other super power. American Presidents in the post-World War II period have been prone to issue their doctrines. In succession to Truman doctrine and Nixon doctrine, now in the wake of Soviet intervention in Afghanistan, the Carter doctrine has been proclaimed which announced the US intention to protect its national interests in the Persian Gulf. How does it help resolve the Afghan crisis? The only concrete action proposed by the US was an offer of $ 400 million military aid to Pakistan, even before Pakistan asked for it. It was rejected by General Zia as "peanuts".

Thus, in this Cold War dominated international scene, whether or not India will be heard and respected will depend largely on the strength and clarity of India's voice. The Cold War in the past was fought in Europe, West Asia and South-East Asia. But since Nehru's time India has adopted two distinct models of response to super power military interventions. Towards the U.S. whether in the case of Dominican Republic or of Vietnam our response has been of open criticism and demand of unconditional withdrawal of troops. But with the Soviet military interventions, whether it was Hungary or Czechoslovakia, the Indian voice was muted. There was neither open criticism nor an unequivocal demand for withdrawal of Soviet troops.

In the light of this past record, three reasons can be advanced to emphasize that our response to the developing Cold War and super power confrontation ought to be completely different than in the past. Firstly, the super power Cold War confrontation has been revived in the 80s in our immediate neighbourhood. Secondly, past victims of super power interventions were mostly aligned nations. This time, the victim of Soviet military intervention is a non-aligned country, and has been traditionally friendly to India. Thirdly, since 1971 after Bangladesh war, India has emerged as the dominant power in South Asia. The dominant power status brings its own responsibilities, sometimes painful. Dominance does not depend upon other's recognition; it has to be maintained by conscious effort to be real.

What has been India's response to the developing Cold War? How effective has it been so far? The Afghan crisis erupted at a time when we had a caretaker government. Caretaker governments are not generally effective in conducting a strong foreign policy. Yet the then Prime Minister Charan Singh, called the Soviet ambassador to his office and expressed India's concern at the Soviet military intervention and asked for an early withdrawal of the Soviet troops. He also told the ambassador that India would like Afghanistan's independence and non-alignment to be strengthened.

But Mrs. Gandhi did not think so when she assumed office on January 14, 1980. A Prime Minister-designate exercises more power and influence than an outgoing one. This was evident from India's stand in the UN two days prior to her formal assumption of power. India's permanent representative in the UN, Mr. Brajesh Mishra, participating in the debate over the non-aligned nations' resolution on Afghanistan, said that the Soviet Union had assured India that it would withdraw its troops when asked by the Kabul government. He further added: "We have no reason to doubt the assurances particularly, from a friendly country like the Soviet Union". However, he made clear India's general opposition to the presence of foreign troops or basis in any country. It was a case of upholding a general principle, while condoning a particular violation of it. The UN resolution for immediate and unconditional withdrawal of the Soviet troops from Afghanistan was approved by 104 to 18, and 18 abstaining. While India abstained 60 out of 96 non-aligned nations voted for the resolution.

Thus, Mrs. Gandhi's initial stand on the Soviet military intervention is in the same category as in the past—one of abstaining from open criticism of the Soviet Union. In international politics, perception plays an important role as reality. In formulating India's response, Mrs. Gandhi lost an opportunity to correct her image as a pro-Soviet leader in international affairs. The Janata Government did not break the "special relationship" this country had established with the Soviet Union by signing the Peace and Friendship treaty in 1971 during Mrs. Gandhi's previous regime. But the pro-west image of Mr. Desai and Mr. Atal Behari Vajpayee had the beneficial effect of creating a relationship of trust and confidence with a large number of nations, especially our close neighbours like Nepal, Pakistan, Bangladesh and Sri Lanka.

With the re-establishment of the tilt towards the Soviet Union, through our vote in the UN, India's foreign policy has suffered a great blow. It is naive to say that we accept the Soviet assurance on troops withdrawal. Have they withdrawn from anywhere in the past?

Would this nation have accepted a assurance of that kind by Britain say in the Suez crisis of 1956? Or by the U.S. in regard to Vietnam? Our UN vote had the effect of our being isolated from our own neighbours. They had voted for the immediate and unconditional withdrawal of Soviet troops. The exchange of views between the government of India and the governments of Pakistan, Nepal, Sri Lanka and Bangladesh has very clearly brought out differences in perception of the Afghan crisis by India and her neighbours. These nations also perceive the Soviet presence in Afghanistan as a threat to their own security. If small nations can say so, what makes us perceive the crisis differently? ...

It has to be India's policy to keep Soviet boundaries far away from our northern borders. For this it is absolutely necessary to work towards the preservation of independence, sovereignty and non-alignment of Afghanistan and Pakistan. India's policy makers have to act as statement who think of the future generations, and not as politicians who only think of coming elections. We cannot afford to buy peace on a short term basis by ignoring the long-term implications to India's security.

Our policy has been neither appreciated by the Afghan people, nor by the present Afghan government, While the people wished for a forthright support for their liberation struggle, the government expected a more vigorous support to the Soviet action. J.D. Singh of the *Times of India* filed this report from Kabul : "The Government would have liked India to take a positive stand in favour of Kabul's known position that the Soviet army came to Afghanistan on an invitation to repel internal and external threats. The ordinary man in Kabul, on the other hand, is critical of India for adopting a pro-Moscow stand and not exercising pressure for the vacation of the Soviet occupation of his country. Even Soviet Foreign Minister Gromyko would have returned to his country with lesser disenchantment with Indian stand when he visited New Delhi in February, 1980 if he had known in advance, through our UN vote, that we support the demand for immediate and unconditional withdrawal of the Soviet troops from Afghanistan.

India's stand is likely to affect its role in the non-aligned movement. At the Havana Conference last year Mr. Castro made his best efforts to convince the non-aligned nations that the socialist bloc is "a natural ally" of the non-aligned nations. This has to be read with the Brezhnev doctrine of 'limited sovereignty' of nations aligned with it and the peace and friendship treaties several non-aligned nations have with the Soviet Union. Our stand in the UN is likely to indicate our acceptance of President Castro's line. Eventually, these efforts by semi-aligned nations might result in a vertical split in the non-aligned movement. Our policy of non-alignment has become extremely relevant with the return of the Cold War. To save the non-aligned movement India should take initiative to restore the non-aligned movement to the period of 50s and 60s when the definition of non-aligned was not diluted to permit bilateral military defence treaties with super powers. Non-alignment ought to mean absence of any special relationship especially with defence overtones with a super power either multilaterally or bilaterally.

Indian policy has gone against the consistent policy followed so far of seeking friendship of the Arab and Islamic world. This policy is aimed partly at neutralizing their support to Pakistan, and partly because of our dependence on Arab oil. There is of course the domestic factor of winning support of muslim minority. Islamic nations have shown their solidarity with the brave Afghan people and unequivocally called for the withdrawal of Soviet troops from Afghanistan. Though the government has made a cosmetic effort to please the Arab world by giving full diplomatic recognition to the PLO, our failure to join our voice with them in asking for withdrawal of Soviet troops from Afghanistan might result in the lessening of Arab goodwill for India.

We cannot afford the luxury of acquiescence in Soviet military intervention in Afghanistan as we did in Hungary or Czechoslovakia as the present Soviet action poses a clear and present danger to our security. In the past there was some justification for a tilt towards the Soviet Union, since undivided Pakistan aligned with the West could create and did create security problems for India. After the 1971 War Pakistan has been reduced to one fifth of India. Since 1979 she has also become a member of non-aligned movement. Pakistan should no longer be considered as a threat. In general, since the Soviet intervention in Afghanistan, Pakistanis have looked to India for support in their "hour of trial". This task is greatly facilitated now by Zia's rejection of American military aid. Indian assurance to Pakistan that India will not exploit the situation created by the presence of Soviet troops on her northern borders to its advantage should also contribute towards developing a joint approach.

What is then necessary even at this stage is an unequivocal call from India for unconditional and immediate withdrawal of Soviet troops from Afghanistan. This will create a unity of purpose among our neighbours in particular and the non-aligned nations in general to work in cohesion. Incidentally, such a declaration will also help us solve the only other threat to our national security, that is from Communist China. Since the process of normalization of relations with China was initiated by Mrs. Gandhi in 1976, it will be another step to convince China that we are not permanently aligned with the Soviet Union her arch foe.

With such a positive step, India ought to move influential powers in the UN to create a UN peace keeping force to be deployed on the Afghan-Pakistan and Afghan-Iran borders. The Soviet Union has made the Afghan rebel threat from Pakistani territories an *alibi* for the induction of troops in Afghanistan, conveniently forgetting the fact that it is the Soviet presence there since April 1978 and massive intervention since December 1979 that created the problem of Afghan rebels in the first instance. The people do not pull the trigger because a gun is given free in the absence of proper motivation. The creation of a UN force will provide a face-saving device to the Soviets to enable them to withdraw their troops and also enable the Afghan refugees to return to their homeland from Pakistan. If the U.S. and Soviet pressure along with world opinion was enough for the U.K. and France to withdraw their troops from Egypt after the creation of the UN peace keeping force in 1956, there is no reason why the combined pressure of the four permanent members of the UN (US, UK, France and China) and world opinion should not be effective in securing a withdrawal of Soviet troops from Afghanistan.

But our government so far has only been telling us that they are trying to 'defuse' the crisis. All recent visiting foreign dignitaries are also said to be appreciative of India's efforts to 'defuse' the crisis. Has Government of India really got hold of the fuse so that it can defuse? People of India have not been told how it is going to defuse the crisis. Until then the term 'defuse' will only mean an agonizing situation of helplessness. This was evident in the belated realization on the part of Government of India, when the External Affairs Minister told the Lok Sabha that the Soviet presence in Afghanistan would not be limited in time" as it was originally thought by the government.

With the other super power, the only issue that has been causing tensions is the nuclear policy of this country. This is one area where the policy of the present government is clear and in keeping with our national interest. During the Janata rule nuclear policy was most unclear. Mr. Desai initially was against all nuclear explosions, and considered the Pokhran experiment unnecessary. However, under the pressure of parliamentary opinion, he attempted to make a distinction between nuclear blasts and explosions and considered that blasts might be necessary for peaceful purposes but not explosions. In an interview with Barbara Walters of the ABC he had said that he would "never go in for nuclear weapons, even if the entire country is destroyed in their absence. But how are we going to manufacture nuclear weapons if we are destroyed?

The fact is no nation can foreclose all its options in international relations. The present government has made it clear that nuclear energy will be used only for peaceful purposes but if necessary nuclear explosions will be carried out. Here our nuclear policy conflicts with the present US policy of nuclear non-proliferation. But this nation has to do what is in its national interest, and what is in keeping with the changing policy of the US. In the 60s the US considered Communist China a security threat, hence, tacitly encouraged the countries on the periphery of China to develop strong security bases and did not openly pressurize them, including India, to desist from nuclear ambitions.

However, with the change in American perception of China, and developing an unwritten alliance between the two, the U.S. no longer feels such a need. It also means that India can no longer bank on an almost immediate support of the U.S. in the event of a Chinese nuclear threat to this country. This was the US policy in 1960s. Lyndon Johnson for instance had said soon after the first nuclear explosion by Communist China in October, 1964 that the U.S. is willing to "respond to request from the Asian nations to help in dealing with Communist China's aggression". With Communist China far ahead of us in nuclear technology and rapidly set to acquire a perfect delivery system by the 80s, we have to keep our option open on going nuclear.

Here we might be trapped by our own past rhetoric. We have been advocating a comprehensive test ban treaty. The super powers have already acquired over-kill capability with their high technology. If they feel in near future that it is no longer necessary for them to conduct any more underground nuclear tests, they may well agree on a comprehensive test ban treaty. This, if we are to accept, might result in freezing our nuclear know-how at the present level, reducing our nuclear know-how to a permanently low level of development.

These are the two most important challenges faced by Indian foreign policy makers. Firstly, military expansionism by the Soviet Union threatening dangerously to move closer to India's north-west borders. Secondly, the American efforts to reduce India to a position of permanent nuclear inferiority *vis-a-vis* the super powers. Hence, the need is for a clear policy to keep the Soviet borders farther away from Indian borders and a clear nuclear policy in national interest. To conclude, I may reiterate what I have said in the beginning. How we conduct our foreign policy and international relations will largely decide our future in the family of nations. Paraphrasing Karl Deutsch, I may say that if our civilization is going to be destroyed in the next fifty years, it will not be destroyed by famine or plague but failures in foreign policy and international relations.

The Radical Humanist, October 1980

Challenge before non-aligned

An important factor responsible for the birth of the non-aligned movement was the Cold War of the '50s. This was reflected in Pandit Nehru's statement that "India will follow an independent policy keeping away from the power politics of groups aligned one against another" However, in the '70s with the Super Power detente and the growing economic, if not military, power of West Germany and Japan, it was not inconceivable to assume that the world was once again moving towards multipolarity. In a multipolar world it could have been argued that non-alignment had become less relevant if not irrelevant.

But in the '80s once again Cold War has returned as though with a vengeance. It has in fact come next door with the Soviet invasion of Afghanistan an old member of the non-aligned movement. The Cold War and Super Power rivalry for expanding their respective spheres of infinence will be conducted in the '80s in the vast arena of the non-aligned nations across the underdeveloped world in Africa, Asia and South America, with this backdrop the conference of Foreign Ministers of non-aligned nations in session in New Delhi will have to review the challenge of the '80s from a longer-term perspective and find an answer to it instead of merely discussing current problems. The challenge needs to be viewed in the larger interest of the very survival of the non-aligned movement in the context of the need to preserve world peace and ensure economic development of the developing nations.

Today the non-aligned movement is facing the gravest crisis of preserving its unity. The nations under its unity wings are a heterogeneous group, consisting of members from different regional groups like the ASEAN, OAS, OAU and the Conference of Islamic Nations and diverse systems like democracy, communism and dictatorship. How externally difficult it is to achieve unity even on broad issues in even smaller groups is evident from the record of the conference of Islamic nations. The 40-nation conference in spite of being bound by the strong bond of religion, was divided like Shia and Sunni, between Iran and Iraq. The Marxist regime of Afghanistan was not invited and policy differences between Libya and Saudi Arabia kept the former out of the Taif conference. As for the non-aligned one can size up the problems faced by the movement if one puts together the differences within all the regional groupings.

Yet unity is not impossible on the broad principles and the direction the movement will take in future if certain steps in that direction are taken by general consensus. This can be done by once again Reiterating the fundamental principles of non-alignment. Firstly, the movement not withstanding differences of views on the form of government believes in the right of each nation to decide its stand on international issues on their respective merits. This forecloses the possibility of an advance leaning towards one bloc or the other. Hence, Cuba's advance of the socialistic bloc as "a natural ally" of the non-aligned has no place in the movement. Any such prior commitment to one or the other bloc will blur the vision of the non-aligned and prevent it from viewing the merits of a conflict with complete objectivity.

Secondly, the movement was originally a negative response to the military blocs led by the Super Powers. Any membership of the multi-lateral military bloc like the NATO or the Warsaw Pact, disqualified a nation from the membership of the non-aligned movement. However, in the '70s, with the detente, the Soviet Union has signed peace and friendship treaties with almost a dozen nations. While there cannot be any objection to simple bilateral treaties aimed at peace and friendship, such treaties with military provisions and/or overtones by a non-aligned nation amount to a dilution of the original principle of absence of military entanglement with one or the other Super Power.

Thus, for instance the Soviet invasion of Afghanistan is justified by the Soviets in terms of Article 4 of their peace and friendship treaty of December 1978 with Afghanistan which provides for the signatories to "consult each other and take by agreement appropriate measures to ensure the security, independence and territorial integrity." In effect, such bilateral treaties with the countries of a region are in no way different from the now discredited multilateral military pacts signed by the US, like the CENTO or SEATO. What the US did in aregion though multilateral pacts, the Soviet Union is trying to do bilaterally.

Thirdly, the non-aligned nations cannot be non-aligned as far as their internal disputes are concerned such as the one betwen Iran and Iraq. They should take initiative to resolve their conflicts among themselves. The longer these conflicts are allowed to go on, the greater would be the Super Power involvement in such conflicts. As it is, in the Iraq-Iran War, it is the Soviet and US weapons which clash, though they have so far maintained an apparent neutrality on the will and bold initiative, it should not be difficult for the non-aligned movement to resolve their conflicts peacefully.

Fourthly, the non-aligned nations are committed to the principle of non-interference in the internal affairs of any other nation. When such interfernce takes place, whether by a non-aligned or aligned nation or even the Super Powers themselves, it is the bounden duty of the non-aligned group to condemn such action. One cannot upload a principle by condoning a particular violation. As the Yugoslavian Ambassador in his address to Indian Council of World Affairs (Mumbai branch) rightly observed: "By justifying one intervention, we invite the other intervention and there will be no end to this vicious circle. Also nothing will remain of the principles." In this context, the non-aligned nations once again need to call upon the Soviet Union to withdraw their military presence from Afghanistan at once, and allow the people of that country to decide their own future.

Fifthly, the non-aligned nations have put utmost trust in the UN as a forum to resolve international conflicts and maintain world peace. It will not be an exaggeration to say that the existence of the UN has been the best guarantee of the independence of the small and weak nations. Today the non-aligned nations form the majority of this world organization. While they have shown a greater degree of willingness to resolve their conflicts through the UN than the major powers, they have to do something more than that in the present context, with the new found money power of some of the non-aligned nations, they help the UN overcome its perennial financial crisis. This will also make the world body less dependent on the Western powers for financial support as is the case now.

What can India, as founder of the movement and host of the current session, do to restore the credibility of the non-alignment movement and persuade the member-nations to go back to the original principles of non-alignment as propounded in the '50s? While India has not accepted Cuba's doctrine of socialistic bloc being "a natural ally" of the non-aligned movement, it has not done much also to oppose that pernicious doctrine. It was almost forced by the circumstances of the Bangladesh War to sign the peace and friendship treaty with the Soviet Union. It may very well try to seek a review of its military consultation clauses, if not an outright abrogation of the 1971 treaty in the near future.

On Afghanistan, India gone a long way from the original stand it took at the UN in January 1980 and its abstention from voting with the non-aligned nations on the resolution asking for immediate and unconditional withdrawal of the Soviet troops from Afghanistan. Indo-Soviet friendship should not come in the way of India telling the Soviet Union openly what it has already conveyed to it privately. It need not be inhibited by its own intervention in the West while East Pakistan on humanitarian grounds because India is the only country having militarily intervened to withdraw its troops almost immediately. The fact that the Soviets and the Vietnamese have not been confident of withdrawing their troops from Afghanistan and Kampuchea respectively amply proves that the regimes imposed by the intervening powers have no roots in the soil of their own country.

Hence, it will considerably enhance India's credibility in the non-aligned movement if it joins hands with the non-aligned countries assembled in New Delhi in demanding immediate and unconditional withdrawal of all foreign troops from Afghanistan and Kampuchea. The strength of friendship lies in telling frankly what vitally affects our interests. One need not fear that such bluntness will sour if the otherwise friendly relations with the Soviet Union. As for Vietnam, our having recognised the Kampuchean Government should in fact lend more strength and weight to the voice in demanding the withdrawals of troops.

The Free Press Journal, 9 February 1987

2

PROCESS OF MAKING OF FOREIGN POLICY: INDIAN & AMERICAN

National Security Adviser in the US: Exit of Richard Allen

Monday, 4th January 1982, was the first working day of the new year in the U. S. On that day, Mr. Richard Allen, President Reagan's National Security Adviser who was on a "voluntary leave of absence" was led to submit his involuntary resignation. This is the first time a National Security Adviser, since the creation of that office by President Eisenhower in 1953, has been forced to seek involuntary resignation owing to unfavourable circumstances. Eisenhower had four different National Security Advisers to serve him during his eight years in the White House. The first to hold that office was Robert Cutler, a Bostonian businessman. When he left the office in April 1955, he left it because he could not be away from his business for a long period. He, as a matter of fact, had another stint as the National Security Adviser, from January 1957 to July 1958, during the second term of Eisenhower. Two of the other three-Dillon Anderson (April 1955 to October 1956) and William Jackson (October 1956 to January 1957) also left for their own personal reasons. The third Gordon Gray, who became the National Security Adviser in July 1958, remained there till the end of the Eisenhower Administration in 1961.

In the succeeding Democratic Administrations of Kennedy and Johnson, and Republican Administrations of Nixon and Ford, two National Security Advisers McGeorge Bundy and Henry Kissinger - stayed beyond the term of their original masters. Thus, after the assassination of Kennedy in November 1963, Bundy continued to serve

Johnson until February 1966; Kissinger continued to serve as the National Security Adviser to President Ford after Nixon, disgraced by the Watergate scandal, resigned in 1974. Walt Rostow and Brent Scowcroff, were two other National Security Advisers, who served Johnson and Ford respectively till the end of their respective administrations. Only President Carter and his National Security Adviser, Brzezinski came and left the office together.

Growing Powers

The position of National Security Adviser was created by President Eisenhower, conceptually with a staff role. During his eight years in the White House, his four National Security Advisers functioned largely in that role, though there were occasional temptations to get into the role, of an adviser and advocate of foreign policy, which is traditionally a role of the Secretary of State.

Whenever the National Security Advisers volunteered their opinions too frequently and too vehemently, they were reminded of their role by President Eisenhower. As Dillon Anderson narrated his experience: "I became mindful early in the game that the only way I could be of continuing service to him was to keep out of an effort to suggest policy to him." But beginning from Bundy in the White House basement, the Nationl Security Adviser gradually has emerged as a competitor to the role of the Secretary of State, as the President's chief foreign policy formulator and adviser.

Dean Rusk, Kennedy's Secretary of State had in a sense of frustration, even expressed the futility of his being Secretary of State when Bundy was dominating the foreign policy-making process in the White House. By the time the Nixon administration was to be inaugurated in January 1969, the position had already become sufficiently powerful and a most coveted one. It was the number one choice of Henry Kissinger, when he was offered a position in his administration by Nixon. Kissinger of course, took the powers of his office to the pinnacle so as to be considered as the most powerful man in foreign affairs, next only to President Nixon. William Rogers, the Secretary of State, was a mute spectator of foreign policy events, in the development of which, he personally had no role. The Vietnam Peace negotiations were entirely conducted by Henry Kissinger, not Rogers; it was Kissinger and not his Secretary of State who accompanied Nixon in his historic meeting with Mao.

Critical

President Carter had promised to make foreign policy with the aid and advice of his Secretary of State, Cyrus Vance. As a matter of fact, he had been too critical of Henry Kissinger's role as the National Security Adviser under the Nixon Administration. Yet his National Security Adviser, Zbigniew Brzezinski, very soon after 1977, began to assert himself in foreign policy making. Though Vance was not Rogers in relation to his powerlessness in the formulation of foreign policy, he was equally frustrated. This finally led to his resignation over President Carter's abortive bid to rescue the American hostages from Teheran, with which Vance disagreed. The rescue plan was supported by Brzezinski, and Vance's resignation was widely interpreted as his defeat in the power struggle. Mr. Vance told the London Observer after his resignation, that the National Security Adviser "should not be the one who makes foreign policy (and) who expresses foreign policy to the public. That is the task of the President and the Secretary of State."

Powers Struggle

What made Allen leave the most coveted office? Apparently he was not sufficiently "prudent" in "not to accept the watch" one out of three watches gifted to him by his Japanese friends because it was received after he became the National Security Adviser. The charge against Allen by Indian standards, is a most trivial one, and even by American standards appears to be insignificant. However, he was cleared of any "wrong doing" in his failure to deposit, in the government treasury, a sum of $ 1,000 received from a Japanese women's magazine.

However, with the help of information available, it can be argued that the exit of Allen was a direct culmination of an intense power struggle that had developed between himself and the Secretary of State, Alexander, Haig, almost from the first day of the Reagan Administration. Even before Mr. Reagan had come out of his inaugural dress, Haig rushed to him with a detailed 15 page memorandum of his proposals on the formulation of foreign policy in which obviously, he provided for himself, an upperhand. Then came the question of who should chair the crisis management team in the White House. In the past, powerful National Security Advisers like Kissinger and Brzezinski have chaired this group. To ward off a possible conflict between the

Secretary of State and the National Security Adviser, President Reagan put the team under the chairmanship of Vice-President, George Bush. It was constitutionally and politically a much sounder arrangement then the previous ones. Yet, over this issue, Haig raised hell as he felt, the team should be headed by himself. He even threatened to resign. President Reagan, to pacify the wounded ego of his Secretary of State, had to issue a public statement, for the second time in less than two months, reiterating that Mr. Haig as the Secretary of State, enjoyed primacy in .formulating as well administering his foreign policy.

Dominant role

But Haig was not entirely off his fear of a possibility of the National Security Adviser, playing a dominant role from his vantage position in the White House. That the conflict between the National Security Adviser and the Secretary of State was an ongoing problem in the Reagan administration, can be shown from several instances. Suffice it for the purpose here, if I cite one instance. Haig saw to it that the US ambassador to Saudi Arabia, Mr. Robert G. Neumann, was forced to resign for his apparent indiscretion in privately saying, to the Chairman of Senate Foreign Relations Committee, that Mr. Haig has not been forceful in condemning Israeli air raids on Iraqi nuclear installations in June 1981, and that he has been too soft towards Israel. As the subsequent actions of Haig indicated, especially his strong support for the sale of AWACS to Saudis, the underlying reason for Neumann's sack was not his pro-Arab views, but Neumann's alleged action of having opened a secret link of communication directly with Mr. Allen in the White House. As a matter of fact, Neumann was a friend and a nominee of Allen. Having been unable to prevent the appointment of Mr. Neumann initially, Haig made use of the ambassador's private outbursts against him to get the ambassador's sack.

Mr. Allen settled the score even with Mr. Haig, later in September 1981, when a nominee of Haig, on Allen's National Security Council staff, Gen. Robert L. Schweitzer, was caught saying in an off-the-cuff speech to the Association of the United State Army, that "the Soviet's are on the move. They are going to strike." The very next day, he was removed from the National Security Council staff by Allen, and reassigned to the Pentagon. Allen was really motivated to get rid off Gen. Schweitzer any how, as the General was Haig's nominee on his staff. This is clear from the fact that another NSC staffer, Richard L. Pipes, had told a reporter that "detente is dead" and unless the Soviet-Union changed from the Communist model, war is inevitable. He was however, not removed by Allen, as he was his own man.

Power struggle

The power struggle between Haig and Allen, reached its climax when Haig told Washington's syndicated columnist, Jack Anderson in November last, that some top official in the White House was conducting a mind-bogging guerrilla campaign to discredit him. That he said, was coming in the way of his being very effective in the formulation of US foreign policy. Though, by all indications, he had Allen in his mind, he went on denying that he had either Allen or any other particular White House aide of the President in mind, when correspondents mentioned them by name. Hence, the press concluded that the top official behind Haig's all troubles, was not a single individual but a hydra headed monster.

The personal rivalry between the two became such a problem for a peace and leisure loving President Reagan-a characteristic common with Eisenhower - that he had to appeal to the good sense of patriotism of the American correspondents, since publishing such stories on the infights in his Administration, would only confuse the foreign governments and would be very destructive to US foreign policy. Such an appeal by the President, only revealed his sense of frustration and inability to restrain his own men in the Administration. Hence, when a thousand dollar opportunity arose, President Reagan grabbed it, and agreed to the removal of Richard Allen as the National Security Adviser, though Allen had been a close associate and foreign policy adviser during his election campaign in 1980.

Imaginary fears

Part of Haig's fears, on the possibility of his being overshadowed by the National Security Adviser, is his own imagination. President Reagan had planned to deemphasise the NSC staff and rely mainly on the Cabinet Secretaries in formulating the policies of his Administration, as done by Eisenhower. That has been true in practice, at least in relation to Richard Allen. He had been playing a secondary role in the formulation of foreign policy, and he was even accused by the President's other White House aides, of not being vigorous enough in presenting national security policies to the President. But Haig lived under the constant fears of the National Security Adviser overshadowing him in foreign policy making. With his long experience in the White House power operations, first as Kissinger's military assistant, then as the Deputy National Security Adviser and later during the crucial days of Watergate scandal as Nixon's Chief of White House staff, he knew that in any power struggle between the National Security Adviser and Secretary of State, it is the Secretary of State who finally loses the battle. He could not fail to forget the fate that fell on William Rogers and Cyrus Vance. Thus, he wanted to pre-empt any threat to his own position as the Secretary of State in the Reagan Administration. In this respect it is a unique victory to the Secretary of State in his power-struggle with the National Security Adviser in the Reagan Administration.

Controversies

Since the '60's the office of the National Security Adviser has been a centre of several conflicts and controversies within the US foreign affairs bureaucracy. President elect Kennedy was advised by Richard Neustadt, a consultant on his staff, to abolish the position of National Security Adviser, as no particular constituency in the country would raise its voice in its favour. Yet Kennedy thought it wise to retain the office. When Johnson had an opportunity to appoint a successor to Bundy in early 1966, he too consulted Clark Clifford, a senior Democrat and a former adviser to Truman and Kennedy, who also advised in favour of abolishing the office of the National Security Adviser. But Johnson wanted an intellectual in his office, and he had Walt W. Rostow, an academic expert of international affairs from MIT.

Future Trends

Where is President Reagan now heading in reorganising his foreign policy establishment? By appointing William P. Clark, a personally trusted aide, but a novice in national security affairs, as his National Security Adviser, Reagan has in one more respect followed the practice under the Eisenhower Administration. Like Eisenhower, Reagan has, in Clark's appointment, chosen a non-expert in international affairs as his National Security Adviser. Only Gordon Gray, amongst Eisenhower's four National Security Advisers had some academic and practical background in national security affairs. But since the

'60's, until the appointment of Mr. Clark in 1982, all National Security Advisers have been academic experts of international affairs.

However, Reagan's emphasis on formulation of policies through the aid and advice of Cabinet Secretaries, and his desire to deemphasise the role of the National Security Adviser as a foreign policy adviser and formulator, and retain him only as a staff assistant, who would prod the administration officials on behalf of the President, to do what they were expected to do, without trying to sell his own policy line on particular national security issues, might prove to be casualties in the new reorganised national security set-up. Because, the President has given new powers to Mr. Clark as his National Adviser, which were denied earlier to Mr. Allen. He will now brief the President every day on national security affairs, deal directly with the President, Secretary of State, Secretary of Defence and the CIA Director. He "will be responsible for the development, co-ordination and implementation of the national Security policy. "

Mr. Clark, before moving over to the White House basement as the National Security Adviser, was Deputy Secretary of State-the second highest official in the State Department. Though, he and Haig got very well with one another, Clark was initially placed in that position by President Reagan to keep a watch on Haig, who did not belong to the group of Presidential intimates. How long the cordial relations, developed between Haig and Clark while they were in the State Department, would serve them well to avoid rivalry and conflicts which troubled Haig-Allen relations ? Given the President's confidence, with enhanced powers Clarks might soon turn out to be a formidable challenger to Haig's constant efforts, to preserve and protect his supremacy in foreign policy making. In that event, his victory-over Allen in the bureaucratic power struggle, might prove to be only a pyrrhic victory.

The Mahratta, 1 March 1982

The Sikh Extremists in the US: Need for Effective Lobbying

As reported in India newspapers, a briefing was held on 11th April, 1985 under the aegis of the Congressional Human Rights Caucus, Human Rights Internet, a Washington based organization, and at least two other groups on, "Human Rights in India : Solutions to the Sikh Problem". It was obviously organized at the persistent lobbying by the Sikh protagonists of so-called Khalistan. This one briefing where a handful of Sikh extremists were able to provide their arguments on violations of human rights in India upset Indian Parliament and the general public opinion. The newspapers have blown it out of proportion. It is evident from some of the headlines given to this news item by *The Times of India.* For instance, it said "U.S. Sikh meet upsets India" (April 17); and "Anti-India lobby wins over U.S. Congress" (April 19). The issue also figured in the Lok Sabha on April 18th When the Deputy Speaker, Mr. Thambi Durai described the briefing as an "interference" in our "internal affairs". Again, *The Times of India* wrote an editorial, "Justified Furore" (April 22), commenting on the discussion in the Lok Sabha.

One must not hesitate to condemn the activities of the Sikh extremists in the U.S. However, the comments made on the briefing so far in the press do not indicate an understanding of two important points. First, an unique feature of American system of government wherein lobbies have direct access to the Law-makers which enabled those extremists to work and succeed in organizing such a briefing in the U.S. Second, our own failure, to meet the challenge of lobbying by the Sikh extremists by positive counter-lobbying. But before I discuss these two points, an objective analysis of when such a briefing constitutes an interference in our internal affairs is necessary.

As a matter of fact today no longer the old division between internal affairs and external affairs holds good. There is in reality only national policy. Bayless Manning some years ago said that international policy and domestic policy have merged into Intermestic policy. In the context of existence of an ethnic or national minority in more than one nation, any of our policy in relation to that minority can and will become a foreign policy problem for another nation. The U.S. has not seen, so far, any racial riots against the people of Indian origin. But Britain has witnessed such race riots more than once. Whenever they have occurred in Britain, for instance, the people of Indian origin have looked to India for help.

In a narrow legal sense, since most of the people of Indian origin affected by racial riots in Britain are British citizens the race riots are strictly an internal matter for Britain. But there are two reasons why India always speaks on behalf of them. First, blood is thicker than the law, and we express our concern at any assault on people of Indian origin anywhere in the world because, we are genuinely concerned about them. Second, affected people have their kith and kin in one or the other states in the Indian Union and these people pressurize government to speak and act to protect people of Indian origin in foreign countries. A democratically elected government cannot ignore such pressures. After all, they are concerned to retain the support of all sections of the electorate.

Thus, when British citizens of Indian Origin, including Sikhs were attacked by the Whites in U.K. in July 1981 there was a furore in this country and naturally the Parliament then too was equally upset. Mrs. Indira Gandhi had deputed Mr. Darbara Singh, the then Chief Minister of Punjab to study race riots against the Indians settled in U.K. and also speak to the British government on their behalf. Mr. Singh was chosen because, amongst the people affected by the race riots most were the Sikhs and Punjabis in Southhall. If today, ethnic riots in Sri Lanka create a domestic stir in Tamil Nadu, in 1981 riots in U.K. created a similar stir in Punjab and elsewhere in the north. If this was not an interference in British internal affairs, how could a desire by some British MPs to visit Punjab be deemed as interference in our internal affairs ? Yet the government of India in 1984 after the Operation Bluestar, refused such a request from the British. The British MPs who wanted to visit India were those who had sizable Sikh population in their constituencies, and now in a reverse situation, British MPs were under the pressure of Sikh voters settled in the U.K.

Hence, the inevitable conclusion is: whenever it is in our interest we do not deem it as interference; but whenever it hurts our national ego or national interest we deem it as interference in our internal affairs. This is a universal reality. All nations adhere to non-interference in others' internal affairs as a cardinal principle of international affairs, only so long as it is convenient to them. Whenever, the national interest demand it, nations do not hesitate to interfere in others' internal affairs.

Now, in the context of the U.S., whenever the U.S. government has discussed foreign aid to India the U.S. Congressional Committees and the Congress have discussed the internal conditions in India, That, strictly speaking, constitutes interference in our internal affairs. Now the Sikhs in the U.S. constitute about one-third of half a million strong Indian community. In some Congressional districts in the U.S. they are influential as voters as well a contributors to the campaign funds to the Congressmen. And as organized groups they do try to influence Congressmen on behalf of the causes they think are important to them.

So, reverting to our first point, that in the U.S. there are several thousand groups working for different causes relating to issues from abortion to Zoo in domestic affairs, and Albania to Zambia in international affairs. In recent years existence of single-issue groups lobbying for a particular cause like human rights, nuclear policy, Non-proliferation or liberation or freedom of some distant land is quite well known. The American government works through a system wherein basically disconnected official, semi-official and unofficial groups work to push one or the other policy for the acceptance by Congress and or the Executive Branch, by forming temporary coalitions. Lobbying is an inseparable part of American system of government. The Congressional groups on different policies lobby for their causes often in league with similar groups outside. Even the White House lobbies for a policy when it has been decided, but needs the acceptance by Congress.

Hence, at no time a policy can either be rejected as unofficial or accepted as official until it is accepted by both the branches of the government and implemented. Because, even at the stage of implementation a policy may be frustrated by some affected groups by lobbying for non-implementation. Sometimes they do succeed. Early in his administration, Kennedy had decided to withdraw Jupiter Missiles from Turkey as they had become obsolete. But Turkish government lobbied with the state department for their retention and they were there to cause some embarrasment to Kennedy while dealing with the Cuban Missile crisis in October 1962.

In this background, if India as nation wants literally to sell its policy preferences, to the U.S. government, it has to lobby effectively for a decision favourable to our interests. This aspect is generally overlooked by the Indian government. Lobbying need not be a dirty word. As individuals lobby for their own interests, we as a nation collectively ought to lobby for our national interest. But we simply do not think of doing any positive lobbying. Whatever little we do only as a reactive and defensive response to a development in the U.S. in a mood of injured ego. This is because we as a people have an inflated ego of being a virtuous people. Since we think our problems are so clear to us, they ought to be equally clear to others as well. Then without trying to explain our policies whenever we find others not accepting our stand, we feel hurt. When without our efforts we feel others have accepted our point of view, we feel as though our virtue has been rewarded.

Thus, it is well known to us, that only a handful of Sikhs in the U.S. are sympathetic to the Extremists' cause. Sitting in the library of Indian Embassy I have watched at least twice during the period often months in 1982 and 1983 that not more than seven or eight people— that include men, women and children— used to be in protest marches at the Indian Embassy. The number of American policemen regulating protesters used to be larger than the protesters themselves! Yet, there is a great sense of relief in the reporting of Mr. J.N. Parimoo when he writes that for the first time the U.S. administration accepted the fact (as they did after the FBI revealed a plot to assassinate Mr. Rajiv Gandhi) that only a small minority of Sikh community in the U.S. backs the demand for so-called Khalistan *(The Times of India,* May 15).

What can be done to counter the lobbying by the Sikh extremists in the U.S.? To be effective, India should volunteer to provide information to any one who wants to know the real situation in relation to the Sikh problems in India. It is unfortunate but true that our Embassy in Washington is generally unimaginative in handling such requests for information. Sometimes lame excuses are advanced for not providing even routine information such as the absence of librarian. It has to be the function of the Embassy to identify the Congressmen and the Senators who are sympathetic to India and provide them with accurate information. They need to do so even with those who are not favourably inclined towards India. The lobbyists for India, not merely the Embassy officials, should try to meet different groups and explain to them how unrealistic is the demand for the Khalistan. Instead, it is reported that the Embassy did not even care to acknowledge let alone respond to the letter, Mr. Robert Mrazek wrote on behalf of 17 influencial Congressmen on March 25, calling for an inquiry into the Delhi riots. Similar lack of information is felt by Congressmen on Indian stand on the ethnic riots in Sri Lanka.

The Government should also send non-officials like journalists, academics, and other social and political leaders to the U.S. to explain the situation in India. A large number of Indians visit U.S. for academic, or business activities without any direct government sponsorship. The Indian Embassy rarely uses them for any public lecturing or group meetings. Such visitors could be used by the Government of India, for speaking assignments at different cities in the U.S. to explain Indian policies in general and not only regarding the Sikh problem.

Another effective step that needs to be taken is to encourage Indian residents in the U.S. to lobby on behalf of their nation. Prime Minister Rajiv Gandhi recently compared non-resident Indians to an asset in the Bank which could be used whenever the need arises. It is true only in a limited sense—to the extent the Government secures millions of dollars through their remittances. But Indian residents in the U.S. are not yet a cohesive group to act as an India lobby. The Government of India has not encouraged the associations of Indian residents in the U.S. to act as an effective lobby for Indian causes. They are, as at home, divided on linguistic and regional lines. When they meet they are either Punjabis or Maharashtrians or Asians but not Indians! The need for and lack of lobbying by Americans of Indian origin can be established by citing at least three instances. Last year, President Reagan's Assistant for Ethnic affairs urged Indians gathered at a Conference in Washington D.C. to be organized and take active role in politics so that they can be effective. Second, Stephen Solarz, the Chairman of an influential House Sub-Committee on Asian and Pacific affairs said in the context of supplying F 16 to Pakistan in 1981 that while Pakistanis effectively lobbied, Indians were not at all effective. Third, a Professor of South Asian affairs, told me with a sense of exasperation that Indians and the Indian Embassy do not effectively lobby at all before a foreign policy decision affecting India is made. They begin to work on it only *after* the decision is announced.

Thus, the need of the hour in this particular case of Sikh extremist activities in the U.S. is to conduct a sustained campaign to explain the real issues involved rather than pretend the non-existence of a problem in Punjab and protest loudly whenever some people succeed through lobbying to organize a partisan briefing on it. That is true of any other issue in which vital interests of India are involved.

The Radical Humanist, September 1985

Foreign Policy Formulation: Need for Open Discussion

I would like to take you to a discussion on foreign policy—an area which has not been so far discussed. It is a difficult task to discuss in ten minutes the achievements or failures of foreign policy in 40 years.

Nehru had a great responsibility in developing both the structure and the substance of India's foreign policy. When India became free in 1947 we had already what was known as the steel frame in the form of ICS to conduct the domestic affairs, but nothing of the sort was left in the foreign affairs or in diplomacy. So Nehru single-handedly had to build from the scratch the entire mechanism for conducting foreign affairs, and also pursue the policy of non-alignment. But Nehru as both Prime Minister and the Minister for Foreign Affairs had exhibited two streaks. He was quite often an idealist but occasionally he was also a realist. Speaking in 1954 in Parliament as a realist, Nehru said, if everything went right in the next forty years, India would emerge as the fourth major power in the world, next only to the United States, the Soviet Union and China. So, a brief question can be asked, to what extent are we nearer to that aspiration ?

Now, Nehru also had the idealistic streak, and which more often dominated his thinking. It seems to me that this idealist streak often came in the way of moving into this goal faster and clear enough. I can't go into the details. But in the mid-50's relying more on non-violence and considering the high principles of non-violence and non-interference as a substitute for building the power of India Nehru learned a hard lesson in the Chinese aggression of October 1962, because he had forgotten India's geophysical compulsions.

But when Mrs Gandhi came to power she appeared to realize these compulsions. She was one person who really realized the role of power in the international affairs and she demonstrated India's ability to understand the geophysical reality during the 1971 war. But in the process, Mrs Gandhi, so to say, saw to it that India's all eggs were put into one basket.

India is today reliant on the Soviet Union in the defence area up to 70% of our requirements. I am putting it on the lower side. Many scholars have said, up to 80%. But the point is that today we have practically lost our position in managing our international affairs in our own best interest. It has been said long ago that there are no permanent enemies or permanent friends; there are only permanent interests. We find that in the international relations our prestige today is not very high. Of course, this view will not be shared by all. In some Soviet bloc countries our achievements and performance may be lauded. But in general even among our own neighbours we are not taken seriously.

Look at our present policy towards Afghanistan. I don't want to go into details. Now when the Government of India makes the effort for the first time to talk to King Zahir Shah publicly, the policy of India is not taken seriously because the Soviet Union has already stated its policies clearly. Neither Pakistan nor Afghanistan seems to be taking India's efforts seriously. This does not mean that we should not be friendly to the Soviet Union. But there is the need to diversify our reliance in the defence field. It was to Mrs Gandhi's credit that she realized this need when she came back to power in 1980 and did take several steps to diversify our reliance on foreign powers. Putting all eggs into one basket does not take much time. But taking them out carefully takes some time. Now the present Government, in my own opinion, tries to diversify, but again here I would refer to what Mr Pal said earlier : our bureaucracy, foreign service bureaucracy which has complete hold over the functioning of the policy-makers does not want India to have a change in India's foreign policy.

I want also to touch upon another important question. Our friendship with the Soviet Union for external compulsions should not be mixed with the functioning of our democracy. In other words, as a democracy we should be clear in our minds as to whether we would like to have the system similar to the Soviet one in our country or we would like a multi-party or two-party system to function as it is now. We have to take care to see that our excessive reliance on the Soviet Union does not influence our domestic policies.

Therefore, in the background I would touch on two important areas where we need to change our thinking so as to be effective in foreign affairs. One very important thing that should be done after forty years is to see that members of Parliament take some interest in foreign affairs. In every country foreign affairs is not a forte of elected representatives. They just defer to the wishes of the few in the executive branch who control foreign policy and therefore, there is an elite management of, foreign policy guided solely by the foreign service bureaucracy. We need therefore, to constitute a foreign affairs committee and a defence committee in Parliament just as we have a Public Accounts Committee or the Estimates Committee.

Mr. Sathe also refers to the need to question. I would fully share his opinion. Here I would like to point out that in 1987 during the discussion on Defence Budget in Parliament one member on the Opposition side asked the question, "Why should we have such a huge defence expenditure" ? The response from the Prime Minister was, "Any one who questions the defence expenditure is anti-national."

Now this is not the spirit in which a foreign policy should be conducted. The foreign policy, like the domestic policy, must be open to discussion and it should be shaped after thorough discussion and criticism. We act first and then try to discuss. That could, to some extent, be checked by having a committee system, which could also function as group within Parliament trained to understand and manage foreign affairs.

The second important thing I like to mention is on the executive side. There is a great need for a policy-planning council on foreign affairs. This policy-planning council should legally be formed by Parliament. It is not to be left to the sweet will of the Prime Minister to contribute a policy-planning council as was done in 1986 only to be disbanded in 1987 when it didn't suit him.

We need to have a body where outside experts would interact with the inside bureaucrats on policies, so that correct policies are evolved based on the discussion weighing pros and cons to the best of our abilities. This body can properly advise the policy-makers. I would also suggest that the policy-makers' exclusive reliance on the foreign service bureaucracy has to be curtailed. We need some sort of a system whereby some outsiders are taken into the policy-making process on a short-term basis. This is called in-and-outer system in foreign countries. Of course, in our system when people go in they do not like to come out. But we have to have a system whereby the policy-makers can bring in their own confidants as advisers in different issues, and with the policy-maker going out the advisers will also go out.

Take the example of the Sri Lanka policy. How much has been discussed ? Has it been discussed in the Cabinet ? Had it been analysed thoroughly before India decided to send the troops into that country ? What are the advantages ? The more you discuss the Sri Lankan policy the more I find that we have completely messed up the policy by ourselves signing the agreement and not making the LTTE or the Tamil militants sign. There are in it such areas where one can go on discussing. These two or three suggestions I have made should help to develop better policy options in foreign affairs.

Parlance, Freedom 40 (IV), May 1988

For Your Eyes Only

The foreign policy-making process is far more overshadowed by the concept of secrecy than the domestic policy-making process.

Foreign policy-making involves the protection of national security and all vital decisions relating to foreign policy involve the consideration of secret information. Thus, divulging of information to the legislature or to the public would enable the State or States in relation to which the foreign policy is made to be forewarned, thus, affecting national security. Thus, for instance, speaking in the Rajya Sabha, the minister of state for defence production, Shivraj Patil, stated on December 1, 1981, that in view of induction of F-16s by Pakistan, India has been 'acting swiftly and in a planned manner'. He could not, however, disclose the specific measures proposed to be taken in the interest of national security.

Thus, information relating to, say, manufacturing of an additional submarine would constitute secret information and the executive claim that it cannot be shared with the legislature is always accepted by the legislature. If the legislature insists on the information in rare cases, the executive comes up with several reasons for denying the information. Often, for instance, the executive branch has argued that legislatures have not developed any methods of guarding such secrets, which might be entrusted to them. In the US, India and in other democracies, often executives have used this argument to deny information to the members of legislatures. The Canadian government 'has consistently acted as though it was frightened of Parliament and MPs...were naughty little boys who could not be trusted with serious issues like security.'

In reality, legislatures have been extra cautious in guarding national security related secrets. This has been testified by the former CIA director, Allen Dulles, when he recorded:

'It is also often said that Congress can't keep a secret. Past history belies this... From almost ten years of experience in dealing with the Congress I have found... that secrets can be kept... In fact, I do not know of a single case of indiscretion that has resulted from telling those (congressional) committees the most intimate details of CIA activities...' In reality, the vital information in relation to a nation's security-preparedness, for instance, is known to its neighbours or others from whom it may want to keep it a secret. This is because of the modern development of the use of satellites in gathering information. If India moves troops closer to Pakistan's borders, Pakistan's intelligence agencies would know it. But it will still be kept a secret from the Indian Parliament under the pretext of national security. All nations do keep national security related information a secret from their own law-makers, even if they are unable to keep it a secret from other nations.

Foreign policy-making also involves negotiations with foreign governments and each step in negotiations cannot be publicly discussed as it would effect delicate positions taken in the bargaining process by representatives of different States. Any public discussion, through Parliament or the media on the complex issues, it is argued would only complicate the process of finding a solution, since the public is ill-informed and their opinion is likely to be charged with emotions.

The secrecy in the making of foreign policy often enables the policy-makers to effectively limit the participation in the process to a few top men within the executive branch. In Mrs Gandhi's cabinet, ministers of foreign affairs were replaced with great ease without effecting the continuity of foreign policy-making, since foreign policy was effectively made by the prime minister with the help of her trusted advisers like P N Haskar (1971-1973), D P Dhar (1971-1977) and others from time to time. So, the change of foreign ministers did not affect the continuity in foreign policy. During the brief Janata rule (1977-79) some members of the Lok Sabha said that foreign policy was made by Morarji Desai with the help of Jagat Mehta (then foreign secretary), A B Vajpayee (minister of External Affairs) was only a translator of policies in Hindi. Mrs Gandhi, in her second tenure as the prime minister (1980-1984), came to rely on G. Parthasarathi, who was not technically part of the prime minister's secretariat (until he was made the chairman of the policy planning committee in the ministry of external affairs with cabinet rank), and her principal private secretary, PC Alexander, in making crucial foreign policy. But it can be said that in a parliamentary system, because of collective responsibility, a foreign minister has a greater say than his counterpart in the presidential system.

President Johnson formulated foreign policy at Tuesday luncheon meetings; the main participants were only four— who came to be referred to as the 'Awesome Foursome'. He even picked up bombing targets in these meetings. Many sub-cabinet officials complained of learning foreign policy decisions through newspaper coverage of the day's developments. Nixon effectively conducted foreign policy within the White House, mainly with the help of Kissinger and a few of his staff members. Nixon's foreign policy-making process has been rightly called the 'Royal Court' model in which King Richard was advised by Noble Kissinger. Thus, secrecy enables the top executives to centralise powers in their own hands. This is done within the executive branch by restricting the information to a few on the need-to-know basis. The secrecy operates within the executive branch through a classification system like 'sensitive', 'top secret', 'secret', 'confidential', 'eyes only', etc.

However, secrecy in foreign policy-making is not merely an American phenomenon, but is found all over the world. As a matter of fact, Americans are less successful in covering their foreign policy-making in total secrecy than their counterparts, say, in the UK or in India. In India even the instructions regarding the use of classification of 'secret' and 'top secret', by the officials in the government departments, is kept a secret from the members of Parliament. After the spy scandal of 1985, then home minister, S B Chavan, said in the council of states (Rajya Sabha) that fresh instructions have been issued on the use of 'secret' and 'top secret' classification. But he could not disclose those instructions in the 'national interest'.

However, the problem is that when classification is indiscriminatingly used to deny information, there is the possibility of the real keepers of secrets being lax in their jobs. If too many pieces of information are classified, naturally too many will have to handle the papers, lowering the secrecy of really vital information. Thus William H Webster, director, FBI, said: "If you have too much that is classified and too many people that have clearance to see that information... there is a tendency to lower your threshold of sensitivity." Such a situation, instead of leading to guarding of secrets, only encourages more international spying and a greater tendency on the part of the bureaucrats to leak the information to outsiders.

In the UK and India, there is a tight control over the information through the Official Secrets Act, under which an official, privy to any secret information, can be prosecuted if he divulges it subsequently even after his retirement.

Secrecy has also been used by the executive to deny information to the legislature. Such denials of information are justified on the grounds of 'national interest' or 'national security'. In India a spy scandal involving government officials at the prime minister's secretariat, defence and the President's office, was unearthed in January 1985. It was alleged that some foreign powers are receiving sensitive information about India's defence planning, nuclear programme among others. When the members of the Rajya Sabha insisted on knowing the identity of the foreign powers, then minister for home affairs, S B Chavan said: "A particular officer attached to a particular foreign mission has been asked to leave at the instance of the Government of India. It will not be in the national interest to disclose his identity as that will hamper investigations and affect relations with a foreign power." Then it becomes a delicate issue to be challenged by the members of the legislature. Any member of the legislature insisting on knowing the details of foreign policy decision-making is likely to fear being branded as unpatriotic. If some members of the legislature do insist on knowing more about foreign policy-making the executive has in recent times made use of the executive privilege to deny information to the legislature.

Executive privilege may be defined as a constitutional claim of the executive to deny information to the other two branches of the government. The use of executive privilege to deny information is typical of the American government. This is because there is no equivalent of the Official Secrets Act in the US. But even in nations where the official acts exist, like India and the UK, occasionally, they do use the concepts of executive privilege or executive prerogative to deny information to the legislature. During the Janata regime in India, there was a controversy about the misuse of the prime minister's position by his son. Some correspondence was exchanged between the Home Minister Charan Singh and the Prime Minister Morarji Desai. When the opposition in the Parliament insisted upon the placing of correspondence on the table of the house, Desai refused to do so claiming the correspondence was a 'privileged document'.

In the US executive privilege has also been used by the top foreign policy-makers to refuse to appear before the Committees of Congress. Thus for instance, participating in the debates over the Dominican crisis of 1965, Senator Joseph Clark, then a senior member of the senate foreign relations committee said:

'The witness who I think should have been called was McGeorge Bundy...Mr Bundy (then national security adviser to President Johnson), in what I consider to be a disregard of the relevant precedents, took refuge in executive privilege and refused to appear before the committee. At one point he said he would come and have tea with us, but then he refused even to do that'.

Bundy was a member of the White House staff who often claimed the protection of executive privilege. But the other officials like the Secretary of State and Secretary of Defence have also refused to share information by appearing before the congressional committees.

In spite of the use of all these methods, if members of the legislature insist on knowing the details of information, the members can be given partial or deceptive information by the executive and the legislature will will at least, for the time being, have no means to double check the domestic information. Thus for instance during the Falklands war, the British navy sank an Argentine cruiser, *General Belgrano*, on May 2, 1982, drowning more than 370 soldiers. This, at that time, helped British foreign policy-makers effectively to kill the Peruvian peace plan, and continue the war. When the issue subsequently figured in the House of Commons, the government justified the sinking of the cruiser by stating that it was menacingly close to the British task force. Hence, in self-defence the cruiser was sunk. It was in fact, completely misleading information given to Parliament, as the later reports showed. As a matter of fact at the time the British navy attacked it, it was moving away from the task force and moving towards the Argentine Coast.

The Illustrated Weekly, 22-28 April 1990

Need for developing foreign policy expertise

For long, the scholars and politicians alike have made a distinction between domestic politics and international politics. They thought that international politics or international relations is too specialised beyond their comprehension hence could best be left to be managed by specialists in the Foreign Ministry. If that is the attitude of the leaders of the society, the general public has always a narrow concern for their immediate problems of economic survival and progress. They are ill-informed and cannot see anything beyond their immediate bread and butter concerns.

This attitude of the general public was well stated by George Jeger, a British MP, who himself had widely travelled abroad and was well-informed on international politics, when he said that his own constituents desired that he take up in the House of Commons the question of a bus shelter which is only a local problem than speak on foreign policy. They told him "that any fool can speak on foreign affairs and no doubt several would" but none of their bus shelter.

Needless to say that in the second half of the 20th century and as we enter the 21st century, international politics is assuming crucial importance. Let me mention briefly only two reasons for this. First, the nations are today armed with nuclear weapons and are able to destroy humankind and usher in nuclear winter. The two super-powers possess the ability to kill each other and the rest, not once but over 33 times. In addition to five nuclear weapons states, at least 20 others have the know-how to develop nuclear weapons and make the world an extremely dangerous one to live. Second, nations big and small, are extremely interdependent for their economic survival and progress as never before. Hence, President Kennedy was only understating the importance of international politics when he said that a mistake in domestic affairs would cost a few lives; but a mistake in foreign affairs could destroy the whole nation. Another scholar, Karl Deutsch has rightly pointed out that in the next 50 years or so if civilisation is going to be destroyed, it will not be destroyed by famine or plague, but by failures of nations in international affairs. Hence, there is a need to develop an awareness of importance of international affairs.

An awareness of importance of international politics can only be created through sustained programme of teaching of international politics at undergraduate and postgraduate levels in the universities. Are the intellectuals and academic policy-makers aware of this vital importance of international politics? During my visit to a University in California, I had extensive discussions with the Chairman of a Political Science Department. He confessed that he did not know much about foreign policy or international politics, as he specialised in municipal administration and local bodies. His preference for local government for specialised study is understandable as he was, stricken by polio since the age of four and naturally his physical handicap prevented him from studying international politics which involves foreign travel.

However, in India even today there are large number of intellectuals who suffer from mental handicap whenever they are required to think of role and importance of international politics. They may not be able to distinguish Iran from Iraq or Pakistan from Afghanistan, but when it comes to a trip abroad the very same intellectuals are the first ones to aspire to go 'foreign'. Our politicians are not different in this respect. For instance, in 1980, a group of legislators was to visit the US during the elections. In a reception arranged in their honour, a video tape of Carter-Reagan 'debate was shown. A legislator, in a low voice pointing to Carter, asked me: "Who is he?" However, when it comes to question of study of international politics in Indian universities a large number of our intellectuals point out that we have got a vast scope to study Panchayati Raj and Indian politics, before we rush to introduce any serious study of international politics. They are ably supported by our politicians. They say resources are scarce and we need to concentrate them on the study of our neighbourhood than on what happens in the relations of nations. Together they have succeeded in practising apartheid of international politics in academic institutions.

Forty-two years after independence, can we, as a nation, afford to continue to cherish and strengthen our narrow attitude and mental handicap towards international politics? Soon after independence, India faced enormous problems of law and order, communalism and economic reconstructions. Yet, Pandit Jawaharlal Nehru, our first prime Minister carved out a niche for India by founding a genuinely native concept of non-alignment. His involvement in international affairs some times made even his close friends to feel that Nehru ignored domestic affairs. This is the impression Maulana Abul Kalam Azad creates in his book, *India wins Freedom.*

For long mass illiteracy and economic backwardness helped to keep even the educated class of the society ignorant of international affairs of our country. No longer we can afford to do so. India has emerged as a pre-eminent power in South Asia and poised to emerge as a major power before the turn of this century. Hence, various facts of international affairs need to be studied and understood as widely as possible.

This need is based on three practical considerations. First, the wall between the domestic policy and foreign policy of a nation is breaking down, if it has not already broken down. Today, there is international elements even in local political issues like schemes of water supply to the city of Mumbai because of the World Bank involvement. Can we neatly categorise either as international or local, a study of impact of the World Bank loan on the working of the Mumbai Municipal Corporation? Bylass Manning, a distinguished professor of MIT, says that there is only one policy which he calls an 'itermestic policy' . In my own forthcoming book on *Foreign policy-making and International Politics* (Radiant Publishers, New Delhi), I have argued that there are no two-policies 'domestic' and 'foreign' but only one national policy. In policy issue there may be more of domestic elements, while in another policy issue, there may be a greater component of foreign policy. The study of international affairs then becomes as important as the study of domestic affairs.

Second, India as an emerging major power will need increased, trained and efficient manpower to manage her international affairs. Today, existing Indian Foreign Service is unable to find enough competent and trained people. Third, as India's role in international affairs increases, Indian democracy needs alert and informed public who can act to check abuses of power, if any, by Indian policy-makers. It must be remembered that most cases of abuse of political power, have their origin in international affairs.

In this background it is heartening to note that the U.G.C since the mid-1980s has begun to give importance to study of international affairs. The U.G.C. Committee on Defence and Strategic Studies has recommended introduction of national security as a paper for study at the undergraduate and postgraduate levels.

The U.G.C. is also strengthening some of the existing departments of political science by providing them assistance.

Free Press Journal, 18 August 1990

Turmoil and Triumph

President John F. Kennedy used to tell his aides that a mistake in domestic policy would cost a few lives, but a mistake in foreign policy could cost the survival of the entire world. The same thought was expressed by the eminent Harvard political scientist, Karl W. Deutsch, when he wrote: "If civilization is killed within the next 30 years, it will not be killed by famine or plague but by foreign policy and international relations."

The fountainhead of American foreign policy is the President. President Richard M. Nixon once said: "I've always thought this country could run itself domestically—without a President; all you need is a competent Cabinet to run the country at home. You need a President for foreign policy; no Secretary of State is really important: the President makes foreign policy." Nixon's assertion could of course have been based on his personal interest, practical experience, and involvement in foreign affairs. But even Ronald Reagan, who came to the White House primarily on a domestic policy agenda, said: "Foreign policy comes from the Oval Office and with the help of a fine Secretary of State."

After an uneasy 18-months relationship with Secretary Alexander M. Haig. Jr., President Reagan replaced him with George P. Shultz for the remaining six-and-a-half years of his presidency. In his memoirs, *Turmoil and Triumph: My Years as Secretary of State* (Charles Scribner's Sons, New York, 1993), Shultz lucidly discusses the world-shaking events that took place during his tenure and his role in those events.

But before we turn to these important events, it is perhaps relevant to explain the "institutional tensions" that forced Haig from office. Shultz writes: "I had heard and read that Haig's resignation was the result of clashes with the White House staff over both style and substance. He wanted to run things himself, but others wanted in—including Ronald Reagan. Haig's bristling manner did not suit the Meese-Baker-Deaver circle, and bureaucratic turf battles were constantly being waged between the White House and the State Department."

Shultz's own role-perception as Secretary of State contrasted with that of Haig. He knew that Haig's "instinct for command had apparently generated many of his problems." For his part, he was willing to "project confidence without arrogance, to be my own man while supporting the President, to speak candidly and substantively without presuming expertise where my background was scanty." He considered "public service as something special, more an opportunity and a privilege than an obligation." He had served in cabinet positions earlier in the Nixon Administration.

The events covered by Shultz's memoirs are indicative of the global reach of American foreign policy. From the beginning, Secretary Shultz had to deal with crisis like the Israeli intervention in Lebanon, the shifting of the PLO headquarters from Lebanon to Tunisia, the Siberian Pipeline dispute with the West European allies, and the Iran-Iraq War, to mention only a few. They all demanded attention and skillful handling.

What stands out as the most significant accomplishment in the management of international relations by Shultz is best expressed in the words of one of the book's chapters, "Realistic Re-engagement with the Soviets." President Reagan initially had refused to hold any summit meeting with the Soviet leaders. In retrospect, it was justified in view of the quick turnover in the Kremlin leadership. Reagan saw in a little more than four years three Soviet leaders die in office—Leonid Brezhnev, Yuri Andropov, and Konstantin Chernenko—before young and dynamic Mikhail Gorbachev assumed political power in Moscow. With Gorbachev as the new leader, it seemed possible for the United States to push ahead new ideas on arms control, human rights, and resolution of regional conflicts.

However, the task was made difficult by hardliners at home and abroad. The intelligence community and Soviet specialists in other parts of the government would tell Shultz "that the Soviet Union would never change no matter how bad their internal economic and social problems were." But Shultz—the professor that he was— turned the Kremlin into a classroom and drilled into Gorbachev these words: "The successful societies are open societies." Gorbachev had decided to focus his attention on domestic reforms; thus, glasnost and perestroika became watchwords of the Gorbachev era.

Beginning with the first summit meeting between Reagan and Gorbachev in Geneva in November 1985, and then the Reykjavik summit in October 1986, the two leaders were able to agree in principle on the INF (intermediate-range nuclear forces) treaty to destroy all medium-range nuclear weapons. They signed the historic treaty at their Washington summit in December 1987. It became a turning point in U.S.-Soviet relations, and Shultz proudly records: "I had done the unthinkable—get the United States and Soviet Union on the road to a working relationship." At the Moscow summit in May 1988, U.S. Soviet relations were further strengthened by the ratification of the INF treaty; by Soviet willingness to improve human rights, to resolve regional conflicts, mainly in Afghanistan and Angola, and to move ahead on reducing strategic long-range nuclear weapons.

Meanwhile, relations within the Reagan Administration were not always smooth. Ironically, some of the institutional conflicts that had characterized the Haig period began to appear once again. A case in point is the secret policy pursued by the White House's National Security Council (NSC) staff of trading weapons for hostages with Iran. These developments not only forced Shultz to offer to resign on the ground of policy differences, they threatened to destroy the Reagan presidency itself.

The catastrophe was averted by Reagan's willingness to change course on Iran policy. This change occurred when the investigations carried out by Attorney General Edwin Meese established irrefutably that proceeds from the sale of weapons to the Iranian government were used to support the Contra rebels fighting against the Sandinista government in Nicaragua. In a section titled "Setback," Shultz discusses in detail how the arms-for-hostages policy came to be pursued, first by National Security Adviser Robert McFarlane and later by his successor, John Poindexter.

Shultz protested that the policy violated America's declared goals of opposing international terrorism anywhere and of opposing arms sales to Iran, which was declared to be a terrorist state. Because of Iran-Contra, as the affair came to be called, public trust in President Reagan dropped to 14 percent, the lowest level of his presidency.

In foreign-policy making, intelligence plays a vital role. However, Shultz exhibited a positive skepticism about the intelligence information he was receiving from CIA Director William Casey. For instance, whenever he met a foreign dignitary either in the United States or abroad, the CIA provided to Shultz a "supposedly advance notice" of what the visitor was about to tell him. Such notices invariably "turned out to be quite wrong." Elsewhere in the book Shultz says that intelligence provided by Casey was "nothing better than Reuters reports...."

The Reagan Administration deserves credit for introducing a positive note in Indo-U.S. relations by inviting Prime Minister Indira Gandhi to visit Washington in July 1982. Although this visit figures only peripherally in this 1,184-page volume, Shultz devotes three pages to Indira Gandhi's funeral on November 3, 1984, which he attended as head of the U.S. delegation.

Rajiv Gandhi's visit to the United States in June 1985 gets more space. The issue highlighted by Shultz in the context of the young Indian Prime Minister's visit is the Soviet pullout from Afghanistan. This was "an issue that was exacerbating Indo-Pakistani tensions....The Indians thought Moscow may be ready to act quickly to get out of their Afghan quagmire. The Indians were ready to undertake a new diplomatic initiative with the Soviets, arguing for a change in Moscow's policy and removal of their troops from Afghanistan."

In sum, *Turmoil and Triumph* provides ample primary source material on the Reagan Administration's foreign policy issues for students and analysts who wish to examine them. The volume also serves as an empirical warning to policy makers that taking shortcuts for expediency could land them in a political quagmire from which they may be unable to extricate themselves. If President Reagan survived the after effects of Iran-Contra, part of the credit must go to George Shultz who at the right moment could tell him: "Mr. President, you are going wrong."

Span, August 1994

A Pledge for Peace

Indian foreign and security policy making has suffered from ad-hocism from the beginning. Under Pandit Nehru it was because of the fact that as a towering personality of the freedom movement, he could easily centralise policy making in his own hands. In the areas of foreign and national security policy, he could exercise almost a free hand as there were not many others who had experience and knowledge of foreign affairs in India. On the other hand, he devoted more attention to foreign affairs than domestic affairs. He has been an internationalist in his approach according to Maulana Azad.

But the subsequent Prime Ministers did not do much to improve the policy making process. It was equally ad hoc under Indira Gandhi who had the second longest tenure as the Prime Minister of India. Though at different times she had different persons as Foreign Ministers, the ad hoc nature of foreign policy making is reflected through an observation of the then Foreign Minister, Dinesh Singh, that foreign policy making during his times (1967-1970) was "one of carrying on, merely responding to situations". The policy making on vital national security issues did not improve in the subsequent years.

In the meanwhile a crop of national security experts was growing in the country. This writer had been the first to have studied the creation and working of the National Security Council (NSC) in the United States. Based on my study, I had written numerous articles to impress upon the policy makers the necessity of developing a formal mechanism for formulating a national security policy. However, the credit for lifting it from the intellectual plane and placing it at the plane of politics, goes to the Janata Dal (JD) led National Front, which for the first time in 1989, promised to create an NSC.

In the 1990s, the establishment of NSC is the one single issue on which practically all national political parties are in agreement. Yet, it is not acted upon by the governments so far. In 1996 elections, practically every political party in their manifests had shown their willingness to establish it. In the elections of 1998, again there is a consensus on the creation of NSC in India. The then Prime Minister, VP Singh, announced on several occasions in the Lok Sabha, his commitment to establish it, each time setting a new date. But he did not really act till September 1990, when his going out of office had become almost a certainty.

The NSC created by him suffered from two drawbacks. First, the NSC supposedly, created for effective and well co-ordinated policy formulation had many unco-ordinated bodies around it. This was done to accommodate many who wanted to be in the new mechanism. Second, he also created it by an executive order and not by an act of the Parliament. This was as though to indicate an ad hoc nature of the NSC which could be disbanded by the next government.

This was exactly what happened when Narashima Rao constituted his government in June 1991. He never said a word about it till he also took the charge of the defence portfolio in March 1993. However, it had become a ritual for the defence ministers every year, while discussing defence ministry demands, to promise the creation of an NSC. Thus, in October, 1991, the then Defence Minister, Sharad Pawar, promised to recreate the NSC to formulate a national security policy. In April 1991, Narashima Rao, then PM, who also carried the additional responsibilities of the defence portfolio, stated in the Lok Sabha that the proposal to set up an "NSC is under review". In 1995, he stated, "I have got the matter examined and we, have come to the conclusion that it should be set up". Though in 1996 he mentioned the need to set up NSC once again, his 'conclusion' was never translated into action.

Then came the government led by a humble farmer from Karnataka, H D Deve Gowda. As he was not then much conversant with the issues of high politics, like security and diplomacy, he had Inder Kumar Gujral, as his Foreign Minister. The first statement by Gujral on assuming the office of foreign minister in then UF led by Deve Gowda, was to announce his intention to establish the NSC. However, nothing was done by him either as the foreign minister or later as the prime minister.

Structure and Functions

The NSC should consist of the Prime Minister as its chairman and other Ministers for External Affairs, Defence, Home, Finance and Commerce as its statutory members. The chairman should be empowered to invite others on the basis of their advice. The Permanent Secretaries of the departments represented at the council level. The three service chiefs as well as the director of Research and Analysis, also need to attend as the advisors of the NSC.

The NSC needs to have a small staff of its own, headed by a Secretary. The staff under its secretary, need to function as effective brain, eyes and ears of the NSC on security matters. They could be drawn from the permanent service on the basis of their abilities or from universities and research think tanks in the country for a fixed tenure of three to four years.

Today, creation of the NSC assumes extreme significance for several reasons. First in the 1990s, since the end of the Cold War and the emergence of the United States as the sole military superpower, security policy making has become complicated and complex. In the past when the Soviet Union was a bulwark against US power, India had the easy option of going along with the Soviet Union. Hence, it is incumbent on the part of the government to examine every policy from various angles before a decision is reached.

Second, today two aspects of national security, external and internal have inseparably mingled together. Hence, national security concerns of the government of India have shifted from the traditional external security, to more on the threats of internal subversion and terrorism of pure domestic origin as well as externally promoted one on ethno-religious grounds. This calls for a greater co ordination between ministries of defence and external affairs on the one hand, and between various ministries dealing with internal security like home and others. In the absence of such co-ordination, ministries cause cacophony by speaking in a conflicting and contradictory manner. This was clearly evident in the Narasimha Rao government even within the same Ministry of Home. On the question of Kashmir, while the then Home Minister, S B Chavan, used the hawkish line, Minister of State for Internal Security, Rajesh Pilot, used to publicly take a dovish position finally forcing Prime Minister Rao, to take over the Kashmir affairs in his own hands.

Third, there is continued need for policy co-ordination between the traditional ministries mainly concerned with national security, viz. External Affairs and Defence. Each of these ministries consider security policy as its ultimate concern whether through diplomacy or defence. The conflicts and competition between the two are unavoidable compelling the need for effective policy co-ordination. This can only be done by an independent body like the NSC.

In recent times, we have the example of Defence Secretary, Ajit Kumar, publicly calling off his visit to Washington DC in October 1997, to attend the meeting of the Defence Planning Group (DGP) on the ground that his US counterpart, Frank Kramer, was only an Assistant Secretary of Defence. But the Ministry of External Affairs publicly expressed then displeasure at the over concern of the Defence Secretary for protocol instead of promoting national interest. Similarly they have publicly aired their differences over the sending of peace keeping troops to Somalia in the past under Rao's tenure.

Fourth, international economic issues have become far more important than international political issues. Hence, states are more interested in geo-economics and geopolitics in the sense that the states go in search of markets and economic conditions conducive to investment than looking for friends to create military blocs. If the powerful states twisted arms of leaders of developing nations for their politico-diplomatic support in the 1980s, today in the 1990s, they twist arms for securing economic benefits. This was experienced by India in 1991 in the wake of economic liberalisation that was forced on her because of an empty treasury that had only enough foreign exchange to buy essentials for just seven days.

Fifth, the world has undergone a transformation in terms of military technology and strategic thinking. It should be the function of the newly created NSC to study the application of technology to needs of guarding Indian security within the means available. In real terms it means creation of a sophisticated armed forces well equipped and conversant with the use of latest technologies with an ability to fight a high-tech war.

Conclusions

If the institution of NSC is so vital for the promotion of India's security, and if major political parties were agreed on its creation, what prevents its establishment in reality? Without going into details, it may be stated here that the idea is not to the liking of the foreign service bureaucracy which does not wish to share policy making with other ministries. India is probably the only country where the higher echelons of the defence forces do not participate in national security policy making. Hence, the idea of NSC was scuttled by the foreign service because it feared losing its power. There has also been a lack of decisive leadership since 1989. The NSC, whenever created, should be created by a law of the Parliament so that no future PM can make it a football to kick around on the basis of his political convenience.

However, creation of an NSC is merely the first step in equipping Indian society to deal with security problems of the 21st century. In the ultimate analysis what will really guarantee the national security of the country is its internal political stability. Such political stability can in turn only come by turning Indian society into a civil society based on respect for human rights, social justice, political fairness, economic equity and religious tolerance and harmony.

One India One People, April 1998

Not the PM's Job

ATAL Behari Vajpayee returns to the Ministry of External Affairs,' (MEA) once again, after 20 years, as minister. But this time with added responsibilities as the prime minister (PM).

Is it in the national interest for Vajpayee to retain the MEA with him? The question is of extreme importance and the ultimate longevity of the government, in my opinion, depends on the answer to the question.

However, he is not the first PM to retain the MEA with him; the most recent one to do so is I K Gujral, his immediate predecessor. Indira Gandhi has done it for a some time. Narasimha Rao did it in effect by appointing an ailing Dinesh Singh as his foreign minister. India's first PM, Pandit Nehru, had done it.

In the case of Nehru, at least initially, it was made out to be inevitable as he was the one with an international bent of mind. But he retained the portfolio of External Affairs till the last. However, only some months prior to his death in May 1964, he had appointed Lal Bahadur Shastri as the minister without portfolio to assist him because of his failing health.

In retrospect, however, he has had much political advantage in supporting his action and covering consequent lapses on his part. Second, the Congress then enjoyed unsurpassed public acceptability as the party that won freedom for India.

But it would have been in the national interest if he had divested himself of is External Affairs portfolio. This would have prevented many blunders in foreign policy formulation which actually took place in his tenure.

He took the Kashmir issue to the United Nations at a time when the Indian troops were driving the Pakistani troops away and were in a position to completely liberate Kashmir. He conceded China's claim for Tibet without considering its significance to India as the buffer state. Even after China's border war with India, Nehru advocated the sealing of China in the UN.

But Vajpayee, as the PM in the BJP-led coalition Government, cannot afford the luxury of retaining External Affairs. It will be in the national interest for Vajpayee to relinquish his hold over the MEA. He needs to be the PM for political coordination. There are at least five strong reasons for this.

First, the biggest task in the government is to coordinate various policy responses. Coordination is popular and without power you can not coordinate. The PM alone can coordinate.

Second, political and bureaucratic conflicts between the various ministries are inevitable. 'Where you stand depends on where you sit' has been stated as an administrative law. Of course, Marxists say 'where you sit depends on where you stand'. Both are right. A minister is placed in a ministry for his views, but he also comes to represent the viewpoint of his ministry.

Third, the PM alone can act as an unbiased referee whenever there are conflicts between the MEA and Ministry of Defence (MOD) which are traditionally unavoidable. In recent times, the MEA and MOD have taken divergent stands on crucial issues.

For instance, in November 1997, Ajit Kumar, MOD secretary, called off his visit to Washington DC on grounds of protocol as he thought negotiating with a United States assistant secretary of Defence was belittling. But the MEA was publicly critical of the stand taken by the secretary, MOD.

If the PM also holds the MEA charge, he can not act without a bias in favour of the MEA. The minister for Defence also will feel inhibited to present the case of the ministry when the PM is also in charge of External Affairs.

The PM also is required to coordinate between the domestic policies and foreign/security policy. Here again, the PM, as the Minister in charge of External Affairs, is likely to see the problem in conflict from the point of view of the MEA leading to a feeling of frustration among the domestic policy ministries.

Fourthly, the National Agenda of the BJP-led coalition has committed itself to establishing a national security council (NSC). Whenever established, the PM ought to be chairperson of the NSC. He can perform the role of chairperson effectively, only when he is without a portfolio of his own.

Fifth, in modern times, the PM and MEA minister have to travel considerably to foreign capitals because of growing interdependence of nations not only in economic policies but security and diplomatic policies as well.

Vajpayee as the Foreign minister under Morarji Desai's shortlived Janata Government (1977-1979), was in India for 717 days while spending 225 days outside the country. As a modest estimate, if the PM also spends an equal number of days abroad, Vajpayee will be away from Delhi for almost eight months in a year!

The sixth and the most important reason for me to make this suggestion is the political compulsion of the BJP-led coalition. The PM will need exceptional abilities to keep his coalition partners together. He needs to be an expert political coordinator to keep his folks together in good humour.

There are so many contentious issues over which partners in coalition might not see eye to eye. For instance, the Shiv Sena and Lok Shakti, over the Maharashtra-Karnataka border issue or Lok Shakti and All India Anna Dravida Munnetra Kazhagam over the sharing of Cauvery waters.

The problems arising from internal contradiction cannot be wished away; but they demand additional energies to manage and build confidence within the coalition, particularly when the margin of the majority of the government is so narrow.

And the Congress has a vested interest in destabilising the government to save the skin of All India Congress Committee President Sonia Gandhi over the Bofors scandal.

The main party in the ruling coalition, the BJP, came to power by proposing to provide a stable government under an able PM in A B Vajpayee.

There is absolutely no doubt about the PM's ability to govern ably. In national and international stature he is like Pandit Nehru but he needs to acquire the shrewdness of Indira Gandhi and Narasimha Rao's ability to transform a minority government into a majority one not by bringing members of Parliament into supporting him by bribing, but by transparency of actions and the compulsive need to provide a stable, clean and non-corrupt government.

These tasks need the PM to give the portfolio of External Affairs to another able leader like Lal Krishna Advani. There are many others in the present cabinet instead of himself limiting to Foreign Policy coordination.

Midday, 3 April 1998

ASSESSING INDIA'S FIFTY YEARS
A foreign policy perspective

In 1787 after the Philadelphia Constitutional convention got over Benjamin Franklin was asked a question by an old woman as to what have they given to them? Benjamin Franklin replied: "a Republic, if you can keep it." Another member of the constitutional convention, Nathaniel Gorham, did not think in 1787, that thirteen colonies which came together to form the United States of America, would survive as a perfect union, 150 years later. Applying these concerns of American founding fathers to the Indian nation after fifty years of its existence, what strikes most — in the context of South Asia as well as the global politics — is the fact that India managed to survive both as a Republic and a nation in integration.

This achievement cannot be underestimated, when we see that Pakistan, formed by partitioning India, disintegrated in 1971 with the birth of Bangladesh. After the end of the Cold War, some nations in Eastern Europe and Africa too have disintegrated. The Soviet Union was divided into fifteen independent states; Czechoslovakia became Czech Republic and Republic of Slovak, Eritrea separated from Ethiopia and Biafra got bifurcated from Nigeria. In this background, despite some of our American academics predicting that India, too will go the Soviet way, Indian nation has stood the machinations of foreign powers who want India disintegrated.

But, going beyond the achievement of preserving India's integrity, what have been other accomplishments of India's foreign policy? There are only a few accomplishments, while, the young nation made numerous mistakes. The most noteable achievement, is the intellectual coup led by the first Prime Minister of India, Jawaharlal Nehru, in providing an alternative option to newly independent nations of remaining non-aligned, of then prevailing two military blocks led by the United States and the Soviet Union.

India's desire to have peace for her economic development was possible only when she was not involved in Cold War conflicts. Additionally, having gained independence from a long colonial rule, India did not wish to lose her independence. The policy of non-alignment, helped India considerably to rise in stature in international affairs, until the Cold War of 1954, when Pakistan joined various military alliances led by the US.

With India's own security being drawn into larger global politics by Pakistan, India was compelled to lean towards the Soviet Union, in international political relations, while maintaining good relations with the US, in other areas such as economic, cultural educational etc. With Britain and the US supporting Pakistan, over the question of Kashmir, in the United Nations(UN), India became dependent on the Soviet veto.

Kashmir crisis became the first major challenge to Indian policy makers in handling India's security and foreign policy. The Indian forces were capable in 1948, to drive away marauding invaders from Pakistan. But it was Nehru's faith in internationalism as represented by the UN, that he complained to the UN on Pakistan's aggression and accepted a ceasefire. The Kashmir crisis, still continues as a major national security threat to India.

It was obvious that until the early 1950's, India, had in addition to geopolitical stakes, economic and cultural interests as well, in Tibet. China's claim over Indian territory, is based primarily on Tibetan and not Chinese documents. Its only after Indian recognition of Tibet, as an autonomous region of China, in the 1954 treaty, that China began to claim Indian territory as their own. Under Nehru, as Dawa Norbu, points out, "Strategically India surrendered Tibet — its outer ring of defence — without gaining in return from China, which penetrated India's inner ring of defence starting with Nepal in 1955." *(Asian Survey,* November 1997).

China's aggression in October 1962, was only an assertion of China's claims over Indian territory by the use of force. A strong China, today says, that Aksai Chin, and other territories claimed by them, belonged to them since ancient times.

India, of course, continued to follow the policy of non-alignment in post-Nehru era, but a diplomatic tilt towards the Soviet Union, not only continued, but became more visible in the 1970s. In 1965 war with Pakistan, the Soviet Union, pursued a strict policy of neutrality between India and Pakistan, particularly during the Indo-Pakistan war, and in subsequent Tashkent agreement. The Soviet Union was aiming to wean away Pakistan, from the US military bloc while acting as a friend of India. But it did not work. During the Indo-Pakistan war of 1971, India's non-aligned tilt to the Soviet Union, was at its peak with India signing the Peace and Friendship Treaty, with the Soviet Union, with military overtones, and US President Richard Nixon asking India to follow the non-alignment.

However, the Indian foreign policy making has not been able to adjust rapidly according to the changing international environment. This was evident in India's continued public adherence to policy of non-alignment, under P V Narasimha Rao. But with the end of the Cold War, non-alignment developed in the specific context of bipolar global Cold War politics, lost its significance and relevance. With the collapse of one of the two poles, every nation in fact, has become non-aligned. The nations are regrouping since 1991 mainly on the basis of their congruent economic interests as evident in the growth of North American Free Trade Agreement between US, Canada and Mexico or Asia Pacific Economic Co-operation (APEC). India, at the formative stage of the APEC, did not vigorously pursue her claim for the membership, which now she claims, but is not granted by its member nations.

Nehru, an idealist and realist, wanted to see India, emerge as a major power. In Lok Sabha in 1954, he said: "If we peep into the future, and nothing goes wrong like war, India will be the fourth major power in the world next to the US, Soviet Union, China." This vision continued to guide, prime ministers Indira Gandhi and Rajiv Gandhi, despite their mistakes in implementation.

Indira Gandhi initiated several steps, to make India self- reliant in defence preparedness. One of her major step was first-ever nuclear test at Pokhran, in May 1974. It was mainly in response to the growing triangular relationship between the US, China and Pakistan against the Soviet Union. Since India, was perceived as leaning towards the Soviet Union; US during the Bangladesh war made it clear to India, that in the event of China intervening on the side of Pakistan, India should not look for the US help. The US had also sent nuclear powered *USS Enterprise* to the Bay of Bengal, to threaten India in the style of old gun boat diplomacy. Mrs Gandhi also gets the credit for India's space programme, its growing naval power, and measures such as conducting the science missions to Antarctica. The greatest achievement of India, under her tenure, was of course, the effective conduct of foreign and security policy during the Bangladesh war. Atal Bihari Vajpayee had then described her as the Goddess Durga. However, great achievements in foreign policy arena had the adverse effect on her behaviour in domestic politics leading to the imposition of national emergency.

Rajiv Gandhi had similar vision of making India a per power, preparing the nation for thc 21st century. While giving new directions to India's foreign policy, he committed a serious foreign policy mistake by sending Indian peace keeping forces (IPKF) to Sri Lanka, thus, deviating from the role of a mediator between the Sri Lankan government and their Tamil citizens. At one stroke, Sri Lanka's problem became ours, and we lost our leverage with the Sri Lankan government thereby losing our abilities to help Tamils. Nothing much has been achieved by the Indian government since 1989. The period since then, has seen only political instability at home, making thc government focus on struggling for their own survival in office rather than conduct nation's foreign policy, to guide it to thc great power status. Domestic political instability, is compounded by the economic crisis that forced PV Narasimha Rao government to go in a big way for economic liberalisation.

For effective foreign policy, domestic political stability is a prerequisite. Foreign policy, is the projection of nation's totality of interests in external relations. In the absence of a stable, strong, and sincere government, in an anarchic world, where each nation has to help itself, weak nations are not heard at all. In this regard, the BJP led government under Atal Bihari Vajpayee had a vision to make India, a great power. The Pokhran II, nuclear tests conducted indicate this vision. But the question is: will his alliance partners, be able to see beyond their state borders? If they can, will the opposition parties, allow the new alliance at the centre to govern for the next four years?

One India One People, August 1998

Shaping foreign policy

Nearly 20 million Persons of Indian Origin (PIOs) are spread throughout the world. These are the Indians who were involuntarily taken away from India by the colonial powers like Britain, France, and Portugal to different parts of the world where they founded their colonies as in Africa or in Asia. If today we have the problems of the PIOs in countries like Sri Lanka, Fiji Islands, we have also opportunities to close relations with these countries by cultivating PIOs. A fine example is Mauritius.

After Independence, there has been a different trend — Indians who migrated to foreign countries in search of greener pastures. They are the Non-Resident Indians (NRIs). There are an estimated 1.5 million of them in the US alone.

Indians who live abroad do perform a certain role in shaping India's foreign policy. When we look at the NRIs in the US, their role has increased considerably in the last decade compared to the 1980s. In the 1980s, when the Reagan administration proposed a $3.2 billion military aid package to Pakistan and under it proposed to supply F-16 planes to Pakistan, Indian-Americans did oppose the US move. Their voice, however, was drowned in the determined effort of the Reagan administration to help Pakistan. An influential pro-India Congressman, Stephen Solarz, said that Indian-Americans did not exert much influence on American foreign policy. Professor Stephen Cohen commented that Indian-Americans begin their lobbying after a decision has been reached and not before.

This has changed drastically since the 1990s. Not only have the Indians doubled in number but their political awareness and organization have also changed. As a highly educated community their contribution to both political parties has increased. Vinod Gupta, a California-based businessman raised $500,000 for the Clinton-Gore second campaign in 1996. He said, "If you don't spend money, you don't get heard."

There are today a few Indians working as political aides to Congressmen and Governors. Kris Kolluri is political director of the minority leader Gephardt in the House of Representatives. During a visit to India two years ago, Kolluri described how Indian-Americans plunged into action once India conducted nuclear tests in May 1998. They rang up their Congressmen to explain Indian compulsions in conducting nuclear tests. During the Kargil conflict, NRIs in the US were active through their political forums. The outcome was very positive not only in bringing about a change in the general attitude towards the threat of terrorism faced by India but also in positively improving the general contours of Indo-US relations.

NRIs have played a negative role too. In the 1980s though a numerically small community then the Sikhs in the US were able to see that the US pressurized Indian government, in particular its armed forces who were violating human rights. It is necessary to recall the negative role played by NRIs in shaping India's foreign economic policy. In 1991, India was forced to take the steps necessary to implement the policy of economic liberalization, privatization and globalization (LPG). Apart from economic mismanagement by the previous governments, one important reason that forced the Narasimha Rao government to go for the LPG in 1991 was the withdrawal of NRI deposits.

However, the same NRIs began to invest in India Bonds and in Indian industries once the World Bank and International Monetary Fund pushed India to go for devaluation of the rupee and vigourously implement LPG. Today India has a foreign exchange reserve of nearly $50 billion, much of it of course being NRI investment.

NRIs can play a negative role in vital security areas as well. During World War II, there were instances of the US using American citizens of Japanese origin against Japan. The possibilities of a major national security conflict between India and the US are almost unthinkable. But there is no guarantee that any country, including the US might not use the NRIs for economic espionage. The government has to be careful in its intelligence gathering and security planning. But that is no argument to shut the door for NRI investment. India needs to pursue a cautious but constructive policy of interaction with the NRIs.

While promoting useful networks between India and NRIs, we need to spread our NRI contacts widely rather than limit to a few rich countries, because they can bring investments. But looking beyond economic benefits, we need to develop and promote cultural and political contacts with the NRIs.

But India has a long way to go in comparison to the Chinese who irrespective of their political affiliation or the country of residence, always think of China as their country: The Chinese are getting maximum investment in their country because of this factor.

One India One People, July 2002

Time to replace Natwar with one having a clean image

Ever since the Congress-led UPA government assumed power in May 2004, Natwar Singh, the minister for external affairs has generated one controversy or the other for Prime Minister Manmohan Singh. The latest one is his alleged receiving kickbacks from Saddam Hussein in the UN-sponsored oil for food programme. The earliest one is his statement in Seoul, South Korea last year, stating that India would not have gone for nuclear weapons but for the folly of the NDA government conducting nuclear tests. "But regret would be futile. You cannot put it back into the tube, it is out" he lamented.

This policy statement was however, disowned by the PM. The PM, then had said that nuclear weapons will stay as part of India's strategic policy and there is no change in that policy because of the new government assuming power. Natwar Singh was in reality not articulating a policy but his anger. Though it was the Congress government under Mrs. Gandhi who had initiated plans to conduct more tests, it was really the BJP that ran away with the credit for conducting them.

During his tenure he was always motivated not so much by national interest in policy formulation but by a burning desire to be something different from the BJP. In November last year he made a comparison between foreign policy making under the UPA government and the NDA government in the past. The Hallmark of the UPA government's foreign policy has been, he said, "consistency in approach" in contrast to the "event-based efforts of the NDA government". The UPA government has adopted a more "process-oriented approach that did not oscillate between euphoria and despair." In this approach "you can only get to the outcome when the process reaches somewhere. By saying that the outcome must be known before to my mind, is putting the cart before the horse."

He was alluding to the NDA's policy making towards India's relations with Pakistan in the above statement. But in fact the UPA government, under Natwar Singh's command of MEA, had diluted the BJP's forcing General Musharraf, through a hard bargain in January 04, to make a firm commitment not to permit Pakistan-controlled territory to be used by terrorists against India. In New York, in September 2004, Pakistan succeeded in avoiding any repetition of earlier formulation. Later when Musharraf visited New Delhi in April 2005 Pakistani commitment to prevent terrorism emanating from their territory was further diluted by stating India and Pakistan would jointly fight terrorism!

The fruits of that formulation are coming to Indian leaders now during Deepavali by way of serial bombing in three places in Delhi on Sunday, 30 October. Pakistan is now offering to help India in joint investigation of terrorist acts by first initiating them! The PM being an economist, Natwar Singh desired to have a better hold of foreign policy making and its expression. As a result, he tried his best to acquire more powers for the MEA so that he can be under greater control of foreign policy process.

The result is there for every one to see. To be on the top of foreign policy making, one need to have proper understanding of the national interest on a given policy issue. One golden rule of policy-making is: never speak-out before you have done your homework. But Natwar Singh has been in the habit of speaking first and then searching for rationale to justify his statement.

Thus, while in New York with the PM this September he asserted that India would support Iran, as though to make it a test case to demonstrate that India is not a stooge of the US. Then he gave the justification of India having a sizeable Shia population majority in Iran are Shiites. When did the UPA government-singing in praise of secularism begin to formulate foreign policy on sectarian considerations?

Does the Iranian government deserve such support from India by going against her own national interest? What the International Atomic Energy Agency is seeking is a confirmation from Iran that it is not going to launch nuclear weapons programme. India with an impeccable non-proliferation record, cannot side with a proliferator like Iran. Iranian President by his irresponsible utterances like the need to wipe out Israel from the face of the earth has only made India's task more difficult in the future.

Now the Committee appointed to study kickbacks involved in the implementation of oil for food programme under the supervision of the UN. Natwar Singh, along with many others, has been internationally accused of receiving kickbacks from Iraq. The Congress Party as a political entity is also supposed to have received kickbacks from the Saddam regime. It will be difficult for the Congress Party to defend itself and clear its name. It will be an additional burden for it also to take up the case of Natwar Singh.

India needs a new energetic foreign minister with a reputation as a clean person. It is therefore time for PM to change the foreign minister before the revelation does further damage. During Narasimha Rao's tenure as the PM, there was somewhat a similar case involving the question of ethics. Madhavsinh Solanki the then Foreign Minister was involved in trying to influence the Swiss Minister in the case of Bofors kickbacks. When the opposition learnt of it, they forced Solanki to resign.

In this particular case of Natwar Singh why should the PM wait till opposition succeeds to build up their case for Natwar Singh's resignation? Already Manmohan Singh had begun his innings as the PM in the UPA government with the question of tainted ministers like Sibu Soren. Now there is a Minister of State, Jai Prakash Yadav being involved in attacking a police station to get his brother freed from the jail! He is also on the run now evading arrest. While keeping some of these tainted ministers within the domestic policy area, at least let us have a clean image in the external affairs!

Free Press Journal, 4 November 2005

Foreign policy must match with national goals

Indian foreign policy makers are well known for their tremendous abilities for cacophony and shooting from hip. Take for instance the manner in which national security/foreign policy makers handled the Kargil crisis. Three days after the starting of air action against Pakistani intruders, George Fernandes said that Pakistani Army hatched the entire Kargil intrusion plan and Nawaz Sharif government had no role in it. But then Home Minister, L K Advani did not think that Sharif was a victim of Army's conspiracy! Under the current UPA government cacophony is created by the Prime Minister (PM) himself, for instance on India-US Civil Nuclear Deal (CND). When their close allies in the Left led by the CPI (M) raised their voice of opposition, in August 2007, he said that the CND is not negotiable. But when the allies mounted their pressure on Man Mohan Singh, a month later he came 180 degree around and said that it is negotiable! Much later, he compromised national interest by stating that CND is important but that is not the only thing that is important to his government.

Before the UPA came to power, the then Prime Minister, Atal Behari Vajpayee had created, most reluctantly, a National Security Council (NSC) to make effective foreign/national security policy in 1998. Till then, there were only four authorities like PM, Foreign, Defence and Home Ministers to cause cacophony in foreign policy making. But now a fifth one is added, in the form of national security adviser (NSA)! India so far had two NSAs-Brajesh Mishra and J N Dixit-both had diplomatic experiences, and were more cautious in publicly expressing their foreign policy views. But the present NSA comes from rich background in policing. But having suffered in silence in performing duties under the police discipline, he got an opportunity to dabble in diplomacy after sudden death of JN Dixit. Now he is doing maximum of expressing his foreign policy views publicly and cause ample cacophony! One example is his recent advice to Sri Lanka to buy their weaponry only from India! Sri Lanka may be comparatively a small country but small nations too have their ego. What we call in international relations parlance as National Prestige! More recently, he is reported to have said that Tamil Nadu and Kerala were home to LTTE's "small pockets of rebel group," only to be denied later by the PM's office. Lack of effective policy making is evident from the fact that after the CND was signed, and 123 agreement was delivered on August 1, 2007 a UPA government committee was appointed to negotiate with the Left-who perform a dual role of 'insider' and 'outsider' who want to eat the UPA cake and at the same time want to spoil the party-by causing the differences within the ruling coalition!

Foreign policy formulation is not like determining price of onions or importing onions in cases of scarcity. Before the foreign policy issue is determined, policy makers need to decide national goal/s in pursuing a policy; have to evaluate pros and cons and nation's available capabilities in achieving the goal/s. It is only then policy makers can pursue effectively the goals set by them before various ministries of the government to implement.

Another unique feature of foreign policy is that it impinges on the jurisdiction of several departments of the government like defence, home, finance to a great extent but generally on every other department of government-whether agriculture, commerce or education.

It is this reason of compulsive need for foreign policy coordination that led to some of us to urge government to establish a National Security Council at the political level with PM as its chairman to coordinate foreign policy with other ministers managing various policy areas.

Since ministers are busiest people in the country pretending to govern the country but also collecting goodies for the next election at the same time, the NSC is supposed to have a small expert staff to work on vetting the policies before the NSC at political level with NSA as its head to consider them.

But ever since what has actually happened since it was created, is that NSC has not been used at all-neither by the NDA nor by the UPA, but they have only used the post of NSA to accommodate one more retired person into the advisory position! It is this fact that has contributed to multiply and magnify cacophony in policy making.

Those who contribute to cacophony say that existing system works well-in other words status quoists Babus in power, as they do not wish to surrender any of their existing power and perks. But if the existing arrangement doesn't work, as its nomenclature suggest, that is part of the game! Thus, for instance, Ministry for external affairs, has a Policy Planning Division, but in reality it is used as a dumping ground for returnees from foreign posting till they can be suitably posted once again abroad! If they hold the post of head of the division for a year or so that's too small a period to think about long-term policies for India.

India's foreign policy has for over 60 years now has been reactive without ever trying to be proactive. Nehru had said in 1954 that if everything goes right India would emerge as the fourth major power after US, Soviet Union and China. But nowhere government is seen to behave, as it wants to pursue the goal of becoming a major power. India can not emerge as a major power, just because the US or other western powers say that we are an emerging major power. But we need to have will to power and act in that direction.

If that is so, we need to give un-coordinated reactive policy made in disconnected mechanism. We need to think big and that is possible only when we have a well developed mechanism to make effective and well co-ordinated foreign policy.

Free Press Journal, 5 April 2008

Is India a major power?

Much of the talk of India as an emerging Major Power is a reflection of India's growing economic clout. It was acquired by India going in for economic Liberalisation, Privatisation and Globalisation (LPG) in 1991 after she was forced by circumstances of near-economic bankruptcy caused by cumulative effects of populist democratic socialism that was practiced by previous regimes. Though Pandit Nehru had said it way back in 1954 in Lok Sabha that "If you peep into the future and if nothing goes wrong—wars and like—the obvious fourth country in the world (after US, Soviet Union, and China) is India," it is more often speculated by foreign powers and think tanks. After 31 years of LPG, despite economic slowdown and projection in the GDP growth at 6.9 percent in the current fiscal year, India's growth rate is still the second highest amongst the world economies.

Conceptual clarity needed

One issue that came up is the need to have a clear understanding about the concept of 'Major Power', its meaning and correct usage. 'Major Power' is essentially a concept in hierarchical classification of states, based on an assessment of their power—tangible and intangible. Thus, in a four level classification of states, the highest category is 'super power,' then 'major power,' third level is regional power, some times also known as medium power and at the bottom is: small powers. Often journalists use these concepts irresponsibly and ignorantly to connote wrong meanings and usage, particularly in regard to the term Super Power or Major Power. For instance, recently (January 16) *The Times of India* carried an item with a heading: "Superpower? 230 million Indians go hungry daily."

In the above hierarchical division, India is not a Super Power. An important characteristic of a super power is its ability to reach out to any crisis and assert its power and if necessary impose a solution of its choice to a crisis. At present, the United States (US) is the only super power since 1991 after the end of the Soviet Union. But now, China can be said to be the only power that aims to achieve the status of a super power. In contrast, a medium power or a regional power has its abilities restricted to a geographical region as in the case of India in the 1980s willing to exercise power in South Asia. On the other hand, a major power has global interests and influence, but do not have power to assert its will globally on every issue. Hence, in the 1980s, the Reagan administration, after Indira Gandhi's visit to Washington, DC, said that India is a major regional power and an emerging major global power. This very clearly brings out the difference between regional or middle power which by definition has its power limited to a region while major powers like Britain or France in the 1950s and the 1960s had global interests and influence but were capable of asserting its power selectively in certain areas where its core values were involved.

China factor

It was again and again stressed with sound reasoning on the need to place India and China in right perspective. It was noted that if India has to emerge as a major power, it ought to be for its own sake and on its own terms and not in competition with China; the need is to decouple India's rise as a major power in competition and in comparison with China. China began its communist capitalism ten years ahead of India. China has the short-term advantage of taking quick decisions towards economic development but India is deterred by democratic debate, discussion, differences and deferences often leading to delay even leading to destruction of plans of development as for instance demonstrated by Tata's experience of putting up a small car plant in Nandigram in West Bengal!

Where is the hurry?

Another question that repeatedly arose is: There are many domestic problems faced by India today, which do not seem to have a solution, at least at the moment. There is for instance the problem of internal security threat, like the one posed by Naxalites and Maoists—running from Nepal to Andhra on the eastern coast right through West Bengal, Jharkhand to Odisha. There is already externally promoted terrorism both by Pakistan and China; a cocktail of two is extremely dangerous affecting economic growth.

Equally important is the present situation on the domestic front. As the above referred ***Times*** report indicated that 21 percent of Indian population is undernourished, nearly 44 percent of under-five children underweight and seven percent of them dying before they reach five years. India is firmly established amongst the world's most hunger-ridden countries. Added to hunger, almost every day there is a report on one imperfect feature or the other of Indian society or the polity. If one day it is a report stating that India is a worst place for girl child, another day it may be health, third day it may be malnutrition! To all this, the government's only action is to call these as shameful!

On the other hand, it can be said that in all cases of powerful states in history so far, in the modern times at least, the poor have co-existed with rich and ultra-rich. The US remained a number one super power since World War II. But the US always had its poor in the ghettoes. During the years of plenty in the US, for instance in the 1960s and the 1970s, Presidents felt that they could afford to have guns as well as buns simultaneously. Despite such tall claims, poor were always there in the US. Hence, it does not mean that Indian nation aspiring to be a major power has to follow 'either or' approach but can have programmers to make India both a major power and raise social and economic status of poor, simultaneously.

Conclusion

In conclusion, however, it was pointed out that what is crucial is the will power to emerge as a major power. It is not enough to possess economic wherewithal to be a major power but willingness to assert power. There was that kind of national will power during the reign of Mrs. Gandhi to assert power to safeguard India's national interest. Though India had nuclear bombs in the basement since the 1980s, necessary will power and diplomatic finesse was provided by the NDA under Atal Behari Vajpayee. It was a widely expressed consensus in the seminar that the will power to emerge as a major power and exercise national power is completely missing at present!

One India One People, March 2012

Should Pravasis be given political Rights?

The Second Pravasi Day was over in New Delhi recently. Since all those Non-Resident Indians (NRIs) and Persons of Indian Origin (PIOs) could not be accommodated at the national meet in Delhi, it is likely and logical that they wòuld be accommodated in the regional fares. This will provide opportunities to local non-Pravasis to interact with the Videshi Pravasis.

Such Pravasi Days are now likely to be held in the state capitals as well. So there would be Maharashtrian Pravasi Divas in Mumbai or Pune, a Gujarati Pravasi Divas in Ahmedabad or Baroda. a Karnataki Pravasi Divas in Bengaluru or Mysore and so on. More the merrier. Philosophically speaking all of us are Pravasis; some are Videshi some are Deshi! On January 3 and 4 Karnatakis living outside Karnataka from all over India met in Mumbai to discuss their problems. These Deshi Pravasis can also be seen as Permanent Deshi Pravasi (PDP) say a Karnataki who is permanently resident in Maharashtra or a Temporary Deshi Pravasi (TDP) like a Karnataki working in Maharashtra for a short period on transfer. Anyhow, it does not take much time for one Deshi to become Videshi! When a territory is conceded by India to another neighbour, overnight a Deshi becomes a Videshi!

I have been an ardent advocate of India cultivating over 20 million of PIOs and NRIs living in various countries. They can be an important lobby to advocate Indian causes in the country of their residence. They can influence the government of the nation where they live. In return the government of India is extending them many concessions like purchase of property, admissions to Indian educational institutions, investment in India and several others.

But the BJP government is thinking of conferring political rights such as voting in elections etc on these Pravasis. Yashawant Sinha said at the meet that whether dual citizenship is to be given to these Pravasis or political rights extended to them or not "is an issue which has to be widely debated in the country...before reaching a decision." Thus the question: Should we favour such a decision?

As Yashawant Sinha rightly observed, democracy "means accountability on a daily basis." Can the Pravasis meet this accountability test, say, having voted to a party into power? Obviously, not unlike our PDPs. A Videshi Pravasi particularly PIO variety who left India centuries ago. holds a foreign passport and visits India occasionally will not be aware of day-to-day affairs of this country. On the other hand, an NRI who still holds an Indian passport but is not a resident of India is more likely in touch with India as a recent emigrant to a foreign country in search of a PIO status. This distinction is useful in discussing the issue raised by Sinha.

In a federal state as we are in India, we do not have a dual citizenship as Americans have. An American is a citizen of state he lives in addition to the Citizen of the US. But in Indian federation, there is always a fleeting population from different states in major urban centres at a given occasion of General Elections. Can a Deshi Pravasi-TDP-say from Calicut in Kerala insist to vote in a national election in Kolkatta? Indians do not enjoy dual citizenship nationally. There is only one citizenship-of India. However, though right to vote is national, voting is done locally-in the locality to which one belongs. If that is so, how can an international Pravasi be allowed to vote in Indian national elections?

Hence, before we consider giving right to vote to Videshi Pravasis let us first devise means to give right to vote to Deshi Pravasis even when he is not a permanent resident of that state. It should be possible now for the Election Commission with Voter Identity Card (VIC) given to every citizen, to permit to vote a Pravasi on the Election Day if he is required to travel.

Then before we consider permitting the PIOs to vote, let us first make it easier to vote for the NRIs from abroad. NRIs are also to be given the VIC to enable them to vote in their constituency by Internet or by some other easier way. The need is to enable and not create obstacles in voting.

But in addition to the above priorities to be attended first, there are stronger and fundamental reasons not to permit Videshi Pravasis of the PIO type the right to vote. If PIOs can vote, can we prohibit them from forming a political party of their own to contest elections? If international Pravasis can vote, why can't they be given the right to hold public office?

As it is, Indians are divided on caste and religious lines nationally, so also they are divided internationally. They are also now divided on their sympathy to one or the other Indian political parties. In the early 1990s when V. P. Singh was dividing the nation on caste lines, then spokesmen of castes likes of Paswans and Yadavs were travelling abroad, particularly the US to extol their caste supporters there to organise themselves into lobbies on caste lines! Once they are permitted to hold office in addition to voting, there would be, not only Pravasi parties like the Pravasi Indian National Congress or the Pravasi Bharatiya Janata Party but also Pravasi Yadavs and Pravasi Bahujans etc!

Giving PIOs voting rights could also pose national security threat to India. In the most unlikely situation of a major conflict between India and a country with millions of PIOs, that nation can use PIOs as intelligence agents to gather information in India. During World War II, the US used American citizens of Japanese origin to collect intelligence in Japan.

After 56 years of Independence we have not yet overcome our colonial mentality of considering everything from the West, particularly those with white skin as the best. Those with brown skin with long imitation of White man are the second best of the lot-so says the White man! Some newspapers have described those who attended the Second Pravasi Day in Delhi as intellectuals and cream of Indian Diaspora!

Then it is possible that powerful nations from the western countries can send a coalition of Pravasi Political parties to rule India without taking recourse to conquering or colonising India once again. After all, newly converted are more loyal than those who were native born. These can colonise India once again without sending their troops. Today it can appear as a fantasyland idea! I am sure, in the 17th century some one stating it when Indians were collaborating with British, might have been dismissed in the similar way!

Free Press Journal, 30 January 2004

Foreign policy: Entirely Modi-Centric

When it comes to foreign policy, apart from content, the media is usually interested in two issues: first, who dominates the process and second, the problems of foreign policy co-ordination. In the six months of the new NDA Government, both these issues have caught the attention of media managers. Currently, public perception is that it is Prime Minister Narendra Modi who dominates policy-making. Last week, the media dubbed External Affairs Minister Sushma Swaraj a 'dummy' If that is indeed the case, then why is it so?

It is not the first time that such a sobriquet has been used to address the foreign minister. During the brief Janata Party rule from 1977-1979, Atal Behari Vajpayee was appointed by the then prime minister, Morarji Desai, as the external affairs minister. Some Lok Sabha members had then said that our foreign policy was actually made by Morarji Desai with the help of his foreign secretary, Jagat

Mehta and all that Vajpayee did was to translate this into Hindi. That was very unfair to Vajpayee as it is unfair to Swaraj now. Vajpayee was the first foreign minister to visit China, in continuance with Indira Gandhi's decision to resume relations with that country, ties which had been in a limbo after the October 1962 border war.

Swaraj is responsible for implementing India's foreign policy. Modi's foreign policy is currently focussed on improving relations with our neighbouring countries in South Asia, engaging the extended neighbourhood in South-east Asia and major global powers. In this pursuit, he has made official visits to Bhutan, Nepal and Japan, the US, Myanmar, Australia and Fiji. He has also played host to the Chinese President, Xi Jinping. He has met at least 45 world leaders. Swaraj too, has made official visits to Bangladesh, Bhutan, Nepal, Myanmar, Vietnam, Bahrain, Afghanistan, Tajikistan, the US, the UK, Mauritius, Maldives and the UAE, either to prepare for Modi's visits or in pursuit of policies independently or accompanying the PM.

In the UPA decade, it was difficult to categorise the making of foreign policy. A Congressman-turned-critic of his party upon expulsion, K Natwar Singh writes in his 'One Life is Not Enough' that Manmohan Singh "didn't have" a foreign policy. Foreign policy "was run from the Prime Minister's Office." As the external affairs minister from 2004 to 2005, Natwar Singh certainly knows what he is talking about. However, what Prime Minister Manmohan Singh considered the best achievement of his tenure was in the foreign policy arena. In January 2014, he said, India's civil nuclear deal with the US was his best achievement.

Yet, in the last two years of Manmohan Singh's government, Salman Khurshid, as the foreign minister made a mess of Indian foreign policy. He conceded a dominant role to China in South Asia without extracting any reciprocal recognition of a similar role for India in South-east and East Asia from China.

Given this background, the rise of Modi-centric policy-making is understandable. This is not unique only to the Indian Parliamentary system. This has happened from time to time with the British parliamentary system as well. The best illustration of our time comes from the period of Margaret Thatcher. She took most of the decisions on war and peace. But it is the Americans who have excelled in moving from one system to the other. During the World War II, it was President

Franklin Roosevelt who decided on issues related to war and peace; he attended all the major international conferences on the conduct of war. During his 13-years tenure as President, he had Cordell Hull as the Secretary of State for eleven years, but Hull had little power in outlining foreign policy. As a reaction to this wartime Presidential dominance of policy during war, the post-war period saw the Secretary of State dictate the policy under Presidents Truman and Eisenhower (1945-1960).

Coming to the matter of foreign policy co-ordination, today, foreign policy affects most domestic policy departments, like agriculture, education, finance, defence, home, science and technology and other sectors. Thus, on the very first day of the Modi Government, external affairs under Swaraj, and home under Rajnath Singh saw a turf war on control of the police force in Indian embassies. It was bearing in mind the cropping up of such issues that the Vajpayee Government had established the National Security Council (NSC) in 1998. It fell into disuse soon after the Kargil War. The UPA-I and the UPA-II too did not use it.

There are no public signs of the present government using it either. The NSC always enables structured decision-making after adequate discussion and participation of all the top brass concerned with foreign/national security policy making. The chairman of the chiefs of staff committee, Air Chief Marshal Arup Raha said in October that PM Modi has one-to-one meetings with the service chiefs every month. Wouldn't it be better if the meetings took place in an NSC setting, with all the other members present—particularly the foreign minister and the defence minister?

While PM-centric policy making is unavoidable, the FM-centric model is weak and can turn disastrous. But broad-based decision-making will always prove beneficial to the long-term interests of the nation.

The Free Press Journal, 10 December 2014

Foreign policy: Centre-State ties count

Prime Minister Narendra Modi assured that a bill would be passed to effect the mutual transfer of Bangladesh-held enclaves within India in West Bengal and Indian enclaves in Bangladesh. The problem is: Bangladeshi enclaves are surrounded by Indian state all around and as a result, Bangladesh cannot provide any services to the people, including citizenship rights. The same is true for residents of Indian enclaves within Bangladesh, who suffer similar inhumanities because the Indian state cannot reach them.

These problems have existed ever since Partition in 1947. Under UPA-II, PM Manmohan Singh had, in 2011 signed a protocol to transfer the land to the respective countries. But this was impeded by the obstinate approach of West Bengal Chief Minister Mamata Banerjee, on the grounds that India was giving away more land to Bangladesh than we were getting in return.

Therein lies the importance of centre-state relations for the success of Indian foreign policy. The nature of centre-state relations depends on, not only the powers of the centre, but also the nature of government at the centre; whether it is ruled by one party or a coalition and whether there is a one-party dominance in the country or multi-party sharing of powers in states.

As far as powers are concerned, our Constitution provides 'exclusive power' to Parliament to make laws in foreign affairs and national security, including internal security policy-making. Wherever there is a 'foreign' element involved, the federal government has been given control over it, like for instance, fishing beyond territorial waters.

But the Indian political process, in reality has gone through two extremes in the last 67 years; in consequence, it has affected the manner in which federal governments in India have seen and worked on relations with states. These are: the One-Party dominance system (1952-1989) and the Multi-Party system' (1989-2014 up to UPA II). These two models differently affect the making of foreign policy. We have to wait to see how the present government will conduct its relations with the states, as even if it has absolute majority in the Lok Sabha, it does not have a majority in the Rajya Sabha and there are different political parties in power in the states.

Thus, during the Bangladesh War in 1971, Mrs. Gandhi informed Parliament of her intention to sign a treaty of Peace & Friendship with the Soviet Union one hour before, on August 9, 1971. But after Manmohan Singh signed the CND with the US and presented a 123 agreement with the US to the Lok Sabha for approval in 2008, there was stiff opposition from the Marxists, who were supporting the UPA-I Government. When the agreement was passed, it did not bring any glory either to the government or the Lok Sabha! It sullied the reputation of both institutions.

The impact of the multi-party system at the federal level on the conduct of foreign policy has illustrated the tremendous pulls and pressures of moving away foreign policy goals from a rational choice. Look at the manner in which the question of Prime Minister's participation in Commonwealth Heads of Government Meeting in November 2013 in Sri Lanka was decided. The two main Dravidian political parties—the DMK and the AIADMK, through a legislative assembly resolution in Tamil Nadu, asked the PM not to attend it in protest against the Sri Lankan Army's violation of human rights during the war against the LTTE. This chorus was joined by prominent Congress ministers, P Chidambaram, A K Antony, V Narayansami and G K Vasan. The PM did not go. Instead, he sent Minister for External Affairs, Salman Khurshid.

The rational choice would have been for the PM to attend, so he could ask the Sri Lankan President to investigate human rights violations and press for a lasting political settlement with the Tamil minority in Sri Lanka. He also had also an invite from the chief minister of the Northern Territories.

As for Mamata Banerjee, in 2011, not only did she not agree to the mutual transfer of enclaves between India and Bangladesh, but she also rejected the then federal government's proposal on the sharing of Teesta waters on the grounds that the proposed reduction in the share of waters of West Bengal from the present 75 percent to 52 percent to raise the Bangladesh quota from 25 percent to 48 percent would cause suffering to farmers in North Bengal.

But now, she has agreed to the new deal over the transfer of enclaves as proposed by the Modi Government. She has agreed to provide land in West Bengal to settle those who will move in from Indian held enclaves in Bangladesh. She might also agree to revisit the water-sharing formula if the Indian Government agrees to re-examine de novo the Teesta water-sharing agreement.

The Free Press Journal, 20 December 2014

Vital role of India abroad

January 7-9-2015 will see a large number of Indians, resident abroad, in various continents, land in Gujarat to celebrate the 15th

Bharatiya Pravasi Din (BPD) or may we call it 'Indian Diaspora Day' (IDD)? What is the significance of this IDD? Is it merely another photo opportunity for a large number of well-to-do persons of Indian origin to mingle with Indian Prime Minister or does the expenditure on this observance make any significant contribution?

Before we answer these two questions, we need to know that primarily there are two kinds of Indians abroad: One those who have migrated in post-Independence period; largely, those who migrated in search of greener pastures and some, who went on service deputations. They are called Non-Resident Indians (NRIs). Second, there are a large number of Indians who settled in foreign lands during the period Indian territories were colonized by the British, the French and the Portuguese. They were taken abroad as indentured labour, to work in plantations and became citizens of the country they were taken to or moved to, like Fiji, Mauritius, Sri Lanka, Trinidad and several others. They are called Persons of Indian Origin (PIO), as they hold citizenships of the country they are residents of and don't have many links to India, while NRIs hold Indian citizenship and have family in India. Even a majority of these NRIs, eventually try to obtain citizenship of the country of their residence. Hence, practically, it would be correct to refer to all NRIs and PIOs as the Indian diaspora (ID).

Since Independence, India's policy towards ID for a long time, as initiated by the first PM, Jawaharlal Nehru, was to ask Indians outside their mother-land, to assimilate with the country they lived in. This policy was followed religiously by Nehru's successors.

The rationale was that when the diaspora assimilated with the native population, whether in Africa or South East Asia or the Caribbean, the US or the EU, charges of outsiders exploiting their former natives could be minimised. Yet, Indira Gandhi did respond to racial attacks in London against Punjabis or Sri Lankan Tamils.

Even those who were politically opposed to Nehru's Congress Party, and later, became short term PMs, like Morarji Desai, Charan Singh, V P Singh, Chandra Shekhar, Deve Gowda or 1K Gujral, largely followed the Congress policy line on ID, because they either had their roots in the Congress or they were in power for a short tune to change the policy into a new direction. Thus Gujral, for instance, while on a tour of South Africa in October 1997, had urged the Indian community there to fully assimilate into the native community.

However, the need for a change in policy was acutely felt by Vajpayee Government, when in May 2000, a democratically-elected government led by Mahendra Choudhury in Fiji Islands was overthrown under the pretext of power to native Fijians. The change was facilitated also by the invention of the internet, which brought the nations closer to one another. Other factors are the end of the Soviet Union and the Cold War; liberalisation, privatisation and globalisation (LPG); by which nations are moving from interdependence to closer to integration of economies and human societies.

Thus, the first NDA Government embarked upon the first celebration of the IDD in 2003. These celebrations are beneficial to India as well as the diaspora. For India, in a globalised world, it provides opportunities to tap into the highly-trained manpower resources in the European Union (EU) and the US, to bring innovative knowhow to fulfil the goal of 'Make in India.' Scientists based abroad can come to India on a long term/short term assignment to transfer latest know how to pay back to their motherland.

Second, events like these help bring in investments. As per available figures, foreign remittances of more than $25 billion were recorded during 2005-06, an amount much higher than Chinese remittances, though the Chinese abroad outnumber Indians. Diaspora remittances constitute 3.8 percent of the Indian GDP today, much higher than what India spends on national security or education. This remittance was a meagre $2.1 billion just prior to the Indian embrace of the LPG in 1991, when it was only 0.7 percent.

Third, more than the intellectual or financial capital that India can gain from the diaspora, international perception shaped by such annual events are very important. The perception of the popularity of the government created by such events amongst foreign governments, encouraging them to invest in India.

However, two precautions must be followed: First in the interest of national security, PIOs that India employs cannot provide information to their country of residence. During World War II, the US had used American citizens of Japanese origin to spy on Japan, despite the fact that the Roosevelt administration had put such citizens into concentration camps.

Second, with the growing importance of the diaspora's role, there is clamour for voting rights to be conferred on them. As long as they are Indian citizens, such rights can be conferred. But it cannot be extended to PIOs, as they are not familiar with the nation's problems at a given time. This applies to the demand that the Minister for Overseas Indians be an NRI, not simply a politician from the ruling party or coalition, on the ground that NRIs would better understand the problems of the diaspora and would be able to find the right solution. Winston Churchill, while he was Chancellor of Exchequer, had famously admitted that his knowledge of finance would not have got him a clerical post in the East India Company.

The Free Press Journal, 1 January 2015

3

AMERICAN FOREIGN POLICY

American Foreign Policy Today

Contemporary American foreign policy is formulated with four important objectives. Firstly, maintaining U.S. supremacy in the Western Hemisphere which is the foremost consideration. The Monroe Doctrine of 1823 is a good example. The doctrine was a warning to outside powers to keep their hands off the Western Hemisphere. Since then, it has been the American sphere of influence. Whenever American interests were threatened, the U.S. has freely intervened in the internal affairs of small Latin American Nations. Secondly, the U.S has been concerned to maintain the balance of power. Until World War II, it was limited to Europe. The US entered into two World Wars, initially on the weaker side led by the U.K., lest the democracies suffer under the onslaught of a dictatorship. Since World War II, the U.S. is also concerned with the maintenance of a balance of power regionally. This explains U.S. interest in Pakistan. In the 1971 Bangladesh war, the great practitioner of balance of power in modern times, Henry Kissinger, believed that the defeat of Pakistan, an ally of the U.S., at the hands of India with the help of the Soviet Union, would disturb the balance of power to an unacceptable level.

Two more objectives have became uppermost in U.S. foreign policy since World War II. Firstly, a desire to maintain the newly acquired status as the world's most powerful super power. The U.S. accepted global commitments to protect nations friendly to it. This was the essence of the Truman Doctrine. When the U.K. withdrew from its responsibilities to protect the security of Greece and Turkey, the Soviet Union was willing to fish in troubled waters. Truman warned outside powers not to interfere in European affairs and assured military aid to those who needed it. The super-power responsibility of the U.S. was stated forcefully by John F. Kennedy in his inaugural address of 1961. He said: "Let every nation know whether it wishes us well or ill, that we shall pay any price, bear any burden, meet any hardship, support any friend, oppose any foe to assure the survival and the success of liberty." Secondly, contemporary U.S. foreign policy is based on an intense anti-communism. Communism ***per se*** is bad, hence, the struggle against it is a normal duty of the U.S. As Fulbright put it, the fear of communism has been a "powerful prejudice".

The cumulative result of these four objectives has been a period of Cold War since 1945. The two main adversaries have been the Soviet Union and Communist China. The U.S. acted as a world policeman willing to put down any communist threat anywhere in the world. In the early 1970s, the U.S. had defence agreements with 42 nations, 2200 military bases in some 33 countries and the military presence of 1.1 million men in foreign countries. Whenever the interests of the Western Hemisphere were threatened by a communist nation, U.S. reactions have been decisive. That was the case in the Cuban missile crisis of 1962. The Soviet Union stealthily introduced nuclear missiles in Cuba, a pro-Soviet country in the Western Hemisphere, only 80 miles away from American shores. This was considered an unacceptable threat to American security, and the Soviet Union was compelled to withdraw the nuclear missiles from Cuba. The U.S. also militarily intervened in the civil war in the Dominican Republic in 1965, mainly because of the fear of communist infiltration and the possibility of the Dominican Republic becoming a second Cuba. The main failure of the U.S. in this period was her inability to distinguish between genuine national aspirations and communist insurgency.

The U.S. in this period pursued foreign policy with great confidence and vigour. The Soviet Union only reacted by issuing warnings in the crisis, outside its own sphere of influence. In 1965, the U.S. also intervened in South Vietnam. This was the first direct military involvement by the U.S. in a crisis outside her sphere of influence. The justification for the U.S. involvement in the Vietnam War was provided by Dean Rusk, the Secretary of State in 1967. He stated "Within the next decade or two there will be a billion Chinese on the mainland, armed with nuclear weapons, with no certainty about what their attitude towards the rest of Asia will be." If Asian nations could, with the help of democratic nations, remain free, they would at least make China learn to live in "peaceful co-existence" and also provide security to the U.S. Rusk failed to see the strength of Vietnamese nationalism.

The Vietnam War became, by the early 1970s, a stalemate. The American people were tired of a pro-longed war. President Nixon, a staunch anti-communist, realized that blind confrontation with the Communist powers did not lead the U.S. anywhere. Instead, he developed the policy of limited co-operation with the communist powers. This policy of *detente* was formalized through President Nixon's official visits to China and the Soviet Union in 1972. He also limited U.S. military protection to the nations of Western Europe and Japan. The Nixon Doctrine asked the Afro-Asian nations to practice self-help, and not to depend on direct U.S. military protection.

An important development prior to the policy of *detente* was a gradual decline of U.S. power *vis-a-vis* the Soviet Union. This decline was not in absolute terms. But the Soviet Union, during the period, was able to catch up militarily with the U.S. The American superiority of power ever the Soviet Union was levelled to parity, and that parity became acceptable to the U.S. The *detente* was also based on the U.S. grasp of the fact of intense rivalry between the two Communist powers—the Soviet Union and Communist China. So long as China considered the Soviet Union its number one enemy, in a triangular politico-military relationship, it was inevitable that U.S. and China could co-operate, if need be, against the Soviet Union.

The period of *detente* has been used by the Soviet Union to further augment its power. The American defeat in the Vietnam War made her realise the limits of power. The U.S. refused thereafter to commit her military power outside her sphere of influence. American will power was constantly probed by the Soviet Union by siding with pro-communist groups in different nations. Thus, in 1975, the MPLA in Angola, with Cuba as the surrogate of the Soviet power, succeeded in moving the country under Soviet influence. The Vietnamese attack on Kampuchea, similarly, was stage-managed by the Soviet Union. The U.S. in these cases merely condemned military interventions; nothing more. The change in the U.S. attitude can be illustrated with another example. The U.S. in 1958 under Eisenhower readily intervened in the Lebanese crisis with 1500 combat troops; but in 1976, President Ford only warned outside powers to keep off when the Lebanon crisis erupted again.

Even the U.S. will to maintain its super-power status at any cost has undergone radical changes. This is evident in the current Iranian crisis. Even as late as in 1975, the U.S. was willing to commit its military power to secure the release of the crew of *Mayaguez* held by Cambodia. But great moderation has been shown by the U.S. in her efforts for the release of 50 hostages held by the radical Iranian students in the American Embassy in Teheran. This moderation is unlikely to last very long.

The developments of the early 1980s are likely to end the *detente* and see the return of the Cold War. However, this new phase of the Cold War will be played by reversing the roles of the U.S. and the Soviet Union. In the first phase, the U.S. had a definite superiority of power *vis-a-vis* the Soviet Union. In the new phase, the U.S. power, independently considered, has moved from the position of parity to inferiority in relation to the Soviet Union. It is now only reacting to Soviet moves. The recent military intervention by the Soviet Union in Afghanistan is a pointer in that direction. This is the first direct military intervention by the Soviet Union outside its sphere of influence.

There are mony internal signs to indicate a return of the Cold War. The U.S. President has raised the military budget considerably. He has already announced the creation of a Mobile Task Force to effectively intervene anywhere at short notice. The CIA, weakened by Congressional investigations in the post-Watergate period, is likely to get back its powers to conduct clandestine activities in foreign countries. The American people are already clamouring for a strong leadership from the White House—a sure sign of Cold War resurgence.

Freedom First, May 1980

American Foreign Policy since Kennedy: A historical perspective

Since the end of World War II the American foreign policy has primarily revolved around her relations with the Soviet Union. The Cold War only intensified the conflict and competition between the two super powers. Ever since then, the result has been that US relations with other nations have come to be seen entirely through a perspective of super power equation. How do the US relations, say with nation X, help in strengthening her over-all power equation with the Soviet Union? Is a nation with the US with the Soviet Union ? These questions have primarily determined the US foreign policy since 1945.

President Kennedy was essentially a cold-warrior. The policy of containment within Europe, vigourously pursued by the previous administrations, was globalized by Kennedy. It is clear from his inaugural address, when he said: "Let every nation know, whether it wishes us well or ill, that we shall pay any price, bear any burden, meet any hardship, support any friend, oppose any foe to assure the survival and success of liberty." However, the strategy of "Massive Retaliation" formulated by the Eisenhower Administration was considered as bringing unacceptable risks of either actually retaliating and suffering destruction or backing out at the last minute and exposing the US impotency. Hence, the Kennedy Administration developed the doctrine of "Flexible Response", the US response to an international crisis would vary according to the nature of crisis.

Containment

The underlying assumption under all administrations, including the Kennedy, was that the US would be able to pursue her foreign policy objective of "containment" on a global basis only when she is able to maintain her economic and military and especially nuclear superiority over the Soviet Union. Hence, the US, under Kennedy launched a massive programme of development of newer varieties of nuclear weapons. In one sense the Cuban Missile crisis of October 1962 can be treated as the Soviet response to the US nuclear programme. Unable to match the US nuclear strength, the Soviet Union decided to place intermediate range nuclear missiles in her newly acquired ally-Cuba. The Super Power confrontation on the Cuban Missiles, finally ended in the Soviet Union agreeing to remove them from Cuba. If however, one accepts the Cuban logic behind the placement of the Soviet missiles in their territory that they had feared then, an imminent threat of the US invasion, and needed additional sense of security, then it is clear that Cuba did gain an assurance from the US through the Soviet Union that it will not directly or indirectly, organize an invasion of Cuba.

Cuban crisis

The Cuban Missile crisis however, is a turning point in the US-Soviet relations and their thinking on nuclear strategy. The super powers realized the reality of the dangers of nuclear destruction and the need to control proliferation of nuclear weapons. The result was the Partial Test Ban Treaty of 1963, and the establishment of the hot line, connecting the White House and the Kremlin for emergency direct communications. In a real sense, therefore, the Cuban Missile crisis can be considered as the beginning of Super Power detente.

The management of the Cuban Missile crisis by the Kennedy-administration, was deemed as a great success for the American power. Imbued with that success, the succeeding administration of Lyndon Johnson perfected American globalism. Johnson personally was confident that those who successfully advised Kennedy in the Cuban Missile crisis will also steer clear his foreign policy. Basically, this attitude of supreme confidence in the American power, led the US to militarily intervene in the Dominican Republic and Americanize the Vietnam War in 1965.

The Vietnam War was increasingly Americanized by Johnson on the basis of fundamentally, three unsound premises. Firstly, top policy makers of the Johnson Administration closely clung to the Domino Theory. The theory believed that the fall of South Vietnam to the communist forces, would have an irreversible impact on other nations, in the South-East Asian region - including India. The nations like Laos, Cambodia, Thailand, the theory believed, would fall like a pack of cards. The policy makers did not take into consideration the reports of the CIA which discounted the Domino Theory. The CIA felt that at the most the fall of South Vietnam would affect Laos. The fact of the fall of the communists in Indonesia, to the military regime in 1965 was also missed by the Johnson Administration.

Chinese factor

Secondly, the Johnson Administration misconceived the Chinese factor. Until the end of Johnson Administration, the policy makers believed that a decisive military result was a pre-requisite to check the Communist onslaught in the South East Asia region. A billion Chinese, by the turn of twentieth century armed with nuclear weapons, would not only pose a threat to South East Asia, but eventually to the United States itself. The military victory in the Vietnam War will make Communist China learn to live in peaceful co-existence with other nations. The Administration obviously failed to note the fact that by then, communism was no longer a monolithic force once conceived to be, and the schism in the Sino-Soviet relations was deepening. Additionally, the Vietnamese were an independent-minded people who would not make themselves a client-state, either of China or of the Soviet Union.

Thirdly, Johnson was worried about the credibility of the American security guarantee to allies within the Western military alliance. If the US did not stand by South Vietnam in their hour of crisis, who would trust the US security guarantees? But the policy makers, never for a moment, pondered or at least did not take into consideration the completely changed internal situation in that country, where the ruling clique was so completely isolated from the people, that in the absence of American power it could collapse any time without even external pressure.

Vietnam

President Johnson had personalized the Vietnam War. He did not like to be the President who lost the war. He was concerned about his place in history. He equated his personal prestige with national prestige. The Vietnam War became thus, not only an American tragedy, but a personal tragedy for a President, who otherwise was a doer of great things for his people. The War, by 1968, had become a test of two wills-American and the Communist-as North Vietnam was aided actively by the Soviet Union and Communist China. It was the Johnson Administration, which ultimately was forced to ask for the conference table in March 1968.

The accession of Richard Nixon to the American Presidency was enabled by an election promise to end the war with honour. Nixon brought about four main changes in the strategic thinking in American Foreign Policy. The first was a realization that, no longer can the US foreign policy be based on the maintenance of US nuclear superiority vis-a-vis the Soviet Union. During the period the US was draining her economic and military power in the Vietnam War, the Soviet Union was bridging the gap in its military power with the US. The US was now willing for nuclear parity with the Soviet Union. Of course, this was not altogether a new development Robert Mc Namara had said in 1967, that every US dollar on the armament is matched by the USSR leaving the US exactly, where it was. As he said : " It is futile for each of us to spend 4 billion, 40 billion or 400 billion and at the end of all the spending, and at the end of all the deployment, and at the end of all the effort, to be relatively at the same point of balance on the security scale..."

Detente

The American acceptance of nuclear parity was formalized by Nixon in his Moscow visit in 1972, when he signed **SALT I** agreement, and Super Power detente became a reality.

Second, President Nixon decided to exploit the growing antagonism between the Soviet Union and Communist China. It was also a military necessity. Since, with nuclear parity, the US alone could act as a nuclear deterrent and provide effective security to the members of the Western Alliance. The Chinese antagonism could be used to countervail the growing power of the Soviet Union in Asia, more particulary in Southeast Asia. Thus, Nixon took his historic decision to normalize relations with the main-land of China. This was the beginning of a traingular military relationship between the US, Soviet Union and Communist China.

Thirdly, the above two changes in the US strategy, were introduced for the main purpose of resolving the Vietnam War. Instead of approaching the Soviet Union and Communist China as complete adversaries of the US, Nixon wanted to enlist their co-operation in getting out of the Vietnam War. This was a basic difference in the Johnson and Nixon approaches towards the Vietnam War. While Johnson was determined to continue with the War to teach Communist China to learn to live in peaceful-co-existence, Nixon's strategy made China a factor in ending the War, as well as in future American strategy.

Strategy

Finally, to make the shrinking American power, yet effective, Nixon proclaimed his doctrine.

According to him, now US nuclear protection would be available to the members of the NATO alliance, Japan and any non-nuclear nation, threatened by a nuclear nation. But in actual combat situations, nations were expected to rely increasingly on self help, though the US was willing to supply them material assistance. All in all, Nixon's bold strategy of opening China for US relations was a radical step, though one may consider the secrecy that shrouded it, as unnecessary.

While Ford continued the policy of **detente**, saw the limited power of the US crumbling under his Presidency, when the North over-threw the South to achieve their dream of a unified Vietnam. The US was unable to save South Vietnam as a model democracy-the original purpose for which the US went into the region. When Carter took over the Presidency in 1977, the US for the first time in the post-World War II period, was living without a War in hand. He had no go, other than pursue the policy of **detente**. However, he strengthened the US relations with Communist China, finally establishing full diplomatic relations in 1978. The next major step in detente was completed by him when he signed the **SALT II** agreement with the Soviet Union in 1979. Though it was not ratified by the Senate, because of the Soviet intervention in Afghanistan in December 1979. There was full awareness, on the part of the Carter Administration, of the need for detente and the fact that the US cannot counter and challenge the Soviet power / influence everywhere in globe. As he had stated in his 'inaugural address'. We have learned that more is not necessarily better, that even our great nation has its recognized limits, and that we can neither answer all questions nor solve all problems.

The limitations of the US power, was obvious in the case of the Soviet military intervention in Afghanistan in December 1979. President Carter characterized it as the biggest single security threat since the second World War. How effective has the US power been in getting the Soviets out from Afghanistan ? The carter Doctrine, issued in the wake of the Afghanistan crisis, clearly left out Afghanistan from the operation of the doctrine which said that the Persian Gulf - constituted "vital interests" of the United States, hence, she was willing to pay a price to retain them.

The Hostages crisis in Iran again illustrates the same point. Call it President Carter's indecisiveness, or respect for international law, or the decline of the US power, but in the wake of the crisis, the US Administration felt impotency of power. The comparison may not be accurate, and it is not in several respects, yet comparison in the mind is inescapable merely to illustrate the US lack of will power to militarily intervene. Even in the 1975 Mayaguez crisis, when the Mayaguez a US ship was captured by Combodia and 39 Marines were held prisoners, President Ford decided to intervene to gain freedom for the ship and its crew. But in the Hostages crisis Carter was unable to act decisively in that direction; when he finally acted the military intervention was a big flop. The Hostages crisis was at least partly responsible to see Carter out of office in the 1980 elections.

President Ronald Reagan has come to office with a slogan, to make the US militarily a mighty power once again, second to none. In that direction he has been talking tough with the Soviets; he has refused the idea of a summit meeting with Breznev; sanctioned new weapons for the military arsenals like the neutron bomb and MX missiles; agreed to support the Afghan rebels; and removed certain constraints felt by the CIA in their conduct of covert operations. In the wake of budget cuts that the Reagan Administration is applying to every government activity, more specifically to those affecting the underprivileged and deprived, he has been reluctant to cut the military expenditure.

But the question is, can the US really afford to aim at the nuclear superiority, she once enjoyed in the sixties? Will it not prompt the Soviet Union to match every new nuclear weapon with equally sophisticated new weapons of its own? Is it not advisable for the US to settle down to a rough nuclear parity with her adversary ? The problem becomes crucial especially in view of the fact that the US no longer enjoys the economic strength she once enjoyed. Though she remains still far ahead of the economic power of the Soviet Union, she is increasingly countering economic competition from her own allies, like Western Europe and Japan.

The US foreign policy has to adapt to new situations, created by the development of new regional power-centres. The old concept of bipolarity of power no longer hold accurate to describe the power distribution in the world today. This is indicated by the assertiveness of independence in foreign policies by the members of the Western alliance, like West Germany or Japan (This holds good even to the Eastern bloc-Poland today is a case in that direction). This needs the US foreign policy makers to develop an alliance system, not on the basis of a perceived threat of a military adversary but on perceived communality of interests. This also needs an ability on the part of the US policy makers, to judge foreign policy issues not exclusively in terms of the US-Soviet power equation, but in realistic terms of regional problems as well. This may be difficult for a super power like the US but in the contemporary world there seems to be no alternative to it.

The Maharatta, 16 January 1982

Games the Republicans play

GEORGE BUSH's prospects of being re-elected seem to be very faint. The latest *Washington Post/ABC* News poll shows that Bill

Clinton leads by 55 percent to 36 percent. Other opinion polls also show the incumbent president running ten to twenty points behind his Democratic challenger. In early February 1991 Bush appeared invincible. Soon after the Gulf War, his rating in the opinion polls was so high that no serious contender for the presidency was willing to stick out his neck to run against Bush. But as of now, only a miracle can make Bush keep his job.

But Americans, particularly of the Republican variety, have no faith in miracles. The party record in recent years show that they are experts at manipulation. It was reported during the election campaign in 1980 that some members of the campaign staff of Reagan allegedly managed to steal a copy of Carter's talking points, for the TV debates in order to be prepared. But that turned out to be only a minor matter in the Reagan-Bush election strategy. The then Reagan-Bush campaign manager, the late William Casey, conspired to get the release of American hostages in Iran delayed till election day in November. Carter himself has said he was quite certain that if the hostages had come home in the summer of 1980, he would not have lost that election. As a matter of fact, if they were released even a day before the elections, he would have won the elections.

Dr Garry Sick who worked on Carter's national security council staff on the Iranian crisis, wrote of this unfair move in an article titled "Toying with hostages: The evidence suggests a scandal" in the *New York Times*. As he has pointed out, the Carter administration was planning for a second rescue mission after the first one failed in April 1980. This information was obtained by the Reagan campaign managers through organised leaks from the Carter administration. In October 1980, Republican leaders talked loud about an 'October surprise' and warned the Carter Administration against any new adventure in the Iranian crisis. But at the same time, Casey, master spy that he was who later became director of the CIA under Reagan, was negotiating a no-release agreement with the representatives of Iranian government with a promise to provide arms and spares through Israel as the conduit. This part of the agreement was subsequently fulfilled by the Reagan administration in early 1981 which was the beginning of the Iran-Contra scandal that became public in Reagan's second term and almost threatened to bring him down..

The underhand maneouvres in foreign policy practised by another Republican president, Richard Nixon, to win the elections have been well documented by Seymour Hersh in his book, the *Price of power.* In Nixon's 1968 campaign, Richard Allen was foreign policy adviser. Henry Kissinger who then was close to the Democratic administration of Lyndon Johnson as a consultant on the Vietnam peace negotiations, was getting information on negotiating positions from the negotiators and passing it to Richard Allen who, in turn, furnished Nixon with the information. These actions by Kissinger greatly influenced Nixon to later select him as his national security adviser. Nixon had sent clear signals to South Vietnamese President Thieu not to agree to the US terms as he would provide better terms if he was elected. A Republican fund raiser, Anna Chennault, was the channel of communication between the Nixon campaign managers and President Thieu. Nixon had campaianed on the theme of ending the Vietnam War with honour. As the war did not end under the Johnson administration and the peace talks did not take off, Hubert Humphrey, then sitting vice-president and Democratic candidate, lost the election.

Nixon started his re-election strategy early in 1970 by planning a dramatic state visit to China in 1972. By arranging the successful opening of relations with China, he not only silenced liberal critics of his Vietnam policy, but ensured his re-election. Nixon writes in his memoirs that Mao told him that he voted for him. With such skilful manoeuvering of foreign affairs, he had no need to worry about his victory in 1972. Taking place under Nixon's instructions was the Watergate break-into gain access to the Democrats' election strategy; that became the Watergate scandal and marked the end of his presidency.

Bush has denied any knowledge of use of delaying tactics in the Iranian hostage crisis in 1980. Also, so far there have been no reports of his use of any foreign policy issue to get elected in 1988, as he inherited Regan's mantle of conservative leadership. But in 1992, when he escalated the crisis in Iraq, many Americans considered it to be linked to his bid to boost his sagging popularity in electoral politics. But his upping the ante in the Iraqi crisis and calling for a no-fly zone in southern Iraq have apparently had no effect on the electorate.

During a TV interview last December Bush said: "I will do what I have to do to be re-elected". Is he going to throw an 'October surprise'? That is what worries many election-watchers today. Dr Garry Sick in his article on the Reagan scandal of 1980 raised an important issue: is it democratic to play politics with national security?

The Stakes may be high; success in manoeuvering foreign policy may be easy on account of the enveloping secrecy. But are such dirty tricks legitimate in a democracy? Especially when the Republicans talk so much more about morality?

The Independent, 19 October 1992

Caution: Superpower looking for trouble

The United States is conducting a military campaign, with the nominal collaboration of the North Atlantic Treaty Organisation (NATO), against the Federal Republic of Yugoslavia, an independent country within the United Nations (UN) system. This is the most brazen use of air power by a military alliance dominated by a leading member of the organisation, and against a member of the UN, in violation of Article 53 of the UN Charter.

Brazen, because the use of force has not been authorised by the UN as was the case in the war against Iraq in 1991. On the other hand, two permanent members of the UN Security Council, Russia and China, vehemently opposed the attacks on a member of the UN as unwarranted and unjustified. Yugoslavia has committed no aggression against any neighbour.

What is the American and NATO rationale for their brazen use of destructive air power against Yugoslavia? The Bill Clinton administration has accused the Yugoslav government, under President Slobodan Milosevic, of gross violation of human rights in Kosovo, a province of Yugoslavia inhabited by Muslim Albanians. This is not to condone the violation of human rights by Serbian leaders, but was there no alternative to the use of blatant force?

The use of air power, which is nothing but an act of undeclared war against Yugoslavia is in pursuance of an American post-Cold War doctrine of foreign policy

Under the new doctrine, the Clinton administration has given itself the right to interfere in the internal affairs of another country, albeit selectively. Addressing newspaper editors in Annapolis, Maryland, Clinton, in early 1993, said: "During the Cold War, our foreign policies largely focussed on relations among nations. Today, our policies must also focus on relations within nations, on a nations form of governance, on its economic structure and on its *ethnic tolerance.*"

In the case of Kosovo, the US and NATO, from the beginning, were itching to use force. Madeleine Albright, US Secretary of State, said long before 24 March: "In case the Serbs do not accept the agreement for K&M (Kosovo & Metohija), they will be bombed, while, if the Albanian side refuses, they will no longer have the help and support." This is exactly what the US forces have done from 24 March onwards.

To pursue the US foreign policy doctrine, more than 500,000 refugees have been created, Belgrade has been bombed — which cannot be rebuilt in the next 10 years — as also all bridges on the River Danube, all to force Yugoslavia to accept the terms worked out by NATO, so far accepted only by the Kosovo Liberation Army (KLA).

What are the implications of the US-led NATO bombings of Yugoslavia for the international society and, in particular, to the many multi-ethnic nations, including India? Without claiming to be exhaustive, three major implications of the US-led NATO bombing of Yugoslavia can be discussed here.

First, the obvious. The bombing has been justified to promote human rights and create a sense of security amongst ethnic Albanians who are now scattered in the neighbourhood of Yugoslavia as refugees from Kosovo. But under the domestic jurisdiction clause, Article 7 of the UN Charter, member nations are prevented from interfering in the internal affairs of another state. US efforts to discuss human rights violations by China in the UN Human Rights Commission (UNHRC) in Geneva have been frustrated by China for the last seven years. No nation allows its internal affairs to be discussed, let alone let action to be taken, by other nations. Why then is the US taking a special interest in Kosovo? This will set a bad precedent.

Second, in recent years the US has come out a little more clearly against state-promoted international terrorism, as opposed to the earlier double standard in which terrorism against the US was treated differently from terrorism against other states. At the NATO summit in Washington, DC, last week, NATO leaders loudly announced their intention to fight international terrorism. Then why are the Americans embracing the KLA, an extremist terrorist force equipped with weapons looted from Albania to fight for an independent Kosovo?

An American journalist, who travelled with Richard Holbrooke in his failed mission to resolve the Kosovo crisis, filed this report for the

New Yorker (January 11, 1999): "In early 1997, following the collapse of Albania, the population looted the government arsenals, making off with an estimated three million grenades and bombs and seven hundred thousand rifles. These arms quickly found their way into the hands of Kosovo guerrillas, who now gather in Albania, train there, and cross the border into their homeland." These very forces are also involved in international drug smuggling.

The Americans, instead of assisting moderate forces in Kosovo, which were willing to settle for genuine local autonomy within Yugoslavia, threw their weight on the side of the KLA. Yugoslavian leadership, for its part, was willing to concede autonomy to Kosovo, even accept NATO aerial surveillance of the implementation of the agreement. But the US and NATO wanted Yugoslavia to accept NATO troops in Kosovo to supervise implementation of an agreement signed only by the KLA and not by Yugoslavia. Yugoslavia, rightly, was not willing to accept the presence of NATO troops on its soil to oversee the implementation of a KLA agreement.

What explains the US behaviour? Within Europe, a unified Germany led the first strike to disintegrate Yugoslavia by recognising Slovenia and Crotia as independent states. Then the US stepped in, to seek the separation of Bosnia from Yugoslavia. Now, the US is pursuing its predetermined policy of separating Kosovo from Yugoslavia. The US, thereby, wants to use the situation to wash off its guilt feeling for not doing much to help Palestinians in the Middle East, and demonstrate a pro-Muslim image to diminish threats from the Muslim world to American interests. Remember, Clinton permitted Iran — declared by the Americans as a terrorist state — to provide weapons to Bosnian Muslims to fight Serbs.

Third, if the NATO plan is allowed to succeed, it poses a severe threat to national security and the territorial integrity of many multi-ethnic and multi-religious societies big and small, like Russia, China, India, Iraq, Turkey and even Sri Lanka.

Why does the US, itself a multi-ethnic, and multi-religious state, consciously follow the policy of breaking all such states? The US, thereby, hopes to maintain its preponderance of power. After the break-up of the Soviet Union in December 1991, American scholars were not lagging behind in predicting the similar break-up of India and China.

Hence, India and other multi-ethnic states need to ponder the implications to their highly pluralistic states. Professor Raju Thomas, an American of Indian origin teaching in Marquette University, US, wrote: "If the West can unilaterally/ draw up and dictate a settlement over Kosovo to the Sertbs and follow it up with a massive NATO bombing campaign enforce it, what will prevent NATO from doing the same over Kashmir (or Tibet, Tamil Eelam, Iraqi Kurdistan Chechenia?"

Though India is not Yugoslavia, strong similarities of the issues involved cannot be ignored. There are fringe groups Kashmir demanding separation from the Indian Union, They are aided, trained, funded and armed externally, as in the case of Kosovo. What the if the US, as a friend of Pakistan decides to have an independent Kashmir, so that there can be peace and promotion of human rights in the South Asian region — particularly now that both India and Pakistan are armed with nuclear weapons?

If this was a theoretical possibility till the other day last week the House of Lords in the UK already discussed the applicability of the new US doctrine to Kashmir. Lord Ahmed and other lords, narrated their moving experience with Kashmiri refugees during their recent visit to Pakistan and pleaded with the UK to turn its attention to South Asia.

"What was right in the Balkans must surely be right in South Asia," Lord Ahmed said in the House.

When George Bush spoke of creating a new world order in the wake of the Gulf War of early 1991, no one thought of the American dream of creating a world order chiselled by American artisans. After the unilateral bombings of Iraq now it is the turn of Yugoslavia to be ordered by Americans. Whose turn is it next?

The bipolarity of the Cold War period had created a balance of power in international relations. If the US, in the exercise of its "arrogance of power," the famous phrase of late Senator William Fulbright Jr, threatened Vietnam, the Soviet Union could help the latter face a superior war-making power. In the absence of such balance, because of the economic weakness of Russia, Americans are using their military muscle to perpetuate their hegemony not only over Europe but over the entire world, clearly demonstrating the dangers arising from a unipolar world.

The major powers, like Russia, China and India, need to assert themselves and create multipolar world so that a degree of sanity is re-established in international relations.

The Sunday Observer, 2-8 May 1999

Politics of US debt to United Nations

The US administration has been doing a fire-fighting operation to retain its voting rights in the UN by clearing partially its debt to the world body — the UN in New York. The US government owes the world body a huge sum of $1.52 billion. Under the UN rules, if a member nation does not pay its regular dues for two years in succession, it stands to lose its voting rights. It has won for the time being. The Republican-controlled Congress and the Democratic White House negotiated the fine details of budget recently. In the fiscal year 1999-2000, it provides for US to pay the UN $926 million as part of their dues. Of this, $351 is to be paid before the end of December 1999. The remaining amount is tied with certain conditions.

The fact that the most powerful country — the only surviving superpower — is in perpetual debt to the UN is something difficult to understand. This is more so, when the US mostly used the UN as an extension of its own foreign policy instrument since the demise of the Soviet Union in 1991. Thus, for instance, US conducted through NATO, completely bypassing the UN, a war against Yugoslavia for over 90 days, spending billions of dollars. To cap it further, US gained UN approval for its plan for peace in Kosovo only after forcing Yugoslavia to accept the terms dictated by them.

This makes one thing clear. US has money, but its government or to be more precise, lawmakers — do not have the necessary will power to contribute their share to the upkeep of the UN as a world body of 188 nations in the creation of which their leaders took a leading role in the 1940s. The US contribution to the UN does not come to even a dollar per head while an average American may spend seven dollars to see a movie. Then, what is the cause behind this, what US ambassador in the UN, Richard Holbrooke described as 'unfortunate incidents of US foreign policy'?

Let me touch upon the past attitude of the US towards the UN. In the 1970s, often with the Third World countries joining hands with the Soviet bloc, the West led by the US were isolated on crucial world issues in General Assembly. Then the US did threaten to withdraw from the UN, as was the case with the US ambassador, Patrick Moynihan. In the 1980s the US did withdraw from some of the UN organisations like the UNESCO on the ground that these squander public money by paying high salaries to their top executives. It was a policy plank of the Republican Party and the US governments were under the Republicans in the 1970s and the 1980s barring four years of Carter (1977-1981).

However, in the 1990s the role is reversed with the end of the Cold War in global politics and reversal of party position in the White House. The Democrats gained the control of White House in 1993. Since Clinton took over the White House, he has favoured the continued and active participation of the US in the UN. But Republicans, having retained their hold over the Congress, have continued to struggle to trim the US participation in the UN. Democrats have vowed to fight this trend of neo-isolationism.

In the present war over the payment of legitimate dues to the UN, the major issue that has dominated the debate is the use of US funds for the promotion of family planning globally by international agencies. It is again an ironic trend in the US. In the 1950s, US administration took initiative in pushing for family planning under the Eisenhower administration. Then the Cold War logic was that if the population grows unchecked, it would be a threat to Western economic security. Eventually, it could be national security threat too. The Republicans generally support the conservative plank of pro-life. Now, the Republicans have taken their pro-life plank to the UN. The Congress had legislated in 1973 not to fund any activities related to abortion in the US. How can then they say that the UN use the funds provided by the US to promote family planning or abortions globally?'

The White House has, through hard bargain with the Republican-controlled Congress, got the US funding of the UN approved in the FY 2000 budget that was already delayed by seven months by them. However, the Clinton administration had to agree to limit funds for international groups that support abortion rights.

The Weekend Observer, 27 November 1999

4

INDIA-US RELATIONS: FROM CONFRONTATION TO CO-OPERATION

Time to reassess ties with Israel

OUR traditional policy towards West Asia has been one of blindly supporting Arab and Islamic nations vis-a-vis their dispute with Israel. This policy has been justified from time to time, on three grounds.

First, we depend on various countries of the region like Saudi Arabia, Iraq, Iran and Kuwait for our oil as we are not self-sufficient in energy resources.

Second, through our support of all Islamic states in West Asia, we have tried to neutralise the possibility of their blindly supporting Pakistan in international fora, on issues affecting vital interests of India, particularly on Kashmir.

Third, in the beginning, there was on the part of Jawaharlal Nehru, a personal fascination of a modernist, secularist and socialist President Nasser of Egypt, who was a co-founder of the Non-aligned movement (NAM).

Thus, the traditional pro-Arab pro-Islam policy has resulted in India not establishing full diplomatic relations with Israel, though we have recognised the state of Israel. All these years we have shied away from establishing full diplomatic relations at ambassadorial level with that country though we have consular relations.

On the other hand, not only we have been — and rightly so — in the forefront of advocating the legitimate cause of a statehood for the

Palestinian people and have accorded recognition to the Palestine Liberation Organisation (PLO).

However, the traditional world in which we pursued our traditional policy has changed radically, first with the end of the Cold War in December 1987, and later, as a result of the recent Gulf War between Iraq and 28-nation alliance led by the US.

The post-war West Asian politics is no longer what it was in the 1960s or even in the 1970s. Islamic nations of West Asia are not necessarily a united lot vis-a-vis Israel or even on matters of supporting the PLO. Thus, for instance, Egypt has full diplomatic relations with Israel.

And other nations like Saudi Arabia and the newly liberated Kuwait might soon recognize Israel. Syria may also initiate direct talks with Israel resulting eventually in establishing diplomatic relations between the two.

Israel may not be able to offer us oil: but as a brave people who withstood four wars in their brief life span, as we faced four wars in the more or less same period, can no longer be ignored. Israel is a democracy as we are.

Hence, in. this changing world scenario. India need to reassess it's traditional policy of ignoring and downgrading her relations with Israel. Now is the right time to establish full-fledged diplomatic relations with Israel.

This does not mean we follow 'either or policy' and give up our support to Palestinian people. Instead, our normal relations with Israel will provide us more diplomatic leverage to act as a honest mediator between the two antagonists. Our record of support to the PLO is much more unblemished compared to even some other Arab or Islamic nations.

There is, therefore, no need for us to feel shy, when even the PLO chief, Mr Arafat himself has indicated his willingness to talk directly with Israel. Should we wait till all other Arab nations recognise Israel before we establish full diplomatic relations?

In this changing unipolar world, our normal relations with Israel will bring us some important gains. First, an immediate upgradation of diplomatic relations with Israel will help us to correct our flawed policy towards the Gulf crisis, which started with the demand for Iraqi withdrawal from Kuwait till war began on Jan 17.

But once Iraqi intransigence led to the war, our political support went to Iraq in the name of our traditional non-aligned policy (whatever that may mean in the absence of a bipolar world).

Second, with our normal relations with Israel, we can certainly turn pro-Israeli lobbies in the US to become, indirectly at least, pro-India in the context of our problems with Pakistan, whether in relations to the latter's nuclear weapons programme which is seen as an 'Islamic bomb', or on the question of Pak-sponsored terrorism in Punjab or Kashmir.

Third, our normal relations with Israel can be a counter-weight to Pakistan in all international fora whenever necessary.

It is worth noting that though Iran has not recognised Israel, it has always, even after establishment of an Islamic order by Imam Khomeini, looked to Israel as a counterweight to check the growing regional power of Iraq. We need to look at Israel as a geo-political counterweight to neutralise effects of US close relations with Pakistan.

The big question is: Are our political parties capable of looking beyond their immediate electoral gains?

Is our caretaker government capable of taking care of our nations interests in this rapidly changing world?

Answer to the second question is yes, better than any normal government, particularly in view of a negative answer to the first question.

Mr Chandrashekhar has in a sense a golden opportunity to rectify national political blunder by establishing full diplomatic relations with Israel, perpetrated by governments so far by not realistically assessing our policy towards Israel.

With the dissolution of the ninth Lok Sabha, he is free from political constraints imposed by the myopic consideration of our political parties of losing Muslim votes. He cannot have any sensible hope of returning as Prime Minister after the next Lok Sabha elections.

But at least he could have satisfaction of upholding India's national interest as he upheld his own prestige by resigning on the face non-co-operation of his outside ally, the Congress.

The Business and Political Observer, 12 April 1991

Opening ties with Israel

The smooth passage of the resolution, on December 17 in the UN General Assembly, annulling Resolution 3379, which had for 16 years equated Zionism with racism, reflects the radically changed international scene following the end of the Cold War and the Gulf crisis.

The November 10, 1975, UN resolution was passed in the context of the strong anti-Israeli sentiments prevailing after the Yom Kippur war of 1973. The move was actively supported by the Soviet bloc and a vast majority of the members of the Non-Aligned Movement (NAM) voted in favour of the 1975 resolution.

Since then, Israel had been lobbying hard to get the UN resolution revoked. The recent Gulf War marked a major departure from the past stand on Israel. It saw most Arab countries aligned on the side of the US. Israel's non-intervention in the war, despite Iraqi provocation, encouraged at least some Arab countries to soften their anti-Israeli posture. This helped the passage of the resolution with the support of 111 countries of 166 UN members, including not only India but some 20 Arab countries and the Soviet Union.

The Organisation of Islamic Conference (OIC), at a summit meeting in Senegal, opposed the move. But the Islamic bloc failed to garner support in the UN to block the resolution repealing the pariah status of Israel. This was due to the desertion of the former Soviet bloc of its traditional pro-Arab position. In fact, Hungary and Czechoslovakia co-sponsored the resolution that revoked the anti-zionist resolution of 1975.

After voting in favour of the resolution, what should be the next logical step for India? A reply to this question requires assessment of the recent developments that affect India directly, especially the new international order in which the US alone is calling the shots. In the past, India religiously depended on Soviet support in the UN on all crucial matters that had a bearing on her vital interests. Now, in the absence of a guaranteed support in global diplomacy, India will have to muster support on crucial issues on a realpolitik and purely quid-pro-quo basis.

India should also take note of the fact that, in the wake of declining US and other western countries' support, Pakistan is now trying to enlist support for such issues as Kashmir from other sources. For instance, Pakistan is seeking to use the OIC as forum to raise the Kashmir question and internationalise the issue.

Thus, India's old ties and emotional loyalties towards Arabs and the Islamic World, needs to be reassessed realistically on the basis of the age-old dictum of Lord Palmerston that nations neither have permanent friends nor permanent enemies; they have only permanent interests.

Our permanent interests are protecting our territory from external and internal threats, achieving rapid economic development, and preserving our democratic institutions. In this respect, our past policy of always supporting the Arabs against Israel has not brought us much returns. It has, by no means, helped India neutralise Arab support to Pakistan in all major Indo-Pak disputes.

Hence, a time has come when India should convey to Israel and the world at large, that she too has re-evaluated her interests. And, her vote in favour of the US backed resolution was only the first step towards establishing diplomatic relations, preferably at the ambassadorial level with Israel.

This will enable India to secure international goodwill in world politics in many ways. First, it will help India to develop closer relations with pro-Israel countries in the UN. Many countries, particularly in Europe,- having a sizeable Jewish population would naturally look favourably at India. Second, it will be helpful in strengthening Indo-US relations. India needs to strengthen her relations with the US which now occupies an important place in our security and economic policies, particularly in view of its ability to rein in Pakistan.

Third, it will also help India in winning friends in US domestic politics. The Jewish lobby in the US is one of the most powerful and influential lobbies and has, time and again, shown its ability to influence US government in favour of Israel and her friends. The powerful Jewish lobby will be on India's side in limiting US aid to Pakistan.

Fourth, Israel's experience in successfully handling terrorism in her country could be useful to India which too is faced with serious terrorist-related problems in Punjab and Kashmir. Indian forces need to develop new tactics for fighting terrorists. Israel has fairly advanced skills in counter-terrorist operations and measures. India will do well to learn from the Israelis their methods of dealing with terrorists who have no respect for democratic values or processes.

The Narasimha Rao government, in its eagerness to promote a liberalised Indian economy, is seeking the help of NRIs in a big way. We must remember that there are over 30,000 Israelis who were born in India. They may not be NRIs in the sense that they do not hold Indian passports, but they have goodwill for India primarily because they suffered no discrimination here, unlike the experience of most Jewish emigres from the rest of the world. India, by normalising relations with Israel will provide them the opportunity to invest in India.

Indian reluctance to upgrade diplomatic ties with Israel shows its unwillingness to change her policy even while the rest of the world is undergoing dramatic changes. That it is unable to keep pace with the rapidly changing political scenario is evident from her belated efforts to talk directly with the Russian President, Mr Boris Yeltsin.

Normalisation of ties with Israel does not mean that whatever Israel has done so far or is likely to do in the future is right and in keeping with India's thinking. Indeed, this is not, and should not be the yardstick for establishing relations with nation states. If that is the yardstick by which India proposes to choose the countries with which it will or will not have ties, then it must rethink its ties with a number of countries.

There can be no moral high ground for relations between states. The only criterion ought to be protection of Indian interests. In fact, having ties with states which are treated as international pariahs often act as a moderating influence. Our normalisation of ties with Israel may indeed result in Israel becoming more open to Indian advice, perhaps even on the question of Palestine.

The Business and Political Observer,
25 December 1991

Hard cheese, big bully

The Cold War ended and the Soviet Union disintegrated. There was hope, in the US and India, that, at last, the two governments were coming closer.

But American policy-makers seem hell-bent on proving these perceptions wrong. It appears that they pick up an issue every weekend to prick at Indian sensibilities. The latest involves trying to force Russia into not providing pocket technology to India as agreed under the 1991 treaty, signed before the Soviet Union disintegrated and Russia became a successor state to the treaty obligations.

The state department spokesperson said on May 3 that the US government would impose penalties on Russia and India if the deal came through.

Earlier, there were other irritants. First, there was pressure on India not to sell a 10 MW nuclear research reactor to Iran. Then came pressure not to sell rice to Cuba. These were in addition to renewed pressures to sign the NPT.

While this was in the security arena, there is pressure building up on Super 301 to open up service industries and to protect US patents, particularly in pharmaceuticals. The US trade representative has already suspended duty-free treatment for exports of pharmaceuticals and chemicals as “a first minor step”. More severe action is held out as a threat.

Why are the US policy-makers so shortsighted as to hinder India’s space programme by forcing Russia to deny cryogenic engines needed to launch satellites? How does one explain this American diplomacy, which is likely to slow down or even act as a setback to improvement of Indo-US bilateral security relations? The credibility of American policy is lost, even in the eyes of its friends in this country.

Three explanations can be offered. First, the US government is perennially, unable to formulate any long-term policy because of discontinuities provided by the constitution which limits presidential tenure to eight years. The separation of powers between the executive and the legislative branch only further complicates the problem.

However, this is inapplicable in this case as the long-term policy of looking upon India as a co-operative regional power goes back to 1985 when the Republican party formed the policy.

The second explanation is the inability of the administration to formulate a coherent foreign policy because of strong bureaucratic politics. Thus, for instance, early this year the Pentagon's plans to knock off India's nuclear installations and develop continued strategic relationship with Pakistan were leaked to the press. However, it was dismissed as conflicting perceptions between the central command under which Pakistan falls and the Pacific command under which India comes. The State Department also dismissed it as a report prepared by low-level official and not reflecting government views. But nothing of this has been mentioned in the case of rocket technology.

The third explanation — which is relevant in this case — is that it is a sign of arrogance. The Americans are anxious to perform the role of world policeman in the post-Cold War period with a monopoly to maintain international law and order.

During the Cold War, despite enormous resources, the US was unable to assert its presence in all crisis situations as it was challenged by the Soviet Union. But now, with the end of the Cold War, bereft of an effective challenger, it wants to relive the role of supercop. The US victory, in the Gulf War in 1991 has only created a superego in the American psyche.

However, the US ought to know that no country is going to accept its bullying for long. Unlike in the past, today she does not have the resources to buy and bully friends or foes.

With the economy in recession, a $400 billion budget deficit and an over $3.1 trillion national debt, the US will not just be able to dominate the world unless the policy-makers have no long-term perspective and simply desire to win a score against India in the election year.

In the changed world, the US can only act to maintain world peace with co-operation of countries like India and not by bullying her.

Midday, 14 May 1992

Shortsighted American diplomacy

In the recent past there have been many irritants in Indo-US relations. First, there was pressure on India not to sell 10 MW nuclear research reactor to Iran. The ostensible reason was to curb the nuclear ambition of Iran. Then came pressure not to sell rice to Cuba, as a part of US efforts to isolate the only communist state in the Western hemisphere now that it has lost its benefactor, the Soviet Union. These irritants were in addition to renewed pressures on India to sign the NPT. While this is in security arena there is pressure built under the Super 301 to open up service industries like banking and protect US patents particularly in pharmaceuticals. Under the special 301 US. Trade Representative has already suspended duty free treatment to Indian pharmaceuticals and chemicals as "a first minor step". More severe action is held out as a threat.

The latest one is imposition of US ban for two years on trade and technology transfers with and to the Indian Space Research Organization (ISRO) and its Russian counterpart, Glavkosmos. What made these space agencies to merit these sanctions? The US had asked Russia not to provide rocket technology to India as agreed under 1991 treaty signed before the Soviet Union disintegrated and Russia became a successor state to those treaty obligations. The US State Department spokesperson publicly had stated that the US government would impose penalties on Russia and India if the sale of technology is gone though as provided in the treaty. Obviously, Russia and India were not willing to go back on their treaty obligations. Not able overlord Russia, the US resorted to trade sanctions.

With the end of the Cold War and disintegration of the Soviet Union in December 1991, there was a widespread public perception in the US as well as in this country that at last governments of two countries are coming closer in their global security concerns in general and regional concerns in particular. This was significant as record of two democracies is long on conflicts and short on co-operation. But the American policy-makers seem to be hell-bent on proving that these public perceptions are wrong. It appears as though that they pick up one issue every weekend to prick at the Indian sensibilities.

What is the US longterm security objective in the region? It was surmised by US-watchers as one of promoting greater co-operation in political, security and economic arena in the decades to come. Way back in 1985, the then US Under Secretary of Defence, Fred Ikle had said, "India could be a power that contributes to world stability as the US will see it, and to want to shape it in 1995 and the year 2025, and a power with which we could work together... to enhance our long-term national securty aims". Later in 1986 Richard Armitage, Assistant Secretary of Defence said, "We recognise India as a regional power and a coming world power". It is this role as a regional power that India played in Sri Lanka (1987) and Maldives (1988). India also co-operated during the Gulf War in 1991 by permitting it to refuel Air force aircraft in Mumbai.

Why then are US policy-makers so shortsighted as to create obstacles in the India's space programme by forcing Russia to deny cryogenic engines needed in launching satellites? How does one explain US diplomacy which is likely to slow down or even act as a setback to improvement of Indo-US bilateral security relations? The credibility of American policy is lost even in the eyes of their best friends in this country.

Three plausible explanations can be offered. First, the US government is perennially unable to formulate any long-term policy because of discontinuities provided by the constitution which limits presidential tenure to eight years. The separation of powers between the executive and the legislative branch only further complicates the problem.

However, this is inapplicable in this case as the long-term policy of looking to India as a co-operative regional power goes back to 1985 and not only the Bush administration belongs to the same Republican Party as that of the Reagan administration that formulated the policy in the first instance, but Bush was very much part of the Reagan administration.

The second explanation given is the inability to formulate a coherent foreign policy because of strong bureaucratic politics. For instance, early this year, the Pentagon's plans to knock off India's nuclear installations and develop continued strategic relationship with Pakistan were leaked to the Press. However, it was dismissed as conflicting perceptions and policy advocacies between the Central Command under which Pakistan falls and the Pacific Command under which India comes. The State Department also dismissed it as a report prepared by a low-level official and not reflecting Bush Administration's views.

But in the presence case of rocket technology nothing of the sort has been spoken of so far. Hence, the relevance of third explanation. In nutshell, it is a case of arrogance of power. The Americans are anxious to cast themselves in the role of World Policeman in the post-

Cold War period with a self conferred monopoly right to maintain international law and order. During the Cold War, despite enormous resources, the US was unable to assert its presence in all crisis situations as it was challenged by the Soviet Union. But now with the end of the Cold War, without an effective challenger the US wants to relive the role of super cop. The US victory, in the Gulf War in 1991 has only created a superego in the American psyche.

There cannot be any other explanation based on any principle or international law. Otherwise, how else can the US think that what is immensely good for her is not good for developing democracies? Many instances can be cited here. But suffice it, if I give one example. The US wants Russia, as a successor taste to the Soviet Union adhere to all international treaties concluded by the two enforce arms control and reduction. The US sent a list of such treaties to Russia. Interestingly it did not include 1972 Anti Ballistic Missiles (ABM) Treaty which limits number of ABMs possessed by each country which cannot be altered. However the US wants to deploy Strategic Defence Initiative (SDI) system which cannot be legally done under the present ABM treaty. Hence, US would like to renegotiate the ABM treaty to enable her to mission! Cryogenic engines needed for India's space" programme, scientists here pointed out, cannot be used in long range missiles for military purposes. India says that US and France were also willing to sell these engines. But the price was the factor that made India to go for Russian technology because they were cheaper by more than one half. If that is so, should the US prevent a democracy like India from developing its own satellite system which is today a monopoly of US, France and Russia? The US then is merely motivated by trade considerations. It is significant to that the Russians have charged the US of waging a trade war.

The American banning transfer of technology to ISRO also goes against their own decision of 1984, taken under. National Security Decision Directive given to all agencies emphasising the need to accommodate Indian requests for transfer of sophisticated technology with a view to build a better US-India relationship. It will be in the US interest to comprehend that she will just not be able to dominate the world unless of course, the policy-makers in the Bush administration are so shortsighted that they have no long term perspective and and simply desire to win a point against Russia and India in the election year. In the changed world, the US can only contribute to maintain world peace and security with the cooperation of countries like India and not by bullying.

The Observer of Business and Politics, 20 May 1992

U.S. India Relations in the Post-Cold War Era

The greatest event in the history of international relations since World War II, was the end of the Cold War in December 1991.' Ever since, the nations of the world are engaged in reshaping their foreign relations. India is no exception. Since the end of World War II, U.S.-India relations were affected by the then prevailing Cold War. The U.S. considered communism as a threat to its own democratic system and to world peace and, after 1971, the Soviet Union as the only threat to its security and cherished values. Hence, her relations with other countries particularly in the developing world were determined by what 1 call as the Soviet Equation.[2] The Soviet Equation in the context of the U.S. can be defined as a consideration by the U.S. as to how its relations with another country help or hinder her global policy of containment of and confrontation with the Soviet Union.

U.S.-India relations were thus, conditioned by the Soviet Equation. It is well known that India was partitioned and Pakistan was created on the basis of religion. This religious foundation of Pakistan and India's continued adherence to secular principles made 'Pakistan see India as the only threat to its security and survival. Thus, Pakistan joined hands with the U.S. in its global efforts to contain communism by promoting military alliances. After the Sino-Indian War of 1962 Pakistan drew closer to the Peoples' Republic of China (PRC). Americans were not altogether unaware of the fact that Pakistan had joined the American-led alliance system to subserve her own regional Cold War with India. This was summed up by the then U.S. Ambassador to Pakistan, Ronald I. Spiers on 20th April, 1982: Most of our past problems, I think have, stemmed from a different view about the purpose and open-endedness of the security ties which have existed between Pakistan and U.S. since the early 1950s. A principal focus of Pakistani concern has been India, the principal concern of the U.S... is the potential threat and pressures from the Soviet Union. This was, however, overlooked by U.S. policy makers in their broader global objective of the 1970s of containing the Soviet Union. For this broader purpose, the U.S. had coopted the PRC on her side as the PRC considered the Soviet Union its number one enemy. By the time of the Bangladesh War in 1971, the U.S. Pakistan-PRC axis on the one side and the India-Soviet Union axis on the other was very clear. The global triangular balance of power had become pentagonal in the South Asian context. This was also the pattern in the 1980's -the U.S. confrontation with the Soviet-Union over the latter's invasion of Afghanistan.

Mrs. Indira Gandhi then Indian Prime Minister, neither condemned nor condoned the Soviet-invasion of Afghanistan. But Reagan began his perception of India in simplistic terms — those not with U.S. are against the U.S. But by the mid-1980s he had changed his view of India. In an interview with Derek Davis and Nayan Chanda, Reagan said: "Mrs. Gandhi has said that India is not pro or anti any other country, but instead is pro-India. We accept that position."

The end of the Cold War has brought about the demise of the global triangular balance of power. As a consequence, the regional pentagonal balance of power also broke down. What has emerged in the place of the bipolar world of the past is today's unipolar world — only in terms of military predominance and the will power to commit coercive force to achieve global foreign policy goals. But in economic and political terms the world can be described as being multi-polar.

Turnabouts in US-India Relations

Even before the end of the Cold War, the U.S. had taken steps to improve its own perception of India. This was done under the Reagan Administration. Since India was perceived as tilting towards the Soviet Union, the Reagan Administration desired to wean India away from the Soviet Union and help it to move towards greater autonomy in the military arena. Hence, the crucial decision by the US's National Security Council, in October 1984 to permit transfer of technology with dual use liberally. This gained momentum after Rajiv Gandhi's visit to the U.S. in June 1985.

Indian Security Concerns and Pakistan

But major changes in U.S.-India relations came during the Bush Administration in March 1990 when it clearly and categorically stated that it did not believe that old UN resolutions are any longer relevant to resolve the Kashmir question and a solution to the problem has to be found within the Shimla agreement of 1972. This was further clarified to suggest that the U.S. does not support any more the idea of a plebiscite in Kashmir. This was subsequently reiterated by the then U.S. Ambassador to the UN, Thomas Pickering.

It is also a significant gesture from the U.S. that it is committed to the maintenance of the territorial integrity of India. This was significant as India faced (what is described by the U.S.) as Low Intensity Conflict (LIC) promoted by Pakistan in India's north-western province of Punjab and in Jammu and Kashmir (JK). Various 'liberation' movements in these two states are demanding secession from the Indian Union on the basis of linguistic and religious sub-nationalism. These separatist movements are funded, equipped and supported by Pakistan. U.S. policy-makers, Congressmen and Senators are now asking Pakistan not to encourage international terrorism in India.

Pakistan has also played its nuclear ambiguity card very well against both the U.S. and India. This is in contrast to India's demonstrated nuclear capability coupled with its political policy of non-weaponisation of nuclear know-how. The U.S. had conclusive proof of Pakistan's nuclear weapons programme before President Bush suspended all economic and military aid to that country in October 1990. The U.S. has maintained pressure on Pakistan to resist from going nuclear. Thus, in effect the U.S. is acting as a security multiplier to India vis-a-vis Pakistan.

Security Concerns vis-a-vis the PRC.

However, in the security arena the greater, though rather remote, threat to India is from the PRC. The two countries have moved a long way from the confrontationist stand of the 1970s to the uncertainties of the 1980s and to develop closer bilateral relations, in the 1990s. Yet there are four main Indian security concerns. First, is the fact that China is a full fledged nuclear power with all weapon systems and delivery systems. Though the PRC recently signed the NPT as a nuclear power, it had hardly any effect on her nuclear behaviour. For instance, when the Indian President was on Chinese soil in May 1992, Beijing exploded a 1000 kiloton nuclear device. What does it demonstrate? The PRC probably wants to show that her signing the NPT does not prevent her from developing further sophisticated weapon systems. Further, she would like to be part of the five-nation conference on nuclear questions affecting South Asia - whenever it is held, as an equal to two other nuclear powers - U.S. and Russia.

Second, there is the unresolved border dispute between India and the PRC. Though the two countries have decided to place the dispute in the backburner, Indian security concerns cannot vanish and normal bilateral relations cannot be established till the border problem is resolved. Till that happens there are still many issues of mutual interest between Pakistan and China to make common cause against India that India cannot relax her security concerns. Then there is the question of Tibetan autonomy and the question of violation of human rights. Though the government of India has conceded that Tibet is a part of China, Indians are not satisfied with China's treatment of Tibetans.

There is a new dimension to the PRC's foreign relations in the post-Cold War in the context of the democratic movement worldwide — her close co-operation with the military dictatorship in Myanmar. The PRC and Pakistan have been the main suppliers of arms and equipment to the military government to suppress the pro-democracy movement. According to Ms. Than Than Nu, "China alone has supplied two billion dollars worth of arms in exchange for essential commodities. There is a Chinese military advisor in Myanmar where they are building a naval base for China on the southern most tip of the country." The remnants of communism and military dictatorship cooperating with one another is a direct security threat to India. The U.S. as a supporter of the democratic movement in Myanmar has also not taken kindly to this development. In all these areas where India has divergent interests with the PRC, the U.S. and India have a general convergence of interests.

Economic Factors

The end of the Cold War and disintegration of the Soviet Union also witnessed India liberalising her economy by removing practically all socialistic controls and inviting foreign investment. This is no mere coincidence because, with the disappearance of the Soviet Union, India had to look for newer markets to sell her goods and seek new sources of supply of defence equipment. In a sense India lost a captive market for her goods but in reality, the very captive market was acting as a disincentive to economic competitiveness in the country.

With the end of the Cold War the major thrust in the world is towards democracy. With the Soviet Equation out of the way democracy itself becomes a natural bond between India and the

US. Hence, wherever the national interests of the two do not conflict promotion of democracy worldwide could become a common global endeavour.

Conclusions

Apart from the major changes that have taken place, one very important development since 1991 is the growing cooperation in defence matters between the two countries. This was signalled through their cooperation during the Gulf War when India permitted U.S. Air Force planes to refuel in Mumbai. In July 1992 for the first time the two navies held joint naval exercises in the Indian Ocean. There are also continuous service to service contacts through seminars and visits by high ranking officials.

It is not that there are no problems in U.S.-India relations. Thus, for instance, India and the U.S. hold divergent views on the nuclear non-proliferation treaty (NPT). The U.S. wants India to sign the NPT. India has been insisting on a time bound agreement for global nuclear disarmament This is a moralistic argument only to retain her nuclear option if the PRC and/or Pakistan force a nuclear war upon her. There are other problems like U.S. efforts to deny India cyrogenic engines for her space programme by pressurising Russia not to supply the engines.

India needs the U.S. more than the Americans need India. It is in this context that there is a lurking fear that the PRC may try to develop a joint front with India against the U.S. particularly in the fields of human. rights and linking development assistance with human rights. Thus, for instance, the communique issued after the conclusion of PRC Prime Minister Li Peng's visit to Delhi in December 1991, expressed their joint concern over the dangers of an "international oligarchy" (a reference obviously to the U.S. along with its Western allies) trying to pose as a protector of human rights, worldwide. Again when the Premiers of India and the PRC met in New York in February 1992, Li Peng said while greeting Narasimha Rao: "We seemed to have consulted each before drafting our speeches at the Security Council, since there was a great deal of parallelism on major issues."[11] It must be said here that Indian violation of human rights cannot be equated with those of the PRC. India is fighting, with its back to the wall in the two states of Punjab and J&K, against externally aided terrorism. On the other hand, in the case of the PRC it is the government itself that violates the human rights of its citizens to suppress political dissidence.

The U.S. and India will have to fine tune their bilateral relations by keeping in mind the fact that in the long run the democratic bond is far more durable than a relationship between a pluralistic democracy and a one-party state.

Freedom First, April-June 1993

No cause For complacency

US President Bill Clinton, instead of celebrating on July 4, their day of Independence, busied himself trying to persuade Pakistan Prime Minister, Nawaz Sharif, to withdraw Pakistani regular armed forces and foreign mercenaries fighting in Kargil. As a result, in a joint statement, Clinton and Sharif affirmed that 'concrete steps will be taken for the restoration of the Line of Control (LoC)' and 'immediate cessation of hostilities once these steps are taken.'

In the meantime, there is a legitimate doubt in India whether Sharif will be able to exercise his authority to enforce his agreement with Clinton. Hence, there has been an intensified effort by the Indian forces to evict infiltrators from every inch of Indian territory. India has reiterated that the nation will not rest until every intruder is forced to quit from the Indian territory. Thus, Indian diplomacy has achieved a degree of success in isolating Pakistan on the international scene.

It all began with the US President expressing his appreciation of restraint shown by the Indian PM, Atal Bihari Vajpayee, in limiting the war to Indian side of the LoC The US President, while appreciating Indian posture, also asked Pakistan to pull out intruders to their side of the LoC. Pakistan tried several tricks to secure international support for their misadventure. First, it characterised their infantrymen, fighting along with some hard core Afghan guerrillas, as 'freedom fighters.' Secondly, when it did not work, Pakistan began to say that LoC is well-delineated in the maps but not clearly demarcated on the ground, thus, effectively trying to push into Indian side of the LoC. Pakistan desired an immediate ceasefire and negotiations with India. It was an obvious ploy to draw a new LoC inside Indian territory. Thirdly, when that too did not work, Nawaz Sharif said that Kargil is a symptom; the real problem is Kashmir, solve it and have lasting salvation! His Minister for Kashmir affairs, Lt General (retd), Majeed Malik, said that

Islamabad could only discuss the whole Kashmir issue with India and rejected the possibility of holding talks only on the Kargil or the LOC.

In between, threat of a nuclear conflict was also held out to draw the friends to pressurise India to be flexible. Yet, US sent their chief of the central command, General Anthony Zinni, to ask Pakistan to withdraw from the Indian side of the LoC. Pakistan protested at the US stand that infiltration in Kargil should end and sanctity of the LoC be maintained as 'not fair and balanced.' A more or less similar stand has been taken by Germany, France, United Kingdom and Russia. The G-8 countries at their summit meeting also issued a general communique, asking for Pakistani withdrawal from the Indian territory. India's friend Russia has also demanded the restoration of LoC. This has been widely welcomed in India as vindication of its stand.

An official from the South Block is reported to have said that it is for the first time that the Western countries have shown an understanding of the Indian stand. By now, it is a well-known fact that the West European leaders have largely gone along with the leadership of the US. The BJP spokesman and general secretary, Venkaiah Naidu claimed it as a diplomatic victory of Vajpayee government and promised to turn it into a military victory. There is a clear message on the part of the US to side with Indian democracy. Since the end of the Cold War and the ascension of Bill Clinton to the presidency in January, 1993, many think-tanks have advocated such a correction of course, vis-a-vis India. Thus, for instance, there is the 1994 Report of Asia Society to that effect. Indian side is also well argued by several influential Congressmen like Gary Auckerman, Frank Pallone and Benjamin Gilman. Yet, India will have to be very guarded on the change of heart on the part of the Western nations.

In the case of Kargil conflict, the following facts make it essential and prudent on the part of India to exercise maximum caution in decision-making.

The essence of the message in this article is: Fully appreciate the US support in independently pressurising Nawaz Sharif to respect the LoC, but do not be carried away by that till more "evidence emerges to confirm the course correction on the part of the US. Second, there are reports on limited abilities of Nawaz Sharif in enforcing his agreement with the US President. India has made it clear that she will believe in the Pakistani agreement only after it is fully enforced. In the event, Pakistani army or mercenaries or both refusing abide by the decision of civil government, the pressure build up on India to take the war to Pakistani territory, either crossing the LoC or opening new front, preferably in Lahore Third, the G-8 countries has already in their communique urged India to sign the Comprehensive Test Ban Treaty (CTBT) and NPT. It is likely that once Kargil conflict ends, the US might, mount pressure on India to sign both these treaties. In the case of Indian intransigence, the US might activate Pakistani factor against India and seek to impose a solution. Fourth, India has always maintained that Kashmir is a bilateral issue between India and Pakistan and has refused to accept a third party mediation. However, already the US Deputy Assistant Secretary of State, Gibson Lanspher, who accompanied General Zinni in visit to Islamabad, had also visited India to brief the Indian officials.

Therein lies the danger of the US trying to mediate between India and Pakistan though US made it clear that their initiative' ought not to be considered as mediation.'

The Observer of Business and Politics, 21 July 1999

US President's visit to India Political Gains

The President of the United States (US), William Jefferson Clinton has returned to Washington, DC after his visit to India. As the President of the only surviving super power, a visit by Clinton anywhere in the world, is an event to be examined and analysed. The visit is of extreme significance to Indian government. What are the gains for India?

For India President's visit is of great political significance. Frank Wisner, former US Ambassador to India says that the visit marks the "possibility of a new age in Indo-US ties." This is already evident after his return to the White House. One clear indication is the fact that, so far, he has not mentioned Kashmir or the Line of Control (LOC) as the "most dangerous region" of the world.

The visit has brought about a dramatic change in the US attitude towards problems faced by India in the subcontinent. If one is overcautious, one may call it as a preparation to change; but change has come about in many areas.

First, Clinton has clearly asked Pakistan to stop all cross-border terrorism in Kashmir. He has clearly told Pakistani military rulers that there can not be a military solution to the India-Pakistan dispute over Jammu & Kashmir.

If Pakistan still maintain that it is only providing moral and diplomatic support to Kashmiri terrorists, he has told them of his knowledge of "some elements within the Pakistani government" supporting the terrorists.

Second, Bill Clinton accepted the Indian position-notwithstanding Ms. Madeline Albright's effort to underplay the subtle change in Clinton's understanding that, useful India-Pakistan negotiations can start only when cross border terrorism ceases and a climate of mutual trust is created.

There can not be negotiations when Kashmiri Hindus and now Sikhs are targeted by the terrorists as a part of ethnic cleansing.

Third, President Clinton has called upon Pakistan to respect the sanctity of the LOC. It has been an important principle developed during the Cold War, that two nuclear powers do not try to alter borders by force. This is step forward from where Bill Clinton had left during his last July 4 meeting with Nawaz Sharif over the Pakistani Kargil adventure. Then Clinton had only asked Sharif to withdraw, without setting out a principle.

Fourth, for the first time, there is a US commitment to develop relations with India or at least take into account the fact that their interactions are between the two democracies - one, most powerful and the second, largest one. The fact that two nations have agreed to institutionalise their contacts on a regular basis at all levels, shows seriousness of interest in the US.

Fifth, the President came to India by calling the subcontinent as the most dangerous place where the Kashmir issue acted as a nuclear flash point between two nuclear-armed nations in the subcontinent. But after his visit, he was only able to say to the Indians that he looks forward to work with India to see that Comprehensive Test Ban Treaty (CTBT) is implemented. The US latest position is because of his own domestic defeat on securing the Senate ratification of the CTBT.

However, though he described South Asia as the tinderbox of a nuclear conflict, it is Pakistan that he entered by using a decoy plane. Obviously, Clinton must have feared a threat to his own life, obviously on account of his blunt message to Pakistan to restore, democracy, conduct a free and fair trial of ousted Premier, Nawaz Sharif and restore Lahore process in its relations with India. Nawaz Sharif is no friend of India. But he is definitely being punished by the military for stopping its Kargil adventure.

Indian gains out of the visit can be better understood only if one recalls the manner in which Mr. Clinton had the twisted arms of Narasimha Rao during the latter's visit to Washington, DC in May 1994.

Between January 1993, when Bill Clinton was inaugurated as President and May 1994 when Narasimha Rao visited Washington, DC, the foreign policy establishment of the Clinton administration mounted continuous pressure on India publicly to create a sense of national insecurity.

There is no space here for the details. But it is suffice to mention a few illustrative instances. The then Assistant Secretary of State. Ms. Robin Raphel questioned the very accession of J & K to the Indian union. She asked India first to cap, rollback, and then eliminate her nuclear programme. She was ferociously vociferous in supporting the human rights of Pakistani terrorists killed while trying to kill innocent people in J & K. But she was totally blind to see and deaf to the cries of innocent victims of Pak promoted terrorism- Hindus and Muslims alike.

Bill Clinton did not lag far behind. He wrote to Kashmir separatist leader, Ghulam Nahi Faki expressing his desire to work with him to establish peace in' Kashmir. He also wrote to Gary Condit, Democratic Representative from California expressing his concern for human right violation in Punjab. To cap it all, he in his address to the UN General Assembly in September 1993, compared then, situation in Kashmir to the situation in Bosnia where Serbs were accused of massacring Muslims with the aim of ethnic cleansing suggesting as though Indian government was practicing ethnic cleansing in Kashmir. But Pakistani sponsored foreign terrorists brutally massacring forty Sikhs in Kashmir valley on March 20 during the visit of Bill Clinton to the Indian subcontinent, must have influenced Bill Clinton the change his heart. This was the second phase of ethnic cleansing of all non-Muslims from the Valley having practically eliminated majority of Hindus from there. This might have convinced the US President as to who in reality is practising ethnic cleansing in Kashmir valley.

Hence, the change of heart has not come at a low cost to India. It is in this sense we need to see the period of seven years prior to his visit to Indian as a part of wasted years. But the US has come around to accept India perspective on the problem of South Asia, and treat India as an equal partner in world affairs. Of course, the change is seen also as in the US national interest.

The US stands to gain economically, considerably by promoting American Investment and trade with India. If during the Clinton administration there is an economic prosperity, and decline in unemployment in the US, it is largely because of their vigorous economic penetration in large developing economies like those their vigorous economic penetration in large developing economies like those of China and India.

The US also has come to believe that she can not afford to put all her Asian security eggs in the Chinese baskets. Placing a few eggs in the Indian baskets might help the US to counter the growing clout of Communist China.

However, real value of political income accrued by India in the ultimate analysis, depends on how the Indian diplomacy maintains the upward trends in India-US relations to grow and cement a lasting mutually beneficial friendship between the two.

The Free Press Journal, 5 April 2000

India-US Relations

Many have asked me, being a long-time observer of Indo-US relations, whether positive changes brought about in the US perceptions on Indian security concerns would last Indo-US relations have never been so good as they are after Clinton's visit. Today, they stand on the ash-heaps of history of past suspicions and mistrust. There is a new beginning. In the light of developments during the visit of Clinton and since then, my answer has been that though unintended, a bipartisan position has developed in the US on security issues affecting India. It is apparent that the US has matured to see congruence in national interests between the two. Three such issues of congruence are worth mentioning.

First, there is a common understanding on the need to fight against terrorism promoted by Pakistan. This is not a totally new development. When George W Bush relinquished presidency in 1993, he had already placed Pakistan on the watch list for declaring it as a terrorist state. It was the Clinton Administration which removed Pakistan from that list. However, there was a clear message from Clinton to Pakistan now. In his interview to Peter Jennings of ABC on 21 March, Clinton said: "I believe that there are elements within the Pakistani government that have supported those who engage in violence in Kashmir".

It follows from the above that fruitful talks can be held between India and Pakistan only when cross border terrorism stops and environment of mutual trust is created. As he put it, "you cannot expect a dialogue to go forward unless there is an absence of violence and a respect for the LoC". On this issue, the US clearly accepted Indian point of view.

Second, another major area of common perception has gone without much comment in this country. Now US concede that India has a right to exist as a multi-ethnic, multi-religious and multi-linguistic state. He, of course, put it in a negative frame. But effect is the same. President Clinton told Jennings: "I don't think we ought to get in the position of saying that we think that an ethnically diverse country like India can't exist anymore. I don't agree with that". In his address to the Joint Session of Indian Parliament also he rejected the thesis that the only way to prevent "different people from killing one another is to keep them as far apart as possible". This, we must remember, came from a president who was responsible for the birth of Bosnia as an independent country in 1994 and conducted a 78-day of bombing Belgrade and other cities in Serbia to get autonomy to Muslims of Kosovo which any way Slobodon Milosevic had agreed to grant.

The president said that the Kashmir dispute could not be resolved by use of force. India and Pakistan should negotiate and find a solution. The Clinton Administration has now made it clear that plebiscite is unrealistic in changed context.

Third, there is a new discovery by the president that India is a vibrant democracy. This came out many a time in his observations in India and even after his return. In his remarks on 21 March he referred to India and the US as "world's two largest democracies".

However, it is not the tall men of Indian politics but simple women of Nayla village in Jaipur, who drove the point of vibrancy of Indian democracy to Bill Clinton. President observed "in India you can prove that people can lift themselves from poverty and at the same time, end discrimination... to work together across tribal and caste-lines because of democracy..." This very thought he mentioned again in Washington in highly appreciative manner when his party held a reception in his honour.

Even in the areas where there was no obvious convergence of views between like CTBT/NPT, the president desired that India sign the CTBT. But despite differences in perceptions his language had changed radically from that of May 1998. Now he wanted India to decide needs of their security. Now he spoke of 'both nations joining the CTBT. Both working 'against proliferation of weapons'.

This was the outcome of talks between two nations and the Senate rejection of the CTBT in last October. But he went on asking: Is India more secure with the nuclear weapons, than before? Other officials in their presentations to seek India to sign the CTBT will now repeat this question.

In early 1993 after he was inaugurated as President, Bill Clinton had created a sense of insecurity amongst Indian policy makers by publicly writing and speaking which was in favour of Kashmiri terrorists and separatists. He wrote, for instance, to a Kashmiri lobbyist, Ghulam Nabi Fai, expressing his desire to work with him to establish peace in Kashmir!

In his address to the UN General Assembly in 1993 he compared the situation in Kashmir to that of Bosnia where Serbs were accused of killing Muslims in an effort at ethnic cleansing. During his visit to Islamabad, he saw banners asking him to act as he did to help Muslims in Bosnia and Kosovo by intervening in Kashmir. Who really practices ethnic cleansing in Kashmir valley should have been clear to him when he learnt on 20 March that 35 Sikhs were massacred in the valley. Another 3.5 lakh pandits are displaced persons in their own country. Proper understanding of the situation then in 1993 and desisting from playing politics with the issue could have saved at least 20 thousand lives in Kashmir.

But this Clinton's education is not without a price. As it was the case in 1994. It was a case in March 2000, too, that the change of heart has came about at an economic price. Indian economic liberalisation has been helpful to the American economy. The attraction has been a huge market — 250 million-strong middle class. A published report of London-based International Institute of Strategic Studies says, from the Western point of view, that Clintons visit may have advanced America's commerical interests, but not international objective.

One immediate benefit of Clinton's change of heart is that other nations who faithfully follow the US lead in international relations, like Britain, Japan and Germany will follow suit. Robin Cook, British foreign secretary, has already indicated this during his visit to Delhi in April. He repeated Clinton's formulation that cross-border terrorism must stop before the serious Indo-Pak negotiations could begin.

Going back to the position taken by former president George Bush on Kashmir once again. one sees that he had moved closer to Indian position of resolving it bilaterally without use of force in mid-1990. He had then made it clear that old UN resolutions are irrelevant in the changed context; and plebiscite is not practical solution. Hence, wait till November elections. If Al Gore is elected, he has promised to continue Clinton's policies. If Bush Jr is elected, he will be at least on South Asia moving ahead from where his father had left.

The Observer of Business and Politics, 18 May 2000

India-US politico-military relations since September 11

For those who are familiar with zigzags in India-US politico-military relations during the last one decade, the news on India -US agreement on high-tech transfer in the areas of nuclear, space and general high tech should not come as a surprise. It is in keeping with trends established after President Clinton's visit to India in March 2000. While delivering an Endowment Lecture under the auspices of Indian Association for American Studies in Pune University in 1997. I had titled my lecture as "Indo-US relations during the Clinton administration: upward trends and uphill tasks ahead."

But after Clinton visit in March 2000 commenting on the status of India US relations, I wrote to predict that in November 2000 elections if Al Gore wins, he would continue Clinton policies. But if, George Bush wins, he would start from where his father, Sr. Bush had left Indo-US relations in 1993 when he vacated the White House in favour of its new tenant, Bill Clinton.

Clinton then however, instead of moving forward the existing trends in Indo-US relations, had taken it two steps backwards, only to move it two steps forward since 1997. Because. Senior Bush had tightened the screw on Pakistan by refusing to provide F.16s, rejecting the plebiscite on Jammu & Kashmir as impractical and placing Pakistan on "watch-list" on the question of its support to cross-border terrorism. This was exactly the position where Senior Bush had left in January 1993.

However, once George Bush became president in January 2001 Indo-US relations began to move forward in every area of international relations-economic, diplomatic and politico-military. What we need to know is that in the ultimate analysis all facets of relations-economic or military depend on perfect political understanding. That under standing was fine-tuned when India and US held military exercises in Ladakh in early September this year. Because the US policy makers consider J&K technically as a "disputed territory." Hence, I was surprised when George Fernandes, Indian Defence Minister stated that there was nothing political in the context of joint military exercises in Ladakh; it was only a military to military relations! Without perfect political understanding no such military to military relations are ever possible. Politics makes or mars the relations. This is evident from the fact that during the first four years of Clinton administration, it was foul mouth of then assistant secretary of state, Ms Robin Raphel that ruined the US political relations with India built assiduously by the previous Bush administration. I remember then India Desk Officer in the State Department. Thomas Krajeski called on me to ask for suggestions to improve Indo-US bilateral relations. I had then told him to impress upon his superiors to get Ms Raphel removed from the post.

Today, there is a congruence in the interests of the US and India in the region—South Asia and East Asia. Even prior to the September 11, 2001, the US policy makers including President Bush saw India as a bulwark against growing power of Communist China in Asia. Liberal Republican, Colin Powell spoke in favour of strategic alliance with India. It served India's interest as well as China's aggressive territorial claims for Spratly Islands and Paracel Islands in South China Sea did not bode well for India. If we say that US-India friendship made China tilt to speed up negotiations on Border dispute during Prime Minister, Atal Behari Vajpayee's June 2003 visit, we will not be very much off the mark. Second, there is an increasing congruence of interest between the US, India and Israel on their fight against global terrorism. It is the US-India political understanding that enabled this co-operation to develop. As a result the US did not object to Israeli sale of 3 Phalcon Airborne Early Warning Control System (AWACS) to India. On the other hand, last year US had forced Israel to cancel a similar deal with China.

Future of India-US politico-military relations rests on three vital issues. First, how consistently the two countries coordinate their co-operation in the global fight over terrorism. The US knows fully that Pakistan is the epicentre of international terrorism. Pakistan while fighting the terrorism promoted by Al Qaeda on the side of the US, promotes terrorism against India. One cannot fight terrorism in the West while promoting it in the East, as Prime minister Vajpayee put it. Consistency of approach in fighting the scourge of terrorism is needed. And much of it depends on the US. The US seem to be backing Pakistan on the assumption of TINA that 'there is no alternative' to General Musharraf; or only other alternative is the growth of Islamic fundamentalism. On the other hand his cooperation with the US against Taliban in Afghanistan has already brought fundamentalist Islamic political parties to power in Baluchistan and North West Frontier Province, increasing substantially fundamentalist vote percentage. Earlier, it never exceced five percent throughout the country. If continues in power for long, it might take only another ten years for Pakistan to be ruled by Mullahs.

Second, two countries might need to co-operate in preventing nuclear proliferation India has never been a party in proliferation of nuclear weapons. On the other hand Pakistan and North Korea have been bilaterally co-operating in nuclear and missile proliferation. As Samuel Huntington argued that US need to change its mindset to accommodate India as nuclear partner in promoting nuclear non-proliferation. It might even help their interests in South and East Asia. Last US as the only Super power naturally would like to retain its status as such. But US inclination in favour of unilateral moves in world politics has created an urge in favour of multipolar world. In this respect, India goes along with China, Russia, France and Germany Even when the world moves in that direction US-India could benefit because of their cooperation. Such cooperation would be strengthened if the US positively supports seating of India as a permanent member of the UN.

The Free Press Journal, 15 October 2003

Major issues crucial for India's foreign policy

As India gets ready for the next General Elections in 2004-incidentally first time an election is being held after government completes its five years in the office since 1996, government faces four issues in foreign affairs. Of course, elections are not won or lost because of handling of foreign policy issues. But if the government mishandles a foreign policy issue it could lose an election. Here are the four issues, which are crucial for India's foreign policy, and my brief comments on each of them as to the direction ought government ought to take.

First, at present the attitude of the West towards India has changed. The best indicator of it is attitude towards Indian nuclear weapons. How should the partnership if it is going to be a partnership with the West be developed? Of course, West means in effect mainly the US. In the unipolar world it is the US that dominates. It is the change of US attitude towards India on various issues like Indian nuclear weapons or the problem of cross-border terrorism that brought about the general change in the West.

Thus, for instance, during his visit to India in March 2000, Bill Clinton exhibited a complete change in the US approach to Indian problems of cross-border terrorism when he stated that "you cannot expect a dialogue to go forward unless there is an absence of violence and a respect for the LoC (Line of Control). Soon after that then Foreign Secretary of the UK, Robin Cook, visiting New Delhi in April said that cross-border terrorism must stop before the serious Indo-Pak negotiations could begin!

Occasionally, the US attitude towards Indian problems of terrorism might hurt Indian sensitivities. Thus, for instance, in the UN General Assembly speech in September 2003, the US president listed terrorist incidents after the September 11, 2001 like in Bali, Mombassa, Casablanca, Riyadh, Jakarta and Jerusalem but left out attack on Parliament in Delhi. Public outcry in India brought a public statement from Condoleeza President's national security adviser to state that India too is a victim of international terrorism. Not withstanding such instances, Indian problem of cross-border terrorism sponsored by Pakistan received worldwide expression of concern only after the US experience of September 11. India needs to continue to make its war against Pak-sponsored terrorism, part of wider light against global terrorism.

The US support for any final solution to J & K conflict, is a crucial and positive input, despite Indian preference to keep third party out of efforts to find a solution to the Kashmir problem. The US holding of Joint military exercises in Ladakh is an indication of its willingness to change its attitude to "disputed territory" status of J & K. India seems to be preparing public opinion in favour of ultimately internationalising LoC as permanent border. Towards this, the US support is of vital importance.

The US support for Indian legitimate claim for a permanent seat in the expanded Security Council is extremely crucial. Other two, Western Permanent members-UK and France will go, to a large extent, by the US signals. Russia has committed its support for Indian claim. In the light of this, it is worth considering for India positively the US request for dispatch of Indian troops on non-combat duties to Iraq especially in the background of unanimous passage of UNSC Resolution of 1511 in October 2003 on multilateral force for Iraq. India has now said that it considers Interim Governing Council in Iraq as the legitimate authority in that country.

While leaning towards the US, we need to maintain a closer relationship with France and EU. France has always taken an independent approach towards the US. It is nowhere best illustrated as its refusal to impose economic sanctions against India in the post-nuclear tests since May 1998. EU is also important, because of its greater emphasis on economics rather than politics as a determinant in foreign relations. Added reason to cultivate France and EU is they are major poles in future emergence of a multipolar world.

The second issue is the policy towards our neighbourhood, including West Asia and South -East Asia. Our current policy towards Pakistan is the most appropriate one. The Government should take incremental steps to improve relations in Low Politics issues while refusing to talk on vital High Politics issues like J & K, till cross border terrorism ceases completely. Its domestic impact within Pakistan is worth supporting/encouraging from New Delhi. If India tried to give legitimacy to Musharraf as President of Pakistan, by inviting him for a summit meeting in Agra, India's refusal to talk should contribute to destabilise Musharraf as military general and President. He has already spoken of deciding the issue of which one of the two hats he is going to surrender in 2004. A weakened Musharraf might be forced to give up his military post. India should talk to democratically elected government on High Politics issues.

With Bangladesh, issue of illegal immigrants and its impact on national security assumes high concern. The concentration of illegal immigrants on the Eastern borders and demand by Islamic groups for a re-demarcation of borders is a cause of concern. The government needs to focus on the issue seriously before another Kashmir-like separatist movement develops in the region.

We need to focus increasingly on South-East Asia-economically and politically. Our Common cultural connections should be exploited. Indian ruling elite for long has been very unconcerned to exploit religious and cultural affinities for fortifying friendly foreign relations in the region. The Government should move to form an India-centric Cultural Association including Buddhist nations of the region.

If Islamic nations could speak through the forum of Organisation of Islamic Countries, why can't India initiate an association of nations of Indian Religionists? With others in the region, issue-oriented co-operation and coalitions, should be encouraged like anti-terror or pro-democracy.

Third, China is India's foremost competitor in Asia. How should we develop this relationship? The Bush administration began courtship of India with a threat perception from China. India also extended support to the US plan for a Nuclear Missile Defence. President Bush and Secretary of State Colin Powell began with a perception of a strategic relationship with India. However, much of it was diluted after September 11, 2001. But a fairly large number of Republicans still see India as a counterweight to China. Pursuing that line without pushing it too far ought to be in India's interest.

China, since Indian nuclear tests in May 1998, has changed its approach to some extent to India as well. While China is a potential security threat to India and a competitor to influence policies of nations in South and South-East Asia, India has an advantage with nations in ASEAN: They do not see India as a security threat while they do perceive a security threat from China. The recent policy of India therefore, of looking to east is a right policy as Asia is going to be the economic powerhouse of the 21st century.

Hence, since there is a greater congruence in India-US interest vis-a-vis China friends in the US might perceive India as a reliable friend, India need not inherently inherit US hostilities, if any, against China. We should increase our economic and cultural interactions with Taiwan, while accepting Chinese claim of one China.

Finally, is the world veering towards a de-facto clash of civilisations? In that event, where should India stand? Clash of civilisations is a fascinating theme. But the nations do well in trying to avoid such a clash of civilisations. India with a huge Muslim population cannot think of anti-Muslim stance.

However, to sanctify such a mental frame-work, Indian parties must stop thinking of Muslims as a vote bank. The BJP is in a position to articulate this approach, as Muslims do not, at present, constitute its vote-bank. It has to, however develop Hindutva as an ideology against pseudo-secularism rather than as an anti-Muslim ideology.

The Free Press Journal, 15 November 2003

Growth of a multi-dimensional India-US relationship

India-USA relations have always been a fascinating subject for study and commentary. The topic chosen by me today for comment has two sharply focussed angles. One, that it is stronger; and second- multidimensional. One unique feature of India-US relations is in contrast to the US-Pakistan relations, that there never have been extreme ups or downs. Of course, ups and downs have been there; but the downs have not created deep valleys and ups have never been like Mount Everest.

But it has been an upward movement since Bill Clinton's visit in March 2000 towards growth in strength and adding new dimensions. George W. Bush, Jr. took it further from where Clinton had left. Bush has taken it to new heights by adding co-operation in areas like nuclear, missile and general technology development. This was announced in January this year.

The two nations are now moving rapidly towards a multidimensional relationship. But the turning point came through the security concerns. Bill Clinton moved closer to India because of the Kargil conflict in the summer of 1999. An important unwritten rule governing the relationship between two nuclear weapons states developed during the Cold War was that they do not challenge each other's territorial boundaries even if they are in dispute. Pakistan violated this rule while India strictly adhered to it. This established India's credentials as a responsible nuclear power. Military take-over in October 1999 only strengthened US inclination to strengthen multidimensional relations with India.

Bush found in 2001 India as a natural strategic partner particularly in the context of US perception of China and his determination to introduce National Missile Defence system. India extended support to the US concept of NMD. There was a congruence of interest on this issue between India and US. Both were concerned with growing powers of China. US saw India a counterweight to China; India projected US as an option for closer ties unless China shows flexibility in its relations with India.

Vajpayee reiterated India and US as natural allies. This concept also meant US moving away from Pakistan. Bush had naturally come to pursue it. But for the intervention of September II terrorist attack, there was a a temporary setback in the public perception. But even after World Trade Centre and Pentagon attacks, the US said it more than once and at different levels that the relations with India are of strategic importance. While those with Pakistan are of tactical out of compulsions of war against terrorism.

The concerns arising from the role of Pakistan are relevant to both India and the US. India has been stating that Pakistan is the epicentre of terrorism. Now of all the persons, Musharraf has also started saying it! Three Years since 2001, Pakistan has moved to take three different approaches. First, for him terrorists were freedom fighters'. Second, there might be some but Pakistan does not have control over them. Finally, the terrorists are bred in Pakistan; terrorism is a danger and must be controlled. Jehad has to end, Kashmir be resolved by dialogue and not War Terrorism. Inter-related issue is of Nuclear Proliferation. In the transformation of Musharraf, apart from domestic compulsions, like three attempts to assassination, American pressure played a major role.

Security was not the only concern of congruent interest between the two. The US needs access to Indian markets and Indian economy needs Foreign Direct Investment. The economic liberalisation, privatisation and globalisation (LPG) introduced under compulsions of crisis in balance of payments, created a new economic relationship. But as the elections in both the countries near the destiny deciding dates, more of economic issues will come into sharp focus in both countries.

But the debate on outsourcing in the US with an element of anti-Indian approach is definitely going beyond the electoral process. If the Americans are concerned only with creating more jobs in the US, maintaining their economic prosperity at the cost of Indians, does the globalisation mean one-way traffic? While politicians sharpen the focus on outsourcing, companies and chambers of commerce will continue to maintain the tempo on economic relations. Hope is, once the elections get over, downward trend.in economic relations would be arrested and move upward would begin once again.

Another important dimension is educational relations, which is going to be growing important. Trade in Services is an unknown concept to Indian policy-makers when they signed WTO agreement. By 2005 higher education has to be opened to global penetration-whether you like it or not. The educational institutions in India now seem to be interested in only one-way collaboration with American institutions collaborating with Indian. However, we need to cater to Indian-Americans in the US particularly those sections of the Non-Resident Indians who still desire to educate their children in Indian universities.

India however, needs to be extremely careful and alert in India US economic relations. While we are in favour of strengthening, adding more dimensions, care has to be taken to see that globalisation does not lead to security dependence on the US. We need to promote multi-polarity, rather than the globe being dominated by the US.

Similarly, economic inter-dependence should not turn into an instrument of decline of Indian economy, increase of poverty and starvation. Multi-dimensional relations do not lead to return of colonialism. We Indians have not as yet even after fifty years overcome our colonial mentality. Hence, the Indians without any opposition might welcome a return of colonialism in new garb.

The Free Press Journal, 16 March 2004

If CPM forces election on voters will Manmohan emerge stronger?

Increasingly the UPA Government, officially led by Prime Minister Manmohan Singh of the Congress Party, but under the supreme command of Sonia Gandhi at the federal level, indicates a growing tendency to zig now and zag later. In recent times-in less than three months period it has shown its inability to take firm decisions in national interest in both domestic and foreign policy making. Two decisions taken by the government has the effect of heaping criticism on the Indian style of governance both inside and outside of India.

First, let me take the decision in domestic policy, taken by the government of India on the Ramsamudram project. It gives an illustration of its acting first and thinking later. It informed the Supreme Court (SC) that Ram or his war with Ravana of Sri Lanka are not historical facts. Then, Vishwa Hindu Parishad called for an all India agitation on Thursday (13/9) and very next day, government goes to SC to say that their affidavit was wrong. Accepting the "mistake" the Law Minister said, "we have withdrawn the affidavit...." and took three months time to resubmit the modified affidavit! Does it mean that a government that consists of legal luminaries like Kapil Sibal and a party spokesman like Abhishek Singhvi could not anticipate political fall out from their submission?

Second, and more importantly, let us see the manner in which it has handled a very vital national security-related decision, loaded with economic—in a wider sense of the term and foreign policy implications. It has of course, very serious domestic implications as well. I am referring here to the manner in which the Prime Minister got the 123 Agreement approved by the Cabinet to further implement the Civil Nuclear Deal (CND) signed by him with the US President George W. Bush in Washington, DC on July 18, 2005.

Having studied foreign policy decision-making in major democracies including India and having written on it widely, I have no hesitation whatsoever to bluntly say that government's handling of the objections raised by the Communist Party of India (CPI-M) does not reflect maturity in foreign policy making by India. The Prime Minister knows that he is leading a coalition government, but he also knows that he is not leading a coalition of like-minded parties with shades of differences. He leads a coalition of parties with right, centre and extreme left parties which have only one common goal of keeping the Bharatiya Janata Party out of power.

Fair enough; knowing these facts, he should have tried to know who could sabotage the CND. If he has no time to think-actually the

PM is paid by the nation for thinking. He has also a national security adviser to think, who should have done his home work before the 123 Agreement was approved by the nation's highest decision-making body-the Cabinet. After the decision is made to approve the 123 Agreement, and the agreement is released to the general public, the anti-democratic party-CPI (M), a major ally of the UPA, raises the objections to the agreement. The CPI (M) is really trying to erode India's credibility in international relations, though it claims to persuade India to follow an independent foreign policy.

Then what does the PM say? Implementation of the agreement is non-negotiable. Later he says, let's talk. Talks are held-giving an impression to the public in India and the nations in the world, that we first decide, then think and later discuss! Then the UPA decided that a Political Committee, with Minister for External Affairs, as its head should examine all objections raised by the CPI (M), including its implications for national security and India's independent foreign policy! This is the outcome after the PM had said that implementation of the CND is non-negotiable. Was that exercise not done before the CND was signed? What was the Ministry of External Affairs doing? What did the Atomic Energy establishment do in India? Are security implications to be examined after firming up an agreement? But the story does not end there. Even before the Committee finalises its report, CPI (M)'s General Secretary, Prakash Karat says that the PM is in bad company of the US. He wants PM "to be very careful about choosing his friends." By calling the US President "the greatest friend of India" the PM has received almost an ultimatum saying that you can have your friend, but if you wish to be with bad company, as Karat says; "We won't be there to help" the UPA "government to "conclude this agreement." If the PM persists, he will go like, other friends of Bush Tony Blair has gone, others like Japanese PM, Abe, Australian PM, Howard, and Pakistan's dictator, Musharraf are on their way out!

No doubt, President Bush is most unpopular in the US, but that does not make the CND against Indian national interest. It is a canard spread by the Left, that Bush wants to claim a foreign policy success to his credit! We are not concerned with the Bush's popularity in his country!

On the other hand, various public opinion surveys have shown that people think that the CND is good for Indian interests. Since the Indian government makes decisions for the good of Indian people, the Prime Minister should go ahead to operationalise the CND. If the CPI (M) is determined to force an election on Indian people, the PM should accept the challenge. Who knows, he may find better company in India! He may also emerge stronger than before to implement the CND.

Free Press Journal, 20 September 2007

5

INDIA-CHINA RELATIONS: FROM PLAYING SECOND FIDDLE TO ASSERTION OF NATIONAL INTERESTS

Too much of a good thing

President R Venkataraman returned on May 24 after a visit to China. The first-ever visit to China by an Indian President was described variously as a "success" and a "landmark" visit. However, a word of caution may be in order to policy-makers in New Delhi before India falls into any trap laid by the Chinese.

Concern stems from the fact that the presidential summit diplomacy set aside the contentious border dispute as a historical legacy from British rule. But China used the occasion to express its unhappiness over the Dalai Lamas activities from Indian soil.

India has repeatedly accepted Tibet as an autonomous part of China, without insisting on reciprocal acceptance of Kashmir as an integral part of India. For China, Kashmir is also a British legacy to be settled between India and Pakistan through bilateral negotiations.

A far more important development is the mega tonne under-ground nuclear explosion by China, even while the Indian President was still on its soil.

This action is a repetition of its behaviour in 1979 when the Chinese attacked Vietnam. The then Indian foreign minister Atal Behari Vajpayee was there. The present nuclear test smacks of a similar arrogance.

India is under pressure from the US to sign the Non-Proliferation Treaty, and to discuss nuclear non-proliferation in south Asia with Pakistan since the latter claims it has at least parts of a nuclear bomb. Who will moderate these talks? Three nuclear powers — Russia, the US and China. The Chinese N-test is proof that signing the NPT has had no effect on China's nuclear weapons programme.

Which, is a major threat to India's security. With its long-range missile in place, China can reach any part of India. What has been our response so far? We have appealed for a comprehensive test ban treaty. China is likely to respond to this by conducting another nuclear test, but India has not expressed fears of a Chinese nuclear threat.

What are our short-term or long-term gains from this ostrich-like behaviour supposed to be? The short-term gain would be a probable thinning out of troops facing each other on the northern borders.

Is it a positive step if China withdraws its troops on the northern borders? Is it a positive step if China withdraws its troops from the line of actual control? Not necessarily. As a nuclear state, China can use atomic deterrents against any Indian effort to militarily alter the LAC. If India reduces its forces it will be at a disadvantage if China advances, since it lacks the capacity for nuclear retaliation.

Secondly, will China provide cryogenic engines — yet untested— for India's space programme? Apparently there is talk of this; maybe, as a part of increasing economic co-operation between the two countries.

But is China less vulnerable to US pressure than Russia? Its signing of the NPT and accepting US demands to comply with intellectual property rights under super 301 are proof that under pressure it will bend before the US. Hence, is it not appropriate for India to convince the US how short-sighted was its decision to derail our space programme rather than get untested cryogenic engines from China?

If India is looking for China's long-term support in the Security Council as a substitute for the Soviet backing of yore, this will again prove illusory, especially against the West's veto.

So far, in the post-Cold War period, China has not vetoed any western proposal; only recently she abstained from voting on imposing limited sanctions against Libya. And, can we reasonably expect China to exercise its veto against Pakistan, the only country from whom we face a security threat — excluding China herself?

In reality, India's going out of its way to highlight the success and gains from RV's visit only helps China to keep the border dispute in cold storage longer than necessary and to get our continued support on issues vital to it. On the other hand, India should maintain correct bilateral relations with China till the border question is resolved on the basis of reciprocity in international relations.

Midday, 8 June 1992

Caution a Watchword

The recent visit of President R Venkataraman ending on May 24 was described as "a big success" by the Chinese President Yang Shangkun; other phrases used were "landmark" visit and opening a "new chapter" etc. However, in "a big success" story introducing a note of caution at this early stage might be necessary so that the policy makers in New Delhi would not get into any trap laid by Chinese dragon to take India-China relations to the days of 1950s.

The ostensible purpose of the visit was to improve further bilateral relations as both are developing countries, neighbours comprising 40 percent of world's population, having "a lot in common" in international relations. If that is so, China has not done it right at least from Indian point of view by exploding a 1,000 kiloton under-ground nuclear device while the Indian President was still on the Chinese soil. This is particularly shocking and disturbing when other nuclear powers like France have announced a stoppage of nuclear tests.

This Chinese action is a repeat performance of their similar behaviour of 1979, when the then Indian Foreign Minister, Atal Behari Vajpayee, was in China. Chinese leaders decided to attack Vietnam to teach it a lesson as they had taught a lesson to India in 1962. The present nuclear test smacks of similar arrogance. India is under pressure from the US to sign the NPT. The US is also pressurising India to sit with Pakistan to discuss nuclear non-proliferation in South Asia as Pakistan claims she has at least parts of a nuclear bomb.

Who will moderate these talks? Three Nuclear Powers Russia, US and China. The Chinese megaton test is a demonstration that she would like to sit with the US and Russia as equal in respect of their own nuclear capability though China started on the nuclear path, at least twenty yeas after the US. China also wants to demonstrate that by signing the NPT she has not foreclosed her nuclear weapons programme.

Who is China's adversary now in the post-Cold War against whose challenge she is arming herself with the latest nuclear weapons? Until the disintegration of the Soviet Union, China armed herself to meet the nuclear threat from the Soviet revisionists, for which she also aligned with the US. But now, Russia or other nuclear Republics-from the erstwhile Soviet Union can not pose any security threat to her. Thus, the only conclusion that can be reached is that China wants to emerge as a number two super power in the world, now that she does not need to balance her power against any adversary with the help of US. This Chinese stance might help the US. which is in search of an adversary now or potential to maintain its role as the number one military power.

But nuclear weapons of China are a major threat to India's security. With her long range missiles fully in place, she can reach any part of India. What has been India's response? President Venkataraman's visit went through as though nothing really happened.

India has only issued an appeal for a comprehensive test ban treaty. China is likely to respond as though contemptuously by conducting another nuclear test. But there is no Indian expression of apprehensions of a security threat from Chinese nuclear weapons. President Venkataraman himself dismissed the nuclear test as "a Chinese internal policy".

What are supposedly short-term and long-term gains to India from this ostrich-like behaviour? First, a short term gain appears to be a probable thinning out of troops facing each other on the northern borders. India may welcome it as her troops are under stress because of heavy deployment in internal security tasks in Punjab, Jammu & Kashmir and Assam. Hence, reduction of troops, on the Chinese border may spare some more troops, but is it a positive step from national security point of view, if China withdraws her troops from the actual line of control? Not necessarily .

As a nuclear weapon-state, China can use nuclear deterrance against any unlikely Indian unilateral effort to militarily alter the line of actual control. But after thinning of military presence by India, if China wants to do a similar trick. India will be at a disadvantage since India does not possess a countervailing power of nuclear deterrance.

Second, it was presented as a Chinese-Indian coming together lest both "would be left behind and bullied by others".

Any way, China has joined other permanent members of the UN Security Council in calling upon all non-nuclear powers to observe nuclear non-proliferation and also observe guidelines of the missile technology control regime at a meeting held on May 30 in Washington, DC.

Hence, it is appropriate for India to negotiate with the US to convince her how ill-timed and short-sighted her decision has been to derail the Indian space programme, rather than get untested cryogenic enginees from China, even though that itself is doubtful.

On a long-term basis if India is looking for China's support in the UN Security Council, as a substitute for the firm Soviet support of the past, it is likely to be illusive. So far in the post-Cold War period, China has not exercised its veto against any western proposals; only recently she too abstained from voting on the question of imposing limited sanctions against Libya. And, can we reasonably expect China to exercise her veto against Pakistan, the only other country from whom we have security threat if we exclude China herself?

In return to these illusive short-term and long-term gains for India, China on the other hand has gained concrete advantages. First, China has effectively drawn India on her side when the Indian President shared the view of the Chinese leadership that human rights is a domestic concern of each country.

Hence, no country should dictate terms by linking development assistance to aid recipient's human rights protection record. This is a milder version of December 1991 Sino-Indian communique issued during the Chinese Prime Minister Li Peng's visit expressing concern over the dangers of an "international oligarch" (reference obvi-ously is to the US with her western allies), trying to pose as protectors of human rights.

The Observer, 20 July 1992

Let's Not Be Emotional About Panchsheel

"Prime Minister P V Narasimha Rao, in his inaugural address at the recent seminar on 'Panchsheel and global diplomacy', said though these principles can be found in the United Nations charter, their 'reiteration' is necessary 'precisely' for the reasons that the world today 'is riven by ethnic, religious and communal conflicts"

The governments of India and China have suddenly discovered the relevance of Panchsheel or the five principles of peaceful co-existence — mutual respect for each other's territorial integrity and sovereignty; mutual non-aggression; mutual non-interference in each other's internal affairs; equality and mutual benefit; and peaceful co-xistence — in the conduct of international relations in the post-Cold War period. That alone explains why the governments thought it necessary to celebrate the 40th anniversary of the signing of the Panchsheel treaty in Delhi on June 28, 1954.

What explains this resurrection of Panchsheel? When they were first enunciated in 1954, Nehru had admitted that there was nothing new about these ideas except their application to a particular context.' Prime Minister P V Narasimha Rao, in his inaugural address at the recent seminar on 'Panchsheel and global diplomacy', said though these principles can be found in the United Nations charter, their 'reiteration' is necessary 'precisely' for the reasons that the world today 'is riven by ethnic, religious and communal conflicts, with the over-hanging menace of encroaching populations, degrading environments and social ills and a disintegrating faith in common human endeavour.' He continued to refer to the dangers faced by humanity today and more specifically referred to antagonisms based on narrowly conceived national interests and a whole range of challenges... threatening the 'peace and welfare of mankind' which necessitates our generation to 'interpret and apply creatively the five principles' to our age.

It must be restated that four of the five principles emphasise the 'mutuality' of interest in servicing the principles. Hence, it appears that two countries, on the face of common problems that could be tackled together, have discovered some utility in playing publicly the great significance of Panchsheel.

There are two issues that are of immediate concern to the governments. One is the US effort to prescribe norms for human rights violations in India and China. Though the nature of human rights violations in India and China are not identical, there is a sense of common irritation at the US policy of lecturing both nations on their dismal record on human rights. Second, China and India both face the problem of the US trying to link social issues to their need for economic assistance and trade. While India faces the US threat of an economic boycott of its carpet industry on the use of child labour, Chinese products are scrutinised closely for the use of prison labour.

In both cases India and China have taken an identical stand — telling the US that respect for and protection of human rights cannot be uniform in developed and developing countries. The West should not try to impose its standards on developing societies. Similarly, the question for developing societies, often is one of choosing between hunger and child labour and human beings always will opt for the latter. The identity of views between the two countries can best be described by quoting what Chinese Prime Minister Li Peng said after his meeting with Rao in New York in February 1992: 'We seemed to have consulted each other before our speeches at the Security Council, since there was a great real of parallelism on major issues.' Earlier in December 1991 the two prime ministers in their joint communique had expressed their concern over 'the dangers of an international oligarchy' (a reference obviously to the US along with its Western allies) trying to pose as protectors of human rights, worldwide.

Since then these positions have been only strengthened because of India's experience in Geneva at the UN Commission on Human Rights earlier this year and China's experience over the US renewal of its most-favoured nation status in June.

The question, however, is: Should India' base her bilateral relations with China on Panchsheel? Can Indians erase memories of the past? China itself did not observe the five principles by committing aggression against India in October 1962. Earlier in 1959, it overran Tibet's autonomous status by making it a region of China as a prelude to her aggression on India. This disillusioned Jawaharlal Nehru about the relevance of Panchsheel and also left the country bitter about China's betrayal.

Even if our leaders try to dump the past into the dustbin of history, China's behaviour in recent years is not reassuring. Her zeal to promote Panchsheel in the post-Cold War period is somewhat suspect. This is because while asking Washington to keep off China, Beijing does not desist from interfering in another nation's internal affairs.

India desisted from interference in Chinese affairs by not uttering a word when pro-democracy students were massacred at Tiananmen Square in June 1989, which even Mikhail Gorbachev 'regretted'. But what has been China's record? No doubt democracy cannot be exported nor can it be implanted by imports. But when people in Mynamar voted for democracy, the indigenous movement was effectively crushed by the military junta with China's support and arms. Now China, in co-operation with the Mynamar military junta is building a naval base in that country. It can only be used to threaten India's national security.

Mutual respect for territorial integrity and sovereignty are the cornerstones of the post Cold War period. India took a weakened position by conceding Tibet as an autonomous region of China. But when it comes to respect for India's territorial integrity, particularly in respect of Kashmir, China is not willing to reciprocate. China likes to maintain that the Kashmir dispute is a colonial vestige — a creation of Western imperialism — and that India and Pakistan should resolve the dispute together.

China speaks in favour of a multipolar world in the post-Cold War era. It is also keenly aware of the fact that the US remains the planet's solitary super-power. In the next couple of years, the US and other Western nations are likely to increase its pressure on the Chinese government to respect human rights and provide autonomy for the Tibetan people. It is on this sensitive issue that China finds the principle of mutual respect for territorial integrity a convenient principle.

It is worth recalling that the late Acharya J B Kripalani said that Panchsheel was born in sin 'to put the seal of our approval upon the destruction of an ancient nation,' Tibet. We have to be careful to see that it is not furthered now to perpetuate that sin. This is not to introduce an element of suspicion in Sino-Indian relations based on past behaviour or present calculations, but to induce an element of caution.

In May 1992 China exploded a nuclear bomb when the then Indian president Ramaswamy Venkataraman was in Beijing. At the same time incidentally that Chinese President Yang Shangkun yearned to go back to the *bhai, bhai* days of the fifties. The Chinese are masters at conducting cold bilateral diplomacy to promote their national interests minus any sentimentality. Beijing now proposes to conduct global diplomacy with Panchsheel. India should not mix her long-term national interests with sentimentality over Panchsheel.

The Sunday Observer, 17-23 July 1994

India needs a Taiwan policy

Communist China, despite the recent visit of President Jiang Zemin to Washington, DC and the talk of developing a 'strategic partnership' be-tween the two, faces continued US pressure to improve its human rights record — though now in a diplomatic way and not in public sermonisation.

Soon after Jiang's return from Washington, Beijing quietly released its greatest democratic dissident, Wei Jingsheng, from his over 17 years' imprisonment.

The US, in its pursuit of quiet diplomacy, has two other important issues to use against China: Taiwan and Tibet.

Prevailing Sino-US contacts have actually made Taiwan bolder than before. In a statement almost coinciding with Jiang's visit to the US, Taiwan's President Lee Teng-hui declared there was no need for his country to declare its independence as it was already a free country for the past 49 years.

Taiwan enjoyed the status of a permanent member in the UN Security Council until it was expelled in '71 once the US started to normalise its relations with mainland China.

But though the US accepted Beijing's claim of one China, it maintains economic, cultural, educational and scientific ties with Taipei, with which it is also the foremost trading partner as in the case of India.

In this scenario, it is vital to assess India's policy towards Taiwan. Nehru, in pursuit of his policy of "defence by friendship" towards mainland China, ignored the diplomatic gains India could reap by cultivating friendly relations with Taiwan, particularly after China's border war with India in 1962.

His successors, irrespective of their party affiliations, have followed the same policy. Today, even after the tardy beginning in establishing an India-Taiwan Association, Delhi's political outlook towards Taiwan is of political shyness in dealing openly in a friendly manner.

Taiwan would like to diversify its overseas portfolio and considers India an attractive investment destination. But the Indian government is shying away from any collaborative ventures.

India is pussyfooting on establishing mutually beneficial ties with Taiwan because of its over-cautious approach to China's sensitivity over the issue. We are bending over backwards in our attempt not to offend China.

The strong pro-China lobby in Delhi which does not want India tilting towards Taiwan should, however, realise that inviting Taiwan to invest in India is not tantamount to extending diplomatic recognition to it.

India has accepted the Chinese policy of 'one China and two systems' which implies political unification along the lines of Hong Kong but with varying economic systems. We neither encourage Taiwan's independence, nor desire a conflict between China and Taiwan over the thorny issue of unification.

It cannot, however, be denied that an interface between India and Taiwan is in the interest of India economically as well as politically.

Taiwan, at the same time, has not been enthused by the way China has handled the question of internal autonomy in Hong Kong, after it was reverted to Chinese sovereignty last July, under the policy of two systems.

Further, there are no attractive incentives for Taiwan to merge with China. Its 21 million citizens enjoy a per capita GNP of US $ 10,600 in contrast to China's US $ 2200.

In the event of Taiwan emerging as an independent country, India stands to gain political and strategic leverage. If Taiwan emerges independent, *de jure,* it can also act as a counterweight against the growing might of China.

Blitz, 31 January 1998

Push the sale of Indian toys in US market

A major issue that is now almost in daily discussion in the American media is the sub standard quality of toys and games for children available in the US markets. That is because, nearly eighty percent of the US children's toys and games are manufactured in China. However, these toys are not sold in the name of Chinese brands or companies. But by the American companies under their Brand names. Though toys mention, if you carefully see, that they are made in China. Major companies that get the toys made in China are the Mettel and Fisher-Price. If you wish to buy a toy or a game in any major toy shop in the US, with a label 'made in the US' it would be either highly time consuming or next to impossible task. Now that holiday season has begun-with Halloween, Thanks-Giving and Christamas respectively, every one is concerned about choices of games or toys they could buy and safety of their children as there were a few cases of children either losing life or being hospitalised.

The gravity of the problem can be understood by the fact that since June and incresingly since August this year, the American toy making giant companies have withdrawn more than 21 million toys made in China. What is the reason? These toys have excessive lead and mercury-based colours which are hazardous to child's health. Worst still for Chinese reputation, it is not only toys which are withdrawn but food products 'made in China' are also affected and include in the 'withdrawn' list.

The result has been not only companies were forced to withdraw toys but there were Congressional hearings on the poisonous toys. In cases where the toys are found to be of potentially hazardous to children's health, companies, under rules, are required to notify the public and Consumer Safety Commission within 24 hours. But in the current cases, companies did not notify for several days. The NGOs are up in arms against the toy companies and government for the current situation. The Mettel Company Chief Executive, Robert Ecket, had appeared before the Congressional Committee and admitted that the company could have done better in overseeing the sub-contractors in China, apologised to the Amercian people, and promised better care would be taken as far as the toys sold in the US markets. In particular, he promised that every toy sold would be tested in the company's own laboratories or the labs certified by the company.

The Bush administration has come under severe criticism as well for reducing the budget of the Consumer Safety Commission. The entire issue is laid at the door of the Bush administration's policy, and rightly, of globalisation, under which the companies are outsourcing the production of toys. Their single aim is: To take advantage of Chinese cheap labour. While in the US, minimum wages are $7.50 per hour, in China workers are paid half of that per day. China is also accused of using child labour and not providing hygienic conditions of work.

But are the companies passing on to the consumers, the extra profits gained because of reduced cost of production? No. Since toys are sold at the same price as if they were made in the US. Hence, it is only helping the companies to make extra profits and give enhanced dividends to the shareholders. The fact that Mettel could withdraw bulk of toys since June this year and still absorb the loss, confirms very high margins enjoyed by these companies. That is what is meant by free trade in America, as the citizens here, sarcastically say.

However, my interest in writing this piece lies in three urgent concerns from the Indian point of view. First it is more than certain that Chinese toys sold in India might contain same unpermissible levels of lead and mercury. Though these toys are sold in Indian market as Chinese toys and poor in India are able to enjoy access to these toys, because they are cheaper than Indian toys, there is absolutely no awareness on the dangers which arise to the health of the children. After all, unlike in the US, life of a human being is the cheapest commodity in India!

That takes me to the second concern. India needs to develop safety standards on the American lines, on an emergency basis. It is also necessary to protect Indian consumers with safety measures and also have safety inspectors appointed with the knowledge of safety standards. To prevent corrupt officials permitting sub-standard toys entering into the country, countervailing checks ought to be provided by the NGOs working in the consumer safety area.

Third, it is a surprise that Indian toy manufacturers have not taken any interest in attracting American big toy companies to develop their toy manufacturing activities in India. In addition to acting as subcontractors to the American toy companies, Indian toy manufacturers have to take a leaf from Chinese innovative measures. India has many ancient games and toys which were popular from vedic times. Such toys and games should be manufactured and sold in the US market independently. The American consumers would also thereby have multiple choices of toys and price ranges. The Indian toy manufacturers should be able to capture the lower middle class market for toys and games in the US. There is absolutely no anti-Indian expressions in the US media, unlike in the 1970s. Indian games and toy manufacturers should take advantage of this to sell their products in the US. This is the most opportune time for Indian toy industry to push itself in the American market. If the Indian government has time, as it is busy managing its own survival from the threat of 'friends of China', it could also think in terms of encouraging Indian toy industry to use the present situation in the US to our benefit!

The Free Press Journal, 10 October 2007

India needs to stand up to China

SALMAN Khurshid was appointed Minister for External Affairs (MEA) on 28 October 2012; he replaced S. M. Krishna. On 10 December 2012 while addressing the annual convention of Indian Association of International Studies in New Delhi organised by the MEA's Public Diplomacy Division, the new minister is reported to have said: "As India and China move forward in "finding resolution to the issues and converting their relationship into a meaningful partnership, India will have to accept the new reality of China's presence in areas that we consider an exclusive area for India and its friends."

Khurshid's newfound love for China was echoed by Arun K. Singh, India's Deputy Ambassador to the US, when he said that it is in the mutual interest of India and China to work together and to reduce uncertainties in their relations; thus, creating an international environment that would help the two countries to carry on with their domestic efforts to transform conditions for economic development. Their simultaneous "emergence...as Asian and global powers" could make them "sensitive to each other's interests and aspirations." This was what Khurshid had also said earlier, in somewhat different words in his address in Delhi. As he had put it, "India's foreign policy... combines the strengths without targeting aspirations of anyone else in the world..." Thus, he hoped India and China "will define Asia's role in the 21st century."

China's India Policy before Khurshid

Khurshid's analysis of India-China relations is completely different from reality today and the earlier policy stance of India during Prime Minister, Manmohan Singh and S. M. Krishna. Singh had spoken about China's "assertiveness" in pursuit of policy in the region. In his address to American Council on Foreign Relations in Washington, DC, in November 2009, he had spoken of "certain amount of assertiveness on the part of Chinese."

China in reality has gone from assertiveness to aggressiveness in its policy toward India. It has in reality surrounded India through, what scholars say: A "string of pearls," all-around India, with its presence in Pakistan and Pakistan occupied Kashmir (POK), details of which could take the space of an article. But briefly stated, apart from its geostrategic presence at Gwadar Port in North Arabian Sea from where China could get easy access to Persian Gulf, it has about 11,000 troops in POK under the pretext of road building. Chinese presence has increased in Nepal since Maoists coming to power. China has constructed railway route to Kathmandu which could easily be used to move troops in case of a conflict with India. China is actively present in Chittagong Port in Bangladesh, enabling it to get quick access to the Bay of Bengal. In Sri Lanka, China is developing Hambantota Port; has its naval presence there, in close striking distance to India. It has similar naval facilities in Myanmar.

Latest intrusion of China in South Asia is confirmed by its successful efforts to have a naval base in northern Maldives closer to Sri Lanka and India. That was in fact, the root cause that led to the military overthrow on 8 February 2012 of the first elected India-friendly government led by President Mohamed Nasheed since 11 November 2008. He was replaced by the pro-China, Mohamed Waheed, who was Vice President under Nasheed. As a matter of fact, recent standoff in December 2012 between India and Maldives over the cancellation of globally won GMR contract to build Ibrahim Nassir International Airport was an act of pro-China President's way of showing gratitude to China by fulfilling its interest in getting into the building of the airport.

Misplaced expectations

India's Foreign Minister, Salman Khurshid has thus, changed fundamental premises of India's policy towards China. The minister's hopes are based on one sided expectations without any indication of a reciprocal change in China's India policy. So far all moves on the part of India have been one sided. South Asia has been a natural sphere of influence of India since independence. Mrs. Indira Gandhi made every effort to keep foreign powers away from the South Asian Region. During Tamil ethnic crisis in Sri Lanka in 1983, for instance, she went to the extent of warning foreign powers to keep off the region. Her pronouncement then came to be called India's Munro Doctrine!

Khurshid appears to reverse it. If Khurshid wants India to accept China's efforts to increase its presence in South Asia, a natural sphere of influence of India or openly embrace its policy of surrounding India, as a fait accompli, has he secured a similar reciprocal concession from China, by making it accept India's presence in South-east Asia? Similar increased India's presence in South-east Asia, which most of the countries in the region wish and welcome, however, is frowned upon by China. In this respect India has been following a policy of silent obeisance to China. During the East Asia Summit, in November 2011, China publicly warned India to keep off the South China Sea where Indian ONGC (Videsh) has been drilling for oil on a contract from Vietnam, on the ground that it is a disputed territory. India did not show any courage to inform China that POK too is a disputed territory though it is militarily present in that area! It is said that ONGC has been instructed to go slow on oil exploration in South China Sea. Recently, when Navy Chief, D. K. Joshi said that Indian Navy is well equipped with aircraft carrier, and nuclear submarines and capable of taking on the adversaries, government underplayed his observation.

Four questions

Further, for clearly understanding foreign policy mess, in public perception, created by Khurshid, it is necessary to find answers to four questions: First, who makes foreign policy? Second, what is the role of the Foreign Minister? Third, what guides a nation's foreign policy? And finally, are Khurshid's observations on China, in keeping with India's national interest? Brief answers are: First, let me make it very clear that in a parliamentary system it is the Prime Minister, even a weak one, who sets the basic tenets of nation's foreign policy, as it is President who in a Presidential system makes it. Then, did this policy change emanate from the prime minister? If answer is yes, Manmohan Singh himself should have made the crucial announcement on the drastic change of policy, with supporting evidence. Nothing of the kind has appeared in public domain. In answer to second question, it is generally accepted that foreign minister only carries out the policy. Then, is Foreign Minister, laying the ground for a change in policy? Third, foreign policy is guided by national interest. It is in India's national interest that as an emerging major power, that she gives up the policy of playing second fiddle to China or as former Navy chief, Sushil Kumar asked in an article, "Why do we always remain on the back foot when dealing with China?" There is absolutely no indication that change in Indian policy is warranted by a change in China's well established behaviour of containing the growth of India and her emergence as a major power.

Conclusion

In the absence of change in the Chinese behaviour towards India, there cannot be any change in India's national interest of maintaining nation's dignity, security and independence. It appears that Khurshid's acceptance of China as a partner in creating 21st century as an Asian century is not made on the basis of its perceived hard national interest.

Hence, consequences of India's China policy are obviously hurting India's national interest. One obvious consequence is that almost all India's neighbours see her as weak, uncertain of its strength and unwilling to assert her power. Hence, not only Pakistan can kill Indian soldiers with impunity by trespassing into Indian Territory and spite at the dead soldiers by beheading and mutilating their bodies, but even a small nation like Maldives can violate international contracts to please China. Hence, solution lies in India cultivating will power to stand up to China. When you stand up to a big bully, small bullies fall in line. India can thus, regain her strength not only by standing up to assert its legitimate role in international relations but also win back her South Asian friends. Only then can China be prepared to work with India to make 21st century as an Asian century.

One India and One People, February 2013

Decisive leadership and Geopolitics at its Best

Two years of Modi's Foreign Policy

When you look at Modi's achievements under the NDA II government during the last two years, what is strikingly evident is that Prime Minister, Narendra Modi has provided the nation decisive leadership and has demonstrated his astute abilities in the use of geopolitics and geoeconomics at their best, to sub-serve the Indian national interest. Nowhere else have these two admirable qualities — leadership and use of geopolitics and geoeconomics - have manifested so well than in India managing relations with China under him. These qualities shine extremely well when contrasted with handling of a similar situation by the former PM, Manmohan Singh during his lackluster handling of India's relations with China.

Decisive Leadership

Discerning observers had a clue even before Narendra Modi became the nation's PM. During campaigning in Arunachal Pradesh in

February 2013, candidate Modi had clearly asked China to give up its "mind-set of expansion" and work with India to avail fruits of "development and prosperity" for both nations. As far as its claim on Arunachal Pradesh goes, Modi warned China that "No power on earth can snatch away Arunachal Pradesh from India."

This was clearly demonstrated in Modi's planned approach to China. In September 2014, soon after taking over as the prime minister of India, he had invited the Chinese President Xi Jinping. Jinping was given a rousing reception in Ahmedabad before he proceeded with Modi to an official engagement in New Delhi. While the two were having unofficial confabulations in Ahmedabad, PLA as in the past, intruded in Ladakh. But demonstrating clear leadership, Modi informed Jinping that economic relations cannot go on as usual if such incidents on the border continue to occur. Since the Ahmedabad warning was not fruitful, it was repeated in New Delhi once again. These signals were effective as China pulled back after eight days in Ladakh. Jinping, while departing, publicly expressed that he was sad about the tension between armies, which "cast a shadow" on his visit. But such incursions have not occurred again.

Earlier, Modi had shown similar decisive qualities of leadership against Pakistani tantrums. After initial bonhomie with Prime Minister Nawaz Sharif on the occasion of his swearing in as the PM in May 2014, his government cancelled a scheduled meeting of foreign secretaries of the two countries on August 25, 2014 on the grounds that government of India cannot accept the fact that while bilateral talks are to be held, Pakistan holds meeting with the separatists who are challenging Indian integrity.

Geopolitics & Geoeconomics

In Modi's conduct of foreign policy, he has achieved an inseparable admixture of geopolitics and geoeconomics — one aiding the other. This became clearly evident in changing approaches. The Manmohan Singh led UPA government was undoubtedly aware of the geopolitical significance of bilateral relations with Vietnam. However, in awe of China on many issues, the Manmohan Singh government was unable to publicly express our concerns on Chinese policies Vietnam. We only claimed to have privately conveyed our concerns to the Chinese. It was a policy of extraordinary deference to China. In all fairness to the former PM, he only continued the policy of Congress governments since Rajiv Gandhi and PV Narasimha Rao's time.

Thus, in November 2011, during the East Asia Summit, China publicly warned India to keep off South China Sea on the grounds that it was a disputed territory, where Vietnam had awarded a block on contract to ONGC (Videsh) to drill for oil. This was despite the fact that the day before this public warning, India had claimed to have privately explained to China that Indian interests in the South China Sea were purely commercial and China should settle all issues of sovereignty according to the principles of international law and practice. But then the UPA government never demonstrated firm leadership or had the nerve to ask Chinese leadership: How could it build roads or invest in Pakistan Occupied Kashmir (PoK), which too is a disputed territory?

Look at the manner in which India under Modi has deftly handled the issues in relation to Vietnam and Iran. When PM Modi was holding his high level meetings with Jinping in New Delhi in September 2014, Indian President Pranab Mukherjee was in Vietnam as a part of regular exchange of visits. Later, on October 28 2014, Modi held high level talks with the Vietnamese prime minister, Nguyen Tan Dang, on strengthening strategic partnership and as a part of growing understanding of importance of bilateral relationship, India agreed to sell military hardware including BRAHMOS missiles, naval vessels. And Vietnam offered two more blocks to India for energy exploration within its exclusive economic zone in the South China Sea!

China is a dictatorship that understands only the language of power; when it uses its power, India too needs to demonstrate its willpower to counter it powerfully. That is the only way to get substantial results from Chinese leaders. We need not and cannot think of matching China in every respect, as Indian economy is only one third of China's. But Indian power deficit can be balanced by cultivating likeminded friends on the basis of shared interests without compromising national interest. Nations make friendship not only on the basis of their perceived congruence in their national interests but also based on their geographical location, perceived specific economic interests in conjunction with geopolitical interests.

Geopolitics and geoeconomics at its best was demonstrated by India as a gift to people to celebrate completion of two years of its superb conduct of Indian foreign policy. Demonstrating a clear vision of future of Indian foreign policy compulsions, PM Modi signed two agreements in Teheran on May 23; it was a commercial contract with

Iran for development the of Chabahar port and a trilateral agreement between India, Iran and Afghanistan on trade and transit. This effectively links India through Iran to Afghanistan from where it is connected to major cities of Afghanistan like Herat, Kandahar, Kabul and Mazar e Sharif through Garland Road.

Chabahar port development agreement is a smart geopolitical and geoeconomic answer to Chinese controlled Gwadar port in Pakistan at a distance of one hundred km west of Chabahar. When fully developed, the Chabahar port will provide easy access to India to Afghanistan bypassing Pakistan. And through Afghanistan to energy rich Azerbaijan, Turkmenistan and other Central Asian nations. Though Iran had offered the development of Chabahar to India in 2003, Modi government signed a MoU in May 2015 and agreement in May 2016. It should adhere to complete operationalisation of the port facilities by December 2016 to free Afghanistan from over-dependence on Pakistan for access to the Indian Ocean. This move on the part of India will also enable it to play a stabilising role in the Gulf region as well as in West Asia.

Conclusion

Indian pursuit of geopolitical strategic partnership with Iran and Vietnam is likely to be extended with moving times as there are clear signs of it. Japan, which shares India's concerns about China's growing assertiveriess, has indicated to India its willingness to financially participate in the development of Chabahar port. The United States, another strategic partner, has also extended its support to the Indian project to develop modern port facilities at Chabahar. Similarly, the US' lifting of economic sanctions against Iran, after the nuclear agreement, is also likely to share Indian concerns behind its efforts to develop the Port of Chabahar in Iran. India could play a role in bringing Iran and the US closer to promote a win win situation amongst the partners.

Another recent development is President Obama's visit to Vietnam and worth a mention as part of a larger geopolitical operation. Was it by design or coincidence that Modi was in Tehran and Obama in Vietnam on the same day — May 23? We may get clear answers after the Modi-Obama meeting which is scheduled to be held on June 7 in Washington, DC. But as much as India shares US' concerns against the growing Chinese security threat in South-East Asia, it also shares deep concerns with Vietnam and other members of Association of South-East Asian Nations (ASEAN) over the Chinese claim of sovereignty over the entire South China Sea which also washes the borders of ASEAN countries. It is this concern, which led the US to speak of 'Asian Pivot'. It is this concern that led Obama to lift the arms sale embargo on Vietnam after his recent visit.

There is thus, a message to the Congress Party in India: Do not criticise geopolitical co-operation between India and the US on the ground that "PM Modi and his government" are pushing "India into a closer, deeper military alliance and become the part of the larger operational designs and requirements of the US in Asia, in Pacific and South China Sea" in response to the government's in principle, agreeing on military logistics support agreement. It is not intrusive and doesn't affect India's non-aligned status. Anyway, non-alignment in its Cold War sense is dead when Manmohan Singh asked the US to stay put in Afghanistan even after December 2014. What now prevails as PM Modi has said is: Congruence of national interest of US and India. I may add that Non-Alignment (NA) has become National Interest Alignment (NIA)!

The Leadership Review, June 2016

Explaining India-China Doklam Standoff and thereafter

What must have prompted China to create a crisis in India-China formal bilateral relations? China's policy has been since 1990s one of asserting its claims over a land or a sea on historic grounds—using ancient linkages or some time its possession of a now disputed territory Way back in 1998, I had called it as "a policy of fixing the flag in a territory that does not belong to it." If a legitimate nation-claimant, but weaker in comparison to China, objects to such a behaviour, China says using gunboat diplomacy, "let us co-develop—Chinese favoured work for joint-development—it; if the nation claiming it doesn't yield to such suggestions, then subdue it with the use of force. This policy ought have been known to nations crying foul today as in 1993 the then strongman of China Jiang Zemin had developed the policy of "forward projection of power"!

However, more specifically, in India since 1991 all governments so far, including the NDA I under Atal Behari Vajpayee (1998-2004), and later UPA governments led by Manmohan Singh (2004-2014) have followed a policy, may be his reading of political ground realities faced by then forced it on to follow it. I have called that policy, as "playing second fiddle" to China.

But Chinese present President Xi Jinping, being a shrewd politician, had a taste of changed approach of India, when he had met Prime Minister (PM) Narendra Modi in Ahmadabad and in New Delhi during his first visit to India in September 2014, when Modi was playing host to Jinping. As their unofficial confabulations were going on, the Peoples Liberation Army (PLA) as in the past, intruded in Ladakh. Then, Modi clearly informed Chinese President that economic relations cannot go on, if such incidents continued to occur. After eight days standoff Ladakh, PLA forces withdrew. Jinping publicly expressed his sadness over the tensions between PLA and India, while departing from Delhi India has also made it clear to China that its assertion of sovereignty over the South China Sea by use of muscle power and gunboat diplomacy is not acceptable to India.

Origin of Doklam Crisis

This time theatre of the Chinese intrusion was in Doklam, within the tri-junction involving India, Bhutan and China. In this tri-junction, India-China part of borders involving the state of Sikkim have already been settled and demarcated. Doklam belongs, according Bhutanese and Indian plans, to Bhutan; but China has disputed it. There have been 4 rounds of talks between Bhutanese and Chinese officials without resolving it. But normal understanding in international relations has been that status quo to be maintained till negotiations complete and a solution is found.

But suddenly in mid-June, China claimed the disputed territory belongs to it and was found constructing a road as the part of its ambitious plans for One Belt one Road (OBOR). OBOR is envisaged as 21st century equivalent historic Chinese Silk Route. It was the brainchild of Chinese leader, Xi Jinping. It proposes to connect nearly sixty countries in Central Asia, West Asia and South Asia, Africa and Europe with a GDP of $3 trillion.

It's a matter of commonsense, that it will provide an investment outlet for Chinese controlled surplus US dollars, bring the nations accepting the OBOR proposal under a long-term debt-trap with China. A part of OBOR is called China-Pakistan-Economic Corridor (CPEC), which passing through China's only Muslim population dominant province of Xinxiang to Pakistan-held Gilgit Baltistan going all the way to Chinese built Gwadar Port in Baluchistan. It will provide an economic and territorial link between Pakistan and China; China will control Gwadar and enjoy direct access to Indian Ocean.

What provoked it?

First and foremost and immediate provocation to China was, provided by refusal of India and Bhutan to join China promoted OBOR. India of course has strong reasons to reject the idea of OBOR, since a major portion of the project was to run through Pakistan Occupied Kashmir (POK). This part of the project called CPEC and involved an investment of $43billion; as the entire Jammu & Kashmir (J&K) had acceded to India Federation as a unit, India said: OBOR violated Indian sovereignty in POK. Pakistan has been very generous to China in ceding a portion of POK —as though to confirm the truth: Thief would always like to have a partner; by sharing the booty, so that he can cement friendship between two as China-Pakistan friendship is said to be all weather-friendship.

Second, Indian action in turn was deemed as a personal affront to Chinese strongman, President Jinping. After all China is self-proclaimed Superpower, its economy is global next only to the US overtaking that of Japan and aspires to emerge as the Numero Uno replacing the US. This urge is strengthened by globally growing sense of nationalism in many of major powers. Though Communists in the Soviet Union during the Cold War and Indian Communists, during the same period, as well now, claim to believe in internationalism, Chinese, then and now were a different kind of Communists: They were staunch nationalists then and now. However, now globally there is a new push towards Nationalism, as demonstrated in the US by President Trump, in Japan by Shinzo Abe and Modi India. Hence, to keep company with them, China is using nationalism, as a tool to compete with rivals!

Only difference is world leaders expressed then and now, their commitment to nationalism. However, when Chinese leaders exhibit their commitment to nationalism, as a key to making a decision does not recognise a similar right to other nations. Soon after Indian nuclear tests in May 1998, China went out in a campaign trail to advice India not to think of restoring past glory, but concentrate on alleviation of poverty masses in India! But it clearly forgot that it was also motivated by the very idea in 1964 when it went nuclear! Then Chinese had same level economic status as India in the 1960s.

As a matter of fact Chinese supreme leader, Xi Jinping is also nationally motivated by a personal desire to rise to the stature of Mao and De Xiaoping. With that goal in mind, he has to emerge as a strong nationalist leader. One of the reasons, why Mao resorted to October 1962war against India. was Mao's sense that he was then losing his grip over the party. But fifty five years later, Xi knows that the option of war is longer available; hence, what he intends to do in pursuit of his personal ambition is to sideline many senior members Politburo and put his supporters in the key bodies in the next Communist Party Congress to be held in October this year. Xi believes that youngsters brought by him in the Politburo would be supporters of great legacy set by him.

Third, then the question is: why did it, go the extent of dragging the crisis if it had a firm policy, not to go to the extent of harming mutual economic interests? I strongly feel that Xi was trying his hand in replying to Modi in his game of global geopolitical alliance against an assertive and aggressive China which had practiced against India what westerners called a String of Pearls by literally encircling her. Without getting into details, during UPA's second term (2009-2014), China had developed an unholy alliance against India making Pakistan as the firm fulcrum at Gwadar port; on the East, Nepal easily falling prey to monetary inducements offered by China, and an uncertain Bangladesh, down south former President, of Sri Lanka, Rajapaksha handed over Southern port Hambantota to China to develop with a right to park its submarine further South with Maldives having a pro-China government—all were on its side. But Modi had weaned away Sri Lanka's new Presideint Maithripala Srisena elected in 2015 with a suggestion not to put all eggs in China's basket. Modi developed a firm relationship with Sheikh Hasina of Bangladesh. Even he was able to wean away Nepal from China. Modi developed a larger coalition with the US, Japan, Vietnam, Australia and Mongolia—even Malaysia joining in it.

Did Xi Jinping have a plan to respond PM Modi's efforts to build a larger coalition of friends globally with a plan of few of India's neighbouring countries to join him in promoting OBOR to cause a geopolitical embarrassment to India? Plan was to wean a way Bhutan from being steadfast friend of India, and make it to develop direct diplomatic relations with China, as he was able to do, albeit, for a short tenure, also with Nepal. China was also perplexed at the globally growing goodwill for India on the Doklam issue and in general against it. The US had called for peaceful settlement of disputes; Japan had openly extended support on the stand taken by India on Doklam issue. China was accustomed to the style of India under Manmohan Singh dealing with China, wherein Indian government showed all deference to Chinese sensitivities in bilateiral relations. But there was no reciprocity on the part of China. I have called elsewhere this approach as playing second fiddle to China. But under the present, Modi government things have changed. India has taken proactive steps to protect its national interest.

Seventy three days imbroglio and Thereafter

What happened to China after steadfastly holding on to impasse on Doklam for seventy-three days, on 29 August to end its standoff with India. There were threats, ridicule of Indian actions, reminding India of humiliating defeat it suffered in October 1962. Campaigns of disinformation bullying Indian policy makers were practised by China. But India stood firm on its initial suggestion that let both nations withdraw their troops simultaneously and resolve the issue later by negotiations.

China seems to have been in a dilemma on the face of Indian steadfast demand for simultaneous withdrawal of forces from both sides and holding of negotiations. The Chinese Foreign ministry had even created a convenient scenario to enable them to withdraw their forces by stating that Indians have withdrawn some troops. But India had contradicted that claim and stalemate had continued. It gives an impression that there seems to be a difference between the PLA and the political hierarchy. It is confirmed by Chinese Defence Minister by stating that they are so firm that mountain may move but Chinese troops are very firm in their resolve! They also appeared trying to expand the Doklam stalemate by asking India what it would do if China opens similar fronts in elsewhere as well!

China has been threatening and posturing but it is unlikely to make border 'live.' Two nations had bilateral trade touching $71 billion and when Modi and Xi had met it was agreed to raise it further. Incidentally trade is adverse to Indian interests. As of now for India it is a trade deficit $53 billion! China is aspiring to the Super Power status; it also considers itself as a developing country as India also places herself in this category.

Hence, it must have thought not rock the economic boat! China when agreed to withdraw finally after 73 days, it must have also been motivated by BRICS summit due on 4 September either Xi must have felt all his domestic compulsions were met. Whatever may be the reasons for ending of impasse, there is no guarantee that China will not raise it once again. Therefore, Indian government, especially the Army, has to be prepared to face its revival again or China could raise similar issue elsewhere! Let us not be carried away by the Chinese bonhomie at the BRICS summit!

RKPN, 26 March 2018

6

INDIA AND ITS NEIGHBOURS

Avoid Past Mistakes In Sri Lanka

The news that Sri Lanka is seeking military assistance from Israel with whom it has just reestablished diplomatic relations is disturbing. Equally disturbing is the news that Pakistan has shown its willingness to help Sri Lanka to protect its territorial integrity and sovereignty (I wish Pakistan had given that promise to India as well). Of course, these developments have occurred after India publicly expressed its unwillingness to militarily intervene in the present crisis of nearly 40,000 Sri Lankan troops being cornered by the Liberation Tigers of Tamil Eelam (LTTE). Foreign minister Jaswant Singh said: "We are not even contemplating military intervention ...we are the beneficiaries of past experience".

The past experience comes from former Prime Minister Rajiv Gandhi's hasty decision to send Indian Peace Keeping Force (IPKF) to Sri Lanka in 1987. I had then argued against India sending troops. This is my position today. India should not do the dirty work for the Sri Lankan politicians. Unfortunately, the then President Jayavardhane considered Rajiv immature and successfully fooled him to induct IPKF to disarm LTTE and establish peace in northern Sri Lanka.

Jayavardhane made Rajiv to agree to induct IPKF by holding a threat of Sri Lanka asking other foreign powers like the United States or Pakistan or Israel to help in the event of India refusing to do so. In the Cold War mindset, it was enough for Rajiv Gandhi to agree to the Sri Lankan demand. By agreeing to bring peace to Tamil areas, India lost her diplomatic leverage till then she exercised as an honest peace broker between Tamils and the Sri Lankan government.

However, then India failed to get Tamils even regional autonomy. Moreover. IPKF was forced to fight Tamils. As a peace-keeping force, Indian army was not armed to fight guerrillas in the jungles. Sri Lanka was also unhappy then as India failed in the primary task of bringing peace to the region. Tamils were so disillusioned with India that instead of getting them their rightful place in Sri Lankan society, IPKF was killing whom they were supposed to protect. IPKF then became Innocent People Killing Force in the eyes of Tamils.

The result was that Premadasa, the successor to Jayavardhane. became a vehement critic of the IPKF. He successfully ran his presidential campaign on the nationalistic theme of getting foreign troops out of Sri Lankan soil. He overlooked the fact in international law that presence of international peace Keeping force does not curtail sovereignty of a nation. But once elected, he even collaborated with LTTE by providing them arms to fight against IPKF! Indian troops then became his greater enemy than the LTTE!

Hence, in this historic back-ground, it is ironic for a Buddhist monk, Elle Gunawansa. to ask for the induction of Indian troops in Sri Lanka to prevent the LTTE from recapturing Jaffna. Buddhists were by and large against IPKF in 1987. Then, Gunawansa was a leading critic of IPKF.

But in politics, consistency is hardly a virtue. Changing perceptions of national interest bring about a change in the stand of politicians. So Gunawansa said: "Yes, I was strongly against the IPKF then; considering the present situation, it is imperative that we invite the Indian army to help halt the LTTE's advance into the Jaffna peninsula".

Does this mean that India now merely watch helplessly when a friendly government in Sri Lanka being cornered by the LTTE which has been declared a unlawful organisation by India? This will neither well reflect on India's role as a regional power nor will it help India to maintain her role as a leader within the South Asian Association of Regional Co-operation (SAARC).

What is the way out? First, India needs today to reissue Mrs Gandhi's 1983 warning to foreign powers to keep off the region. If India does not wish to send troops to kill Tamils in Sri Lanka, she would not like their being killed by Israelis or Americans or in the least by Pakistanis. We do not want these foreign powers to get a foothold so close to the southern tip of India.

Second, India need to reinitiate its diplomatic efforts to bring the two warring parties together to find a lasting solution to the crisis. Now objections might be raised as to how India could talk to LTTE, which has been declared as an unlawful organisation. This technical objection can easily be met. India is now willing to talk to anti-national separatist organisations like All Party Huriyat Conference (APHC) which is the political face of 23 separatist terrorist groups in Kashmir. If India can talk to these terrorist leaders, among whom some are self-confessed assassins, India could in the interest of peace in South Asia, talk to the LTTE.

Before these talks are initiated with the LTTE, it is necessary and prudent for the government to consult and keep positively informed the Congress leadership as the main opposition party. Because it is an emotional issue for many; since the LTTE is held responsible for the assassination of Rajiv Gandhi, former Prime Minister.

In this context it is also necessary to make it clear that India does not entertain any territorial designs as far as Sri Lanka is concerned. Wild suggestions, for instance, as floated by Subramaniam Swamy, the president of Janata Party, that Sri Lankan government ought to pass a resolution seeking to confederate with India, as Island State is not viable' should be scotched. This, according Swamy, would also enable Indian army to help Sri Lankan government.

Dr Swamy's idea of free border between India and Sri Lanka is premature and his comparison of his suggestion with the Sikkim's merger would be further suspect in the eye of Sri Lankans. Indian starting point has to be as has been always the case that India is committed to Sri Lankan unity and integrity. However, Sri Lanka should first fulfill Tamil aspirations for self-rule by giving them a provincial council.

Once the Tamils are brought into the governing process, Sri Lanka should seriously consider turning the Island into a federation rather than govern it as a unitary state. Sri Lankans' main worry has been that giving Tamils statehood within Sri Lankan federation could be the first step towards their eventual secession. On the other hand, it will be the only step to keep territorial integrity of the Island state intact. Devolution of powers to regional and grassroots level is a compulsion of modern needs of globalisation. More powers you transfer to local bodies, better you can attend to global issues.

One man's ego in the LTTE, the blunders of a series of leaders of Sri Lankan governments, and Indian mistakes of the past intervention have cost several thousand lives of Tamils, Sri Lankans and Indians. It is the time now to reinvest in diplomacy to put an end to this bloody conflict.

The Observer of Business and Politics, 11 May 2000

No Grand Designs

It is ironic for Buddhist monk, Elle Gunawansa to ask for the induction of Indian troops in Sri Lanka to prevent the Liberation Tigers of Tamil Eelam (LTTE) from recapturing Jaffna. Buddhists were by and large against Indian Peace Keeping Force (IPKF) in 1987. Then, Gunawansa was a leading critic of IPKF. But in politics, consistency is hardly a virtue. Changing perceptions of national interest bring about a change in the stand of the politicians. So Gunawansa said, "Yes, I was strongly against the IPKF then but considering the present situation, it is imperative that we invite the Indian army to help halt the LTTE's advance into the Jaffna peninsula."

Sri Lankan main opposition party -United National Party (UNP) has also asked their president, Chandrika Kumaratunga to seek military assistance to overcome the present military imbroglio faced by their army. But the army itself has said that there is no need for them to be evacuated from the region. But it is a fact that 40,000 Sri Lankan troops are cornered by the LTTE in Jaffna.

India need not and should not do the dirty work for the Sri Lankan politicians. This was my position then in 1987 and it is today. Old Fox that Jayavardhane was, he considered Rajiv immature and successfully fooled him into sending the IPKF to disarm LTTE and establish peace in northern Sri Lanka.

Bait for Rajiv

Jayavardhane got Rajiv to agree by threatening to ask other foreign powers like the United States or Pakistan or Israel to help in the event of India refusing to help. In the Cold War mindset, it was enough for Rajiv Gandhi to agree to the Sri Lankan demand. By agreeing to bring peace to Tamil areas, India lost her diplomatic leverage which she enjoyed, that of an honest peace broker between Tamils and the Sri Lankan government.

India was neither able to get Tamils the regional autonomy they wanted nor was she able to establish peace. Sri Lanka remained totally unhappy. Tamils were unhappy that instead of getting them their rightful place in Sri Lankan society, IPKF was killing those it was supposed to protect. Indian peace keeping force then became Innocent People Killing Force (IPKF) in the eyes of Tamils.

The result was that the successor to Jayavardhane, Premadasa who was prime minister under the former, became a vehement critic of the IPKF. He successfully ran his presidential campaign on the nationalistic theme of getting foreign troops out of Sri Lankan Soil. He overlooked one simple fact- presence of international peace keeping force does not curtail sovereignty of a nation. But once elected, he even collaborated with LTTE by providing them arms to fight against IPKF! Indian troops the became the greater enemy.

Say no to arms

Given this background, India should neither provide arms nor soldiers to Sri Lanka. Any possibility of Sri Lankans trying to play their card of inviting foreign troops of Israel or Pakistan or the US or China could be effectively answered by India by issuing "a hands off" warning.

Does this mean that India should watch helplessly as a friendly government in Sri Lanka is cornered by the LITE ? This will not reflect well on India's role as a regional power nor will it help India to maintain her role as a leader within the South Asian Association of Regional Co-operation (SAARC).

What is the way out? India needs to re-initiate its diplomatic efforts to bring the two warring parties together to find a lasting solution to the aspirations of Sri Lankan Tamils. Just how can India talk to LTTE, which has been declared as an unlawful organisation? This technical objection can easily be met. India is now willing to talk to anti-national separatist organisation like All Party Huriyat Conference (APHC) which is the political face of 23 separatist terrorist groups based in Kashmir.

Before these talks are initiated with the LTTE, the government must consult and keep the Congress Party leadership informed, as the main opposition party. Such consultations are also necessary, as it is an emotional issue for many; since the LTTE is held responsible for the assassination of Rajiv Gandhi.

Absurd

In this context it is also necessary to clarify that India does not entertain any territorial designs as far as Sri Lanka is concerned. Wild suggestions, as for instance that floated by Subramaniam Swamy, Janata Party president that Sri Lankan government ought to pass a resolution seeking to confederate with India, as "Island State is not viable" are unacceptable. Dr Swamy's idea of free border between India and Sri Lanka is premature and his comparison of his above suggestion with Sikkim's merger would be further suspect in the eyes of Sri Lankans. India's starting point should be that it is committed to Sri Lankan unity and integrity. However, Sri Lanka should first fulfill Tamil aspirations for self-rule by giving them provincial council.

Once the Tamils are brought into the governing process, Sri Lanka should seriously consider turning the island into a federation rather than govern it as a unitary state. Their main worry has been that by giving Tamils statehood within Sri Lankan federation, it could be the first step towards their eventual secession. On the other hand, it will be the only step to keep territorial integrity of the island state intact. Devolution of Powers to regional and grass roots level is a compulsion of modern needs of globalisation. More the powers you transfer to regional local bodies, you can attends to global issues.

Midday, 13 May 2000

What can India learn from Musharraf's domestic reforms?

There is a remarkable identity of views in India on the fact that Musharraf's Speech of January 12 hugely focuses on domestic reforms and there is very little that meets the Indian concerns. This is the opinion of Jaswant Singh as well as George Fernandes. Home Minister L.K. Advani also shares the same view.

In our own concerns for checking cross-border terrorism, getting extradition of 20 terrorists, and getting Pakistan to foreclose the option of using terrorism as an instrument of foreign policy and proxy war, it is likely that we might ignore effects of Musharraf's domestic reforms. These effects can be examined from two angles. First, their effects on Musharraf himself and second, whether there any thing India can learn from these reforms.

Let me briefly recapture some of the important domestic reforms Musharraf listed. All Mosques need to be registered and no mosque to be built without a clearance from the government. Similarly, all madrassas need to be registered and new ones cannot come up without the permission of the government. They also need to teach modern scientific subjects to gether with religious texts. No foreign national could be enrolled without the clearance from the government.

These are extremely welcome measures as the madrassas and mosques have been breeding grounds for Jihadi elements to fight in Afghanistan and Kashmir. The Americans have driven out Jihadis from Afghanistan. But though Pakistan will never get Kashmir, Pakistani Jihadis, cannot remain jobless. Their unemployment is largely due to the reforms announced by Musharraf under the US pressure. Now after so many years of brainwash, they cannot segregate their fight against India from their fight against Musharraf. It is possible that an Osama or several Osamas might emerge from the ranks of Pak Jihadis.

One cannot ignore parallels. Osama was trained by the American CIA on Pakistani soil to fight against the Russians in Afghanistan. Once that Jihad was over, he began to think of a larger movement to establish pure Islam in Saudi Arabia and in the rest of the Muslim world. He perceived himself as a Khomeini who after decades of exile in Paris returned to Iran to establish an Islamic state. In the like manner, Osama dreamt to return to Saudi Arabia to establish a pure Islamic state.

In the like manner, Pakistani Jihadis trained to fight in Afghanistan and Kashmir might pose threat to Pakistani leaders. What else then, these trained Jihadis would do? Their number is quite large. After all next to Afghanistan, Pakistan has emerged as the Global University to train in the art and science of terrorism. Then, what can we learn from steps proposed to be taken by Musharraf? There are lesson for all Indian political parties including the ruling BJP and the government. The madrassas are proliferating in a big way in the country. In recent reports newspapers highlighted the fact that on India Pakistan borders their number is growing. In Kutch District alone there are 323 of them. Every year they have been growing by at least ten more. On the Nepal-Bihar border there are 200 while on Pak-Rajasthan border their number is said to be 129.

As there are not enough teachers to man them, teachers have come from far away places like Kishenganj in Bihar, Murshidabad in west Bengal and Faizabad in UP. According to Intelligence agencies, these madrassas are being used to train anti-India terrorists. On the other hand, like Musharraf in Pakistan, their supporters in India have justified their existence on the ground that they provide education to poor Muslims. But if the teachers come from far away places to work in these madrassas, it can only be because they are committed to such schools, in their missionary zeal. They are also reportedly getting foreign funding. It is this aspect that has already made intelligence agencies to alert the government that growth of these institutions as "undesirable." But in pursuit of vote bank politics, political parties do not speak about it or against it. What is interesting is that the BJP that is perceived by Muslims as against them also seem to have decided to follow the vote bank politics of other parties. This was evident in last year's call by the President of the party to Muslims to join them instead of pursuing a difficult path of winning the Muslim support by taking progressive steps to improve their lot.

Large segment of Muslims in India want to get secular education, good jobs and lead a decent life. Hence, the government need to provide special educational opportunities to Muslims in poor localities in the country by offering them free education. The opportunities should be in the regional language schools and English medium schools. After the school education, the students should be provided opportunities in different state universities for higher education as it is being done now to students from North East.

The governments in the country should also ask these madrassas to register with the government and introduce prior clearance before they could start new ones. They also should be extended government aid to teach subjects taught in the regular schools and be subject to regular inspections. The students from these schools also be permitted to appear to the state school leaving examinations.

At present the madrassas may not be centres of breeding anti-national activities. But if these are allowed to grow without regulation, it may not take long for them to proliferate and produce students who may not be able to do anything except agitate in the name of religion. But the task is not easy, if Nepal's experience is to serve the country as a warning. The Muslim leaders there are opposing the government efforts to regulate madrassas. India has to initiate these steps now to prevent the future growth of universities of terrorism.

The Free Press Journal, 12 February 2002

Peace lies in the corridors of learning

People to People relations has become the buzzword in India-Pakistan relations ever since Prime Minister Atal Bihari Vajpayee spoke in April 2003 of one more—and, in his tenure, last—effort to bring peace and friendship between the two countries. It's not that there were no such contacts in the past. But those were mostly limited to Track II diplomacy where some retired diplomats, military generals and politicians tried their hand in bringing peace between the two nations which they could not do while they had been in office!

But what is now happening is an unprecedented upsurge in movement of people who arc unconnected with governance or politics across the borders. School children, patients in search of treatment, relatives from separated families, players, performers and a variety of people have criss-crossed the frontiers. This urge is much higher and intense amongst the Pakistanis than amongst the Indians. One main reason for it, according to Pakistani scholars, is: almost 20 percent of all Pakistanis still have relatives in India. In Islamabad last May, I heard professors and poets, scientists and hotel employees all recalling their roots in India and longing to see their relatives once again.

If people to people contacts are really to catch on, we need to invest in the younger generation to remove misconceptions in the minds of the young who are going to take up the rudders of that state in the future. Pakistani distortions of Indian history, society and life are many. One way to address misconceptions amongst Pakistanis is to offer them fellowships to study in India. I suggest that India consider instituting peace fellowships. We may call them the Mahatma Gandhi Fellowships to students from Pakistan and other SAARC countries to study in our colleges and universities Indian anthropology, history, literature, society, politics, law, etc. The programme can be easily managed by existing agencies like the University Grants Commission and the ICSSR. These could be an Indian version of the Fulbright Programme. That programme was started in 1948 during the Cold War mainly to encourage students from communist countries to visit American universities. I had two sessions with Senator Fulbright in Washington, DC on its efficacy in removing misconceptions about American society in closed societies. The Gandhi Peace Fellows after their education in Indian universities would be like our informal ambassadors in Pakistan to explain India to their people.

The Indian Express, 6 January 2004

Institute Gandhi Fellowships to promote peace in South Asia

'People to people' relations has become the buzzword In India-Pakistan relutions ever since Indian Prime Minister, Atal Behari Vajpayee spoke on 18th April 2003 of one more and in his lifetime, last effort to bring peace and friendship between the two countries. It's not that there were no such contacts in the past. But those were mostly limited to Track II Diplomacy where some retired diplomats, military generals and defeated politicians tried their hand in bringing peace between the two nations which they could not do while they were serving their respective nations!

But what has now happened is an unprecedented upsurge in movement of people who are unconnected with governance or politics across the borders. School children, patients in search of treatment, relatives from separated families, players, and performers and a variety of people have criss-crossed the divided frontiers. Suddenly two governments too have remembered to release fishermen held in their prisons as well as young boys put behind bars because they strayed into each others lands.

This urge is much higher and intense amongst the Pakistanis than amongst the Indians. One main reason for it, according to Pakistani scholars I met, is: almost 20 percent Pakistanis still have their relatives in India. During my visit to Islamabad in May 2003, I heard professors and poets, scientists and sweepers in hotels all recalling their roots in India and longing to see their relatives once again.

Two years ago after the Pakistan-trained terrorists' attack on Indian Parliament and subsequent mobilisation of troops on the India-Pak borders, such a people to people contact was unthinkable. In January 2000 General Musharraf told an American correspondent, Mr. Weymouth, of the Washington Post about his belief that possession of nuclear weapons will allow them to "push India to the brink and the US will bail them out." Subsequently he also spoke of using the nuclear weapons if driven to wall. But the fact remains that nuclear weapons are unusable and on the other hand, they impose an additional constraint of not permitting violation of existing boundaries by the use of force even if it's a disputed one. This was one very important reason that made Clinton to force Pakistan to withdraw from the Kargil in 1999. An unwritten rule since nuclear weapons developed is that nations with those deadly weapons do not try to alter the boundaries even when they are disputed.

Hence, two nations need to invest in peace. This investment for peace must come from India and in a big way. If people to people contacts are really to catch up, we need to invest in the younger generation to remove misconceptions in the minds of young who are going to take up the rudders of that state in the future. Pakistani distortions of Indian history, society and life are many. Lord Bhikhu Parekh, a few months back narrated a story of embarrassment experienced by a Pakistani host when a child referred to an Indian visitor to their home as Hindu dog!' Obviously child had paid back what it learnt from the grown ups!

One way to fight the misconceptions of Pakistanis is to offer them fellowships to study in India. I suggest that India consider instituting peace fellowships. We may call them the Mahatma Gandhi Fellowships, instead of the Gandhi fellowships, to distinguish from Indira Gandhi or Sonia Gandhi. These be offered to students from Pakistan and other SAARC countries to study in our colleges and universities Indian anthropology, history, literature, society, politics, law etc.

The programme can be easily managed by the existing agencies like the University Grants Commission, ICSSR, ICHR and other institutions. These could be Indian version of Fulbright Programme. The American Fulbright programme started in 1948 during the Cold War period by Prof. William Fulbright mainly to encourage students from communist countries to visit the American universities. The programme was extremely successful in achieving its goal. One can make out that when one reads about one or the other newly elected East European leader being referred as having studied in the American University.

I had two sessions with Senator Fulbright in Washington, DC on its efficacy in removing misconceptions about American society in closed societies. The Mahatma Gandhi Peace Fellows, after their education in Indian universities would be like our informal ambassadors in Pakistan to explain India to their people. There could be a situation when Pakistan and other countries of SAARC might come out with similar programmes of their own as when Prime Minister proposed Indian offer of certain number of opportunities for Pak children to receive treatment in India, Pakistan also offered certain number of grants to Indian children in their hospitals. Why not? If Pakistan comes out with its own Jinnah fellowships. Indian scholars can visit Pakistan and learn how that country has portrayed Jinnah and how is it different from Indian portrayal.

But we cannot accept non-portrayal of historic events as suggested by Pakistani Foreign Minister, Kasuri. He suggested that Indian war films like LOC do not square up with Indian efforts towards peace. No. Mr. Kasuri, without distortion, story must be told and lesson must be drawn. After World War II, Germany and Japan became good friends of the US. But Hollywood never stopped making War films! But unlike Germany and Japan you were not vanquished. You are in a win-win situation. If Bollywood makes war films, let your country make them too. But without distortions!

The Free Press Journal, 10 January 2004

India-Afghanistan Relation's: The US and Pakistan as Conditioners

Historically, prior to Indian independence, India and Afghanistan had very close relations. However, these cordial relations between two countries were upset by the emergence of a new nation—Pakistan, carved out from undivided India by the British Imperial government. Today, Pakistan has common borders with Afghanistan on its north-west. Hence, practically Indian relations with Afghanistan are subject to whims and vagaries of Pakistan. Afghanistan which had common borders with undivided India has now become for India a state beyond borders—in terms of Chanakya, its neighbour's neighbour as a friend.

India's friendly relations with Afghanistan, however, were affected by the Soviet military intervention in Afghanistan in December 1979. Then though government to government relations were officially cordial because the Soviet Union was an important international prop of India then, Afghan people were unhappy with Indian support to the Soviet Union on its military occupation of their country. Hence, today India is not an altogether free player in Afghanistan. Indian relations with Afghanistan are not only impacted and influenced by Pakistan's game plan in Afghanistan but also affected by the US presence in Afghanistan after it dismissed then ruling Taliban government led by Mullah Omar in 2001.

If we consider India's relations with Afghanistan as the central issue of our discussion, the discussion is conditioned by the US—irrespective of whether one considers it as an occupier or a liberator of Afghanistan. But it's also influenced by Pakistan, as a neighbour of Afghanistan, and an adversarial neighbour of India. But Pakistan also is an important player as an ally of the US in its international war against terrorism. Though my focus is on India-Afghanistan relations, and it is conditioned by Pakistan and the US, China as an all-weather friend of Pakistan on the primary consideration of enemy's enemy is a friend, also influences India-Afghan relations, to some extent.

In this paper, I intend to examine mainly India's relations with Afghanistan in the 21st century that saw terrorist attacks on the US on September 11, 2001, which propelled US into Afghanistan and Pakistan. Thus, though my discussion is mainly on Indian relations with Afghanistan, since Pakistan is tied to US war against International terrorism, India has to give due weightage to the US presence in Afghanistan and Pakistan's concerns, hope and expectations from it. Hence, in the next four subsections, I am going to briefly analyse, the impact of the presence of the US, Pakistan and China in the Neighbourhood of Afghanistan.

US in India's Neighbourhood

The US is an extra-regional power in South Asia but as a super power with its global reach got involved in India's near neighbour, Afghanistan and next door neighbour, Pakistan. The US involvement in Pakistan and Afghanistan has had a direct impact on India's relations with Afghanistan. Hence, in contemporary times, discussion on India's relations with Afghanistan cannot be complete without a detailed discussion on the impact of the US presence on India-Afghan relations.

However, the US entanglement with Pakistan goes back to the period soon after India's independence on August 15, 1947. Because of the beginning of the Cold War, the US was in search of friends to be roped into military alliances. Pakistan was too willing to join hands with the US in military alliance so that through that it can collect military aid theoretically in the name of fighting communism, but to fight against India in reality. This was demonstrated during Pakistan's attack against India in 1965.

Be that as it may, the US role in Afghanistan and Pakistan saw a quantum jump after the Soviet Union's military intervention in

Afghanistan. Of course this evolved during the US policy of drawing China into its orbit in 1970 with Pakistan's help that was fully reciprocated by the US during the Bangladesh War of 1971; the hallmark of that co-operation is the US sending nuclear-powered USS Enterprise into the Bay of Bengal to threaten India. Later both Richard Nixon and Henry Kissinger took credit for saving West Pakistan from Indian attack! Nixon wrote: "By using diplomatic signals and behind-the-scene pressures we had been able to save West Pakistan from imminent threat of Indian aggression and domination."

Since then, the last thirty years, the US has been the mainstay of Pakistan. However, the US has played 'In and Out' policy towards Pakistan; Afghanistan has been the factor responsible for the US to pull Pakistan in its orbit and also, to push it out as well. In 1979-1980 the US was keen to make Pakistan frontline state to pump-in massive arms, money and Mujaheedins into Afghanistan to force its then arch rival, Soviet Union out from Afghanistan. Having achieved that goal in 1989 and also seeing the demise of the Soviet Union, Americans abandoned Pakistan to develop as a university to train terrorists for the globalizing world and Afghanistan to their warlords!

The geopolitical location of Pakistan has given it that power to pull and push the US in and out as and when it is convenient to it. Each time when Pakistan's relations with the US deteriorate and touch the lowest level, it is rewarded by the exigencies of global geopolitics, to move closer to the US. Thus, with Pakistan emerging as the epicentre of global terrorism, Al Qaeda organised terrorist attacks on the US, made it to violently return to Pakistan and Afghanistan in 2001.

Hence, I may say that Osama Bin Laden forced George W. Bush to get himself invited in 2001 into Pakistan to hunt him in Afghanistan! In this period of the last thirty years, Pakistan received a bounty of over $40 billion in military and economic aid. It also got large unaccounted prize money as an extra bonus for killing or capturing and handing over to the US, most-Wanted resident-foreign-terrorists or Pakistani terrorists. Musharraf for instance, proudly claims in his *memoir* that during his rule Pakistan "captured 689 and handed over 369" terrorists to the US and "earned bounties totaling millions of dollars."

Osama as a common link between US, Pakistan and Afghanistan

It was George W. Bush who had vowed to capture Osama Bin Laden dead or alive as a response to Al Qaeda organised attacks on the US on September 11, 2001. George Bush had intelligence of likely Al-Qaeda attacks at least a month before. On July 9, 2001 a detailed report appeared from Islamabad by a TV correspondent, Bakr Atiani of Middle East Broadcasting Centre to the effect that he was called to meet Osama Bin Laden. According to his narrative, though Bin Laden was present, his close aides did much of talking. Bin Laden smiling these aides told him in clear terms: "There would be attacks against American and Israeli facilities within next several weeks." But George Bush did not act; apparently, it was not taken seriously.

But once 9/11 attack took place the US trained their guns on Afghanistan's Taliban controlled government for protecting Osama. Taliban was a byproduct of the US-Pakistan covert War in Afghanistan during the 1980s. But when the US threatened an attack against Taliban, Pakistan did not effectively intervene to pressurise Taliban to accede to the US since it had for the first time secured a foothold in Afghanistan as a friendly country. Afghanistan was seen by Pakistan as providing it 'strategic depth'. After 1971 Bangladesh War, every military chief in Pakistan has invested his time and energy in increasing 'strategic depth' of Pakistan by trying to control Afghanistan.

It is the US and Pakistan that really reaped benefits of their changing relations with Osama. However, his presence became a liability for Afghanistan after Taliban was defeated. An American spy, Lt Col. Anthony Shaffer, who has published his exploits in Afghanistan in a work called *Operation Dark Heart: Spycraft and special ops on the frontlines of Afghanistan* says that despite ground operators and his stating that the intelligence "indicates that the most of leadership [of 9/11 terror] is... now in Pakistan" their superiors forced them to focus on Hindu Kush mountains—winter safe havens of main operatives of Al Qaeda.

In reality, President Bush had lost political interest in capturing Osama since latter had helped him to get elected for a second term by issuing a threat message of terror attack on October 29, 2004. To put it in simple language, till that date, sixty percent of voters considered Bush as competent to protect US security while 60 percent of voters considered John Kerry as capable to improve economy and people were more concerned of economic situation than security. But Osama's message threatening imminence of another attack helped Bush to win November 2, elections by making security once again a main issue. Having won a second term, thanks to Osama, Bush spared the life of Bin Laden.

Contrary is the case with Obama's search for Osama. President Obama, was determined to see that another 9/11 type Al-Qaeda attack just does not take place in the US. His concerns and planning were focused on to continue the Bush policy to search and kill Osama. From day one after he became President-elect, he was briefed on Al-Qaeda and hunt for its top leaders. The description of it has been fascinatingly narrated by Bob Woodward in his *Obama's Wars*.

Thus, the US stunned the world by announcing their successful extermination of Osama Bin Laden in Abbottabad, less than 40 miles away from Pakistan's capital Islamabad on May 2, 2011. Pakistan had maintained that Bin Laden was not in Pakistan but he could be in Afghanistan. Pakistan always resented the American allegation that despite it being an important ally in the US war against global terrorism is not doing enough to get him dead or alive!

Often American actions or inaction in tackling terrorism at the source of it—Pakistan, is frustrating to Indian observers. But reading through *Obama's Wars* indicates that information available with the US policy makers so accurately reflecting situation in Pakistan, yet the US is forced to use Pakistan as an ally because of its geopolitical location though it should be really considered as enemy number one—in its war against international terrorism!

Pakistan's Pretence of Ignorance:

Pakistan of course was not informed by the US before launching its mission to kill Osama. The reasons are very simple and crystal clear. Pakistani President Asif Ali Zardari said in Abbottabad: "Some in the US press have suggested that ...we were disingenuous and actually protected the terrorists we claimed to be pursuing. Such baseless speculation may make exciting cable news, but it does not reflect facts." Poor president! He made almost similar naive unbelievable statement soon after the 26/11 Mumbai attacks when he denied totally involvement of the Pakistan, let alone of ISI, attributing it to non-state actors. Whereas the linkage between the ISI, Army, and their protege Lashkar-e-Taiba (LeT) as one of few terrorist arms, is globally well established both by the trial of the only surviving Pakistani terrorist Kasab captured in Mumbai after 26/11 and testimony of David Headley in the trial of Rana in Chicago!

It has been presented as a two-pronged intelligence failure for Pakistan. First, Pakistan's military and military controlled ISI didn't know whereabouts of Osama while he was living so close to them. Second, they had absolutely no clue that US elite forces—SEAL would conduct a special operation to eliminate Osama for ever—thus, technically violating Pakistani sovereignty.

Soon after the US extermination of most wanted international terrorist, Osama Bin Laden on May 2, 2011 in Pakistan, CIA Director opined that Pakistan was either involved in protecting Osama or incompetent. According to Wikileaks published a week before Osama Bin Laden was finally exterminated by the American elite forces SEAL, had said he was running for his life for months soon after September 11, 2001 in Afghanistan. In reality he was enjoying a comfortable life in his well-protected within a structure located in compound.

Humans lie and since governments are made of humans, governments lie too. During the Vietnam War under Johnson administration an official claimed a right to lie in the interest of national security. Under the broad parameters, how is the US government is coming out with the truth? Is May 2nd the earliest they could get at Osama? Or is it reasonable to surmise that time of assassination of Bin Laden, is timed to suit the electoral purposes at a time when revival of declining economy has become a dire need?

China in Afghanistan

China is the most prominent country which was critical of the US violating Pakistan's sovereignty. China shares Pakistan's concerns on Indian presence in Afghanistan, while it would not like to leave Afghanistan entirely as an exclusive sphere of influence for the US Hence, China has increased its economic and political presence in Afghanistan in recent years.

An Analysis

What explains quadrangular presence of India, Pakistan, US and China in Afghanistan? Though the US is the farthest of four nations under discussion has at present interest as the super power and as the victim of 9/11 that initially led it to attack the Taliban regime. Now, the US President Barrack Obama, after almost a decade of the US presence in Afghanistan, has announced on June 4. 2011 his plans to withdraw troops gradually from Afghanistan—ten thousand during the current year, 23 thousand by 2012 and complete withdrawal in 2014. Though this decision is mainly driven by unpopularity of war domestically and its economic constraints of international debt of $14 trillion.

But on a long term basis, the US scientists and technologists have estimated that the mineral wealth of Afghanistan is expected to range between $one to $three trillion. Geologists and technologists have identified important minerals like, iron, gold, copper, cobalt and industrial metals like lithium. Naturally US looks for a reasonably stable, peaceful and friendly Afghanistan that can allow it a major share in exploitation of it mineral wealth.

But the close ally of the US in its war on international terrorism—Pakistan also looks for a stable and friendly Afghanistan so as to provide it what its generals have called 'strategic depth' against its arch enemy—India! In the 1980s, however, it thought 'strategic depth' as a relevant strategy also against the Soviet Union, but now it is pursued by Pakistan clearly only against India. This was clearly expounded by the present Army Chief, General Kayani. In a rare meeting with foreign media correspondents, he said: "We want Afghanistan to be our strategic depth..." It sounds as though he meant Afghanistan as Pakistan's client state. But he clarified: "The way we understand it, if Afghanistan is peaceful, stable and *friendly* (emphasis added), we will have 'strategic depth' because our western border is secure..." The strategic concept is pursued by Pakistan mainly in relation to India. Thus, it means that in an event of Pakistan-India conflict, it can move its movable war-making and sustaining assets to farthest in Afghanistan.

Hence, towards India, Pakistan as of now has only one policy: Of keeping India out of Afghanistan. Earlier it had organised terrorist attacks against Indian Embassy in Kabul, on Indian construction engineers involved in road building. In the initial years of Obama presidency, Pakistan tried its best to link its continued co-operation with the US with its forcing India to pull out of Afghanistan. Initially when Obama appointed Ambassador Holbrook as his Af-Pak special envoy. Pakistan tried to make the position to reflect Af-Pak-India, so that it can use its concerns with India as bargaining chips to extend its support to US in Afghanistan. But Indian resistance to the idea finally killed the concept.

Along with 'strategic depth'. Pakistan is also working to see that India does not play *any* role in Afghanistan. India has been invited to play a role by the US in the economic and infrastructural reconstruction in Afghanistan. It must be noted that India has committed a soft loan of $2 billion in Afghanistan. While Bush administration had an unwavering and positive approach to Indian presence since 2001, during the first two years, Obama has sent confusing signals on Indian presence. The US also has been over-sensitive to Pakistani concerns in Afghanistan. But post-Osama extermination, the US is unlikely to accept any veto from Pakistan over Indian presence in economic and infrastructural development of Afghanistan. If India is willing this American attitude might even extend to India extending non-combat military role as well.

These signals were also picked up by Pakistan rather Pakistan contributed to that by tacit attacks on Indian interests in Afghanistan. It has used the growing clout of Lashkar-e-Taiba a creation of Pakistani Army and its Inter Services Intelligence. It is also joined hands by the Pakistani Taliban or Tehereek e Taliban. This has been highlighted by Robert F. Willard, commander of the US Pacific forces, when he expressed concern to US Congress about the LeT's reach, warning that it is no longer focused on India and South Asia. The US had evidence of LeT presence and the greater Asia-Pacific region. LeT has declared holy war against the US and its forces in Afghanistan, as well.

China—a long time friend of Pakistan, has asserted its role in South Asia by attending SAARC meetings as an observer—thanks to the help of Pakistan. China has already won a bid for Ayank copper mine in Logar province. China employs all tricks of trade including heavy bribing as in the case of copper mining. Afghan minister for mines was accused of accepting $20 million bribe to award the mining contract.

Americans fear openly and Indians quietly that a resource-hungry China might try to dominate Afghanistan. But at the same time, today, American troops also provide security to Chinese mining activities! The US while seeking presence of India in Afghanistan for infrastructual development, there is also finding of oil and gas blocks in Afghan-Tajik basin. This provides an nopportunity to Afghanistan to achieve great economic development to raise its total GDP from 12 billion to several fold more.

Pakistan is in favour of the US withdrawing from Afghanistan so that it can play again a major role in internal affairs of Afghanistan. China is a sophisticated player in the region. If it continues, to remain in Afghanistan, it can continue to derive essential advantages to safeguard its interests in the region. But it is today India alone which has a position contrary to the one of Pakistan.

India alone is firmly for the US to continue to work to the establishment of political stability and peace in Afghanistan. If the US withdraws its majority of troops by 2012 and completely by 2014, Pakistan is likely to release the terrorists groups pampered, paid and protected by it to hit Indian interests in Afghanistan. As of now it is one hundred eighty degree turn around in Indian foreign policy where earlier under her nonaligned policy, she tried to keep the US away from the region. But now, while professing its faith in nonalignment, India wants the US to continue to play a role in Afghanistan!

But learning from the experience of the US withdrawal from Afghanistan since the demise of the Soviet Union, when it abandoned Afghanistan to the warlords who ultimately saw the emergence of Taliban, the US is unlikely to withdraw completely even after 2014. The US is committed to train "Afghan security forces" take the charge of its security. The US has expressed its desire to hold talk with all forces in Afghanistan, including Taliban, if they abide by the Constitution.

This is indicated by the US understanding that post-Osama problem as one of forcing Pakistan to rein in the terrorist forces it has created within Pakistan to fight in Afghanistan—the Teherek-e-Taliban or Pakistani Taliban. The US has improved its technical capabilities in Afghanistan. Thus it has increased the drone attacks on terrorist camps in Pakistan's Federally Administered Tribal Areas (FATA). The US is also likely to continue to pressurise Pakistani civilian government to undertake control of Pak-produced terrorist groups, operating in Afghanistan, like Haqqani brothers.

That might be some what easier to civilian government today than ever before. With Pakistani military being discredited by its patronage to Osama and Al-Qaeda and other anti-Afghanistan and anti-US terrorist forces, the US is likely to support the build up of democratic structure in Pakistan along with Afghanistan. In Pakistan's FATA, has been stronghold of Pakistani Taliban and a shelter for terrorists. Pakistani President Asif Zardari has for instance, recently moved to tame control militancy there that could bring tribal population into political mainstream in FATA.

What India Needs to Learn and Act?

First, India can best improve its counter-intelligence abilities by enhancing level of its co-operation with America. In the aftermath of Osama's elimination India need to tell the US policy makers that Al Qaeda, though from its perspective is still the main terrorist group, and it is determined to destroy it, experience since 9/11 and 26/11 clearly indicate that all terrorist groups, Particularly: like LeT, Jaish e-Mohammad (JEM) other anti-India terrorist groups are all interlinked with the Al-Qaeda. Al-Qaeda is using Pakistanis with foreign passport holders from UK, US to carry out these attacks. Hence, until LeT and its other affiliates are not eliminated world is not safe for democracies that includes Afghanistan.

Second, ultimately self help is the only help India can get in international relations. But unfortunately Indian ruling class has not learnt this lesson from British, though they have learned from them: How to fool public all the time in domestic politics. Hence, India needs to create a body of intelligence analysts with skills in intelligence operations. India must increase cooperation with the US in counter-terrorism operations.

Third, India should not hesitate to increase its cooperation with Afghanistan by getting involved in training of their Army; providing them necessary weapons systems, including, aircrafts and helicopters along with continued and vigorous cooperation in the areas of strengthening of democratic roots in Afghanistan. By this, it does not mean that their ancient institutions of tribal councils for democratic consultations at the grassroots level are set aside. As an off shoot support for democracy in Afghanistan, India must also see her actions support stabilisation of democracy in Pakistan; especially when military is waiting in the wings to jump to capture power again as its offer to step in to restore peace and tranquility in Karachi as ethnic conflict has already taken a toll of 87. Though rider must always be remembered that democracy survives only when its domestic roots are strong and deep rooted and cannot survive with external promotion and props!

As an extension of the idea it should not be considered as propaganda of the US when it speaks of promotion of democracy every where globally, including China. China should also realize that the its interests in the region are better served by making a common cause with India at least on war against terrorism, checking growth of Islamic extremism and exploitation of mineral resources. In the days of growing multi-polarity, it cannot think of putting all its eggs in Pakistani basket, when is visibly porous and leaking.

Finally, a major feature to be noted is of transformation in Indian policy of nonalignnment: During the Cold War India aimed to see that if the US is kept farther away from South Asian borders, better it is for India; but now in the 21" century, India wants and works to see that the US continues to remain as an active player in the South Asian region! Our policy, making an orientation should be fine-tuned to this changed reality!

FPRC Journal No. 7, 2012

A new step for Pakistan, a new hope for India

Nawaz Sharif, leader of the Pakistan's Muslim League-N (PML-N) has been elected to Pakistan's Federal Parliament in May 2013 general elections. He was twice elected earlier, but on both occasions his term was cut short by the intervention of the Army. Sharif's third term is extremely significant for democracy in Pakistan and the spread of democracy, globally and more specifically in South Asia in several ways. It has in particular direct impact on India-Pakistan bilateral relations.

Improving content of democracy

First, it is the first time in the history of Pakistan that a democratically elected government is handing over power to another democratically elected government without any hitch. Second, the outgoing government for the first time has the unique record and honour of completing full five years' term. Third, for the first time, a democracy succeeds another democracy through a democratic election. In the past, an elected government has always been succeeded by a military government through a coup, most of them accompanied by spilling of blood. Subsequent elections have always been held because of global pressure on military and military's own sense of fatigue in running the government that led to the holding of an election. Hence, this democratic succession should be a cause for celebrations all over the world at least by those who are committed to spread and success of democratic rule.

South Asian Perspective

The South Asian Association for Regional Co-operation (SAARC) was formed in 1985 for accelerated economic development and prosperity through regional co-operation. But India-Pakistan conflicts and regional rivalries have always overshadowed issues of economic and trade cooperation. Though the SAARC Charter prohibits discussion of any bilateral issues, India and Pakistan being two large countries, their rivalries have created frustration amongst the smaller SAARC members, thereby stunting regional cooperation. An effort to break old habits of conflicts was made by the former Pakistani government led by Pakistan's People's Party (PPP). It had taken a bold step when the then Prime Minister, Yusuf Gilani announced his decision to grant Most Favoured Nation (MFN) status to India as India had unilaterally conferred MFN on Pakistan in 1996. But PPP government could not carry out its decision under Pakistani Army-inspired opposition to India getting MFN status manifested by its terrorist stooge, Hafiz Sayeed and his instrument of terrorism— Lashker-e-Toiba. If Nawaz Sharif's government carries out this decision, it could strengthen Pakistani democracy further by promoting bipartisan approach to India-Pakistan bilateral issues. At the same time, it could increase India's positive attitude towards the Pakistani government. This should also help Pakistan in arresting their sliding economy.

India and Nawaz Sharif

There is so much for India to be happy at the recent developments in Pakistan and to look forward for better bilateral relations between the two countries. It is particularly so, because as the Prime Minister for the second time in the 1990s, Nawaz Sharif was determined to improve relations with India. Prior to February 1999 visit of Atal Behari Vajpayee, the then Indian Prime Minister to Lahore, Nawaz Sharif in January 1999 had said: "While 1998 was the year of world reawakening over Kashmir, 1999 will ...be the year of solution of this issue." This was despite the then BJP stand that India is asking "Pakistan to give up Pakistan Occupied Kashmir (POK) prior to any negotiations." It was, of course, a bargaining stand. However, then leaders from both the sides had spoken of turning of Line of Control into international border between the two. During his campaign in May 2013, Nawaz Sharif pronounced his stand that he would like to maintain cordial relations with India. Kashmir issue apart, Sharif is a man completely committed to democracy. After he was sworn in as the PM, his statement included a strong commitment to preservation of democracy. He said: "We should strengthen democracy to close all doors for dictatorship" to reemerge, When he said it, he appeared convincing as he was deposed by General Pervez Musharraf in October 1999, a person whom he had appointed as his chosen man by superseding a few other generals! In another sense, Sharif should thank Musharraf because though he deposed, jailed, and banished Sharif to Saudi Arabia, he spared his life—albeit owing to American pressure so that he could one day see the same military general that tormented him, jailed and eventually banished from Pakistan! This is in great contrast to what Zia-ul-Haq did to another elected Prime Minister—Zulfikar Ali Bhutto in 1978 who was deposed, imprisoned and executed through a judicial verdict. Present development, in retrospect, is also a part of gradual rooting of democracy in Pakistani soil! Yet, Sharif has reasons to be angry with Musharraf, for he remembers how he was handcuffed, and imprisoned; while living a banished leader's life in Saudi Arabia he was refused permission to return to Pakistan when he lost his father. It is natural for Nawaz Sharif to be bitter against Musharraf.

Another issue that Sharif has legitimately raised is the role of Army in Pakistan. He has promised to tame the Army and limit the ISI—notorious Inter State Intelligence. He has promised to investigate the role of Army in the Kargil War, ISI role in 26/11 and hold talks with Taliban. On these counts, Pakistani analysts are skeptical on the abilities of Nawaz Sharif, in the background of failed similar efforts of Zardari in the previous government. But there are two factors which might help Sharif, if he moves gradually, to a greater extent than his predecessors like Gilani or Zardari. First, Army and ISI were considerably discredited by the US expose on Pakistani Army's duplicity in maintaining Osama bin Laden in an Army's hideout right under the tight security of military cantonment area at Abbottabad, while denying any knowledge of his whereabouts! Second, Sharif has retained with himself portfolios of Defence as well as Foreign Affairs. Another major problem he would face is his plans to reach a negotiated settlement with terrorists led by the Pakistani Taliban.

Conclusions

But question is will he be able to go ahead with his plans? Domestic issues which plague Pakistan are: Economic recovery, acute shortage of power with a 14-hrs load shedding, and the issue of galloping prices of gasoline. These seem to be more pressing to the government than foreign policy issues in relation with India. India will also do well in not rushing through early negotiations with Nawaz Sharif for a variety of reasons. Primarily because of past experiences with democratic governments, Pakistani Army's warning to Nawaz Sharif to go slow on his impulses to improve relations with India. Pakistan's policy towards India and Afghanistan are considered as core issues of interest by the Army. The present Indian domestic situation also seems to be non-conducive for resolving major problems in India-Pakistan relations. Though for next general elections there is still eleven months, government seems to have been reduced to a lame duck government so early in its tenure. This may also be a blessing in disguise, in view of the Prime Minister's one-point programme of his long innings in government: To go down in the history of India-Pakistan relations as the one who resolved, for all time to come, all long pending problems with Pakistan. If that is too idealistic, at least he would like to resolve, the thorny problem of Kashmir. But Nawaz Sharif will do well to wait, till he sees out Zardari in September and General Pervez Kayani, present Army Chief in November 2013 before plunging into a radical change in his India policy!"

One India One People, July 2013

7

ISSUES IN INDIAN FOREIGN POLICY

India Vision

India's new President K R Narayanan, few days before assuming office, expressed his belief that "India could well emerge in the 21st century as a major power in the world". This, he said, is not an "idealistic" but a "practical vision".

While everyone who feels pride in being an Indian would like to share Narayanan's practical vision, realistically the question is: are there today in practice, conditions which support, holding of such a vision? As we prepare to celebrate the golden jubilee of Independence, no such practical condition exists either in foreign affairs or in domestic politics to justify such a vision.

In foreign policy, we lost much ground after 1989. We have to deal with nuclear adversaries on our northern borders - Pakistan and China - who are clearly armed with missiles to deliver nuclear weapons on most of our northern cities. Chinese missiles, of course, can hit any city in India. We never protest publicly whenever China conducts a nuclear test or provides M11 missiles to Pakistan.

Pakistan is increasingly posing as a security threat, with US-supplied weapons and Chinese-provided missiles and technology. Recently, Pakistan tested Chinese-supplied Hatf III missiles with a range of 800 km, which can hit most cities in northern and western India.

General (Retd) Aslam Beg says Pakistan would like to acquire capabilities to hit South Indian targets as well.

As it is, in many ways, we play second fiddle to China in international affairs. Now, we are also trying to underplay the threat from Pakistan. Prime Minister I K Gujral expressed doubts as to whether Pakistan by itself can develop long-range missiles. But how does it matter whether you are hit by indigenously developed Pakistani missiles or by Chinese built, Pakistani fired missiles? It is worth recalling Robert McNamara's phrase: "Missile is a missile" in the context of Soviet missiles placed in Cuba in October 1962, which triggered a crisis in relations between the two super powers.

Pakistan's growing confidence in her ability to checkmate India is evident in her behaviour. She first promoted low intensity conflicts in Punjab and later in Kashmir, because of the cover of a nuclear umbrella. India is unable to retaliate, though it knows the exact bases where terrorists are trained. India is reduced to this impotency, because of the fear of Pakistan's retaliation by nuclear weapons.

India, instead of responding to this new missile threat which can carry nuclear weapons with the development of Agni with further tests and acquisition of deterrence capability, our policy-makers sing swan songs of keeping open nuclear and Agni options. Options do not remain for long unless translated into concrete facts at the right time.

Nehru too had an idealistic vision. In 1954, he said in the Lok Sabha: "If you peep into the future and if nothing goes wrong - wars and the like - the obvious country after the US, Russia and China is India." But in the 1950s it was based on the then strong role played by India in world affairs. Then what went wrong in later years, particularly in the 1990s?

Of course, the first and foremost ground for the loss of India's power in world affairs was the end of the Cold War. It proved to be the death-knell of non-alignment, which had circumstantially increased the power of India in world affairs, more than her capabilities. With everyone pursuing independent foreign policy, India became more vulnerable for arm-twisting by the only surviving super power. It is clear for discernible students of international affairs, how the United States twisted P V Narasimha Rao's arms while on a visit to Washington DC in May 1994. India was forced to shelve the Agni missile, go slow on Prithvi, co-sponsor the Comprehensive Test Ban Treaty and a treaty to cut off production of fissile materials in return for US investment in India which India then badly needed to revive her economy.

Second, total collapse of India's economy by the early 1990s made it inevitable for India to borrow from the International Monetary Fund and World Bank. While past socialistic rhetoric and as a part of it, loan melas and loan waivers to farmers - initially contributed to the nation's bankruptcy, later scams involving crores of rupees as a result of economic liberalisation further contributed to the economic fall of the country.

It is now capped by wide publicity given to the fact that India is the eighth most corrupt country in the world which will only deter many foreign investors. Liberalisation so far has meant invitation to foreign multinationals to invest rather than a free hand to Indian investors and companies to expand without facing bottlenecks of licence, quota and permits. Thus, multinationals have brought new brands of whisky, toothpastes, soaps, televisions, fridges and cars without strengthening infrastructure like roads, power and port facilties. The result has been that the net outflow of funds has been more than the inflow.

Third, and the most important factor is domestic political instability. No state can pursue a strong foreign policy if it is not endowed with a reasonably stable government. Alas! US President George Bush (1989-1993), during his one term dealt with four Indian prime ministers! His successor, Bill Clinton, in his four and half years in office, has already dealt with four prime ministers. Current political manipulations in New Delhi indicate that he will deal with three more before the world moves into the 21st century.

But there is no hope for better days in New Delhi. It is because of increasing fragmentation of political parties on caste and communal lines thus, denying any political party, even a working majority. Those, while in power try to rationalise by stating that the days of one party rule are over and coalitions are with us to stay, are only fooling the public.

They do not think about the basic cause of political instability: voter mobilisation on caste and communal lines. Unless they give it up there is no end to political fragmentation and instability.

Nehru had an idealistic vision. It was based on the situation then. Where are the practical conditions to bring back that vision of a strong India, marching into the 21st century as a major power? Nehru's successors have already reduced India to a fourth grade power in international relations.

Midday, 12 August 1997

Don't 'rogue states' need moral leadership?

Prime Minister Atal Bihari Vajpayee was too obliging to the Congress party when it asked him and the BJP not to take credit for India's nuclear test.

Since then he has been giving all the credit to scientists and engineers — deservedly — who were responsible for India's status as a nuclear weapons state. Though the nuclear tests of 1998 are conducted by the scientists — as was the case in 1974 test, what the BJP provided is the political will, which was sadly missing in the governments which came to power since 1989.

It is evident from the admission of former President R Venkataraman — who said that in 1983 under Mrs Gandhi, he as the then Defence Minister had personally gone down into the testing pits in Pokhran, but had to abandon the tests owning to international pressure.

Similar efforts were made by Narasimha Rao in 1995 and as per the boasting of Mulayam Singh by the United Front Governments under Deve Gowda and I K Gujral.

It is significant that after stating in the Lok Sabha that there was I no compelling national security compulsion for the government to test nuclear weapons when he demitted the office in March, he has now justified tests in this interview to the *New York Times* correspondent.

What Vajpayee has done is to create a reasonable hope in the minds of millions of Indians to fulfil the earnest expression of Jawaharlal Nehru, who said in 1954:

"If you peep into the future and nothing goes wrong, like wars, the fourth major power next to US, Russia and China is India". Chinese are right in their reading of Indian history when they said: "A review of Indian history makes two facts clear; India was once a world power. It is obsessed with a desire to be a regional and world power again."

What were the pressing compulsions for the government of India to give up its policy of nuclear ambiguity, despite having conducted a nuclear test in May 1974, and declare herself as a nuclear weapon state?

In his letter to US President Bill Clinton, Prime Minister Atal Behari Vajpayee cited security threat from China as a compelling factor. But when the letter was leaked by the White House to please the Chinese, China reacted violently. The Prime Minister tried to placate China by stating his intentions to improve the relations with it.

Now that India has declared herself as a nuclear weapons state what has to be the policy beyond Pokhran?

Some urgent steps to be taken can be highlighted here.

First, India has identified its nuclear tests as a preparation to China's emergence as a potential national security to India. All our journalist friends have spat venom at George Fernandes for his characterisation of China as a potential security threat. However, they need objectively to know that a Chinese document, "Can Chinese Armed Forces win the next War?" written by some anonymous scholar/soldier identifies India under the heading "potential, large threat - India."

Second, for a credible status as a nuclear weapons state and for a credible nuclear deterrence, India needs to expeditiously develop the medium range — 4,500 to 5000 kms — missiles to that the nuclear weapons can be targeted towards Chinese cities. Thus, there is the need to develop Agni missile.

Third, at present there is no need to deploy nuclear weapons on Indo Pakistan borders. It will be too provocative.

In the absence of strategic depth for Pakistan, the nuclear capability should serve as a credible deterrence, for leaders like Bhutto who had advocated a pre-emptive strike against Indian nuclear establishment.

Fourth, we need to seriously offer to sign a no-first-use of nuclear weapons by all nuclear weapons states as well as threshold states like Pakistan and Israel.

The only state to have used nuclear weapons so far is the United States which steadfastly refuses to agree on a no-first-use of nuclear weapons.

So long as the Soviet Union existed, its preponderance in conventional force gave some legitimacy in the US perception, tactically to their refusal. But now, it should be forced to join other states in agreeing to a treaty on no-first-use of nuclear weapons. As a matter of fact, this treaty should precede the proposed Fissile material cut off treaty.

Fifth, India should negotiate with the US and other major powers on renegotiating the CTBT. Though India is willing to accept its non-comprehensive nature as it permits, computer simulated laboratory tests, so called sub-critical tests, India should make its acceptance of the CTBT and NPT conditional to certain gains to India. Thus, for instance, the US must be asked to extend its support for India's claim for a permanent seat in the UN Security Council.

Sixth, India should also seriously pursue from the position of strength, the nuclear disarmament.

All countries including China need to reduce their number of nuclear weapons to the needs of an effective deterrence and not to the extent of overkill. Even after the end of the Cold War, the US spends about $35.1 annually to maintain nuclear weapons.

The US as the leading power, need to lend its moral leadership to the would be, what it calls, rogue states.

The Free Press Journal, 21 August 1998

Erect Statues in other States too

Recently one Mr. Joe Eruppakkatt, Society of St. Paul, New York has initiated on internet, a Public Interest Litigation (PIL) against the Maharashtra government's plan to erect a statue of Shivaji in the Arabian Sea. The PIL speaks about waste of resources involved in an expenditure of ₹ .350 crores to erect the statue, which is bound to escalate once the work really starts. PIL makes a strong case in the background of insufficient rains and consequent drought in over 27 districts in Maharashtra.

I understand that petition has been submitted to the Mumbai High Court. A similar public plea was made by Kumar Ketkar, Editor of Lok Satta in his editorial on June 4, 2008. Its English version 'All the problems have been solved. Now let's build a statue' appeared in the Op-ED page of the Indian Express on June 6. I was highly impressed by Ketkar's critique of Maharashtra government's plans to erect a statue of Great Maratha warrior in Arabian Sea. However, in his criticism of the Maharashtra government's proposal he saw it purely from a domestic perspective and made a convincing case that it was a waste of scarce resources when there were hundreds of suicides of farmers, cases of death by malnutrition and thousands of children were denied the benefit of free education. When I read it initially I was inclined to accept Ketkar's argument of waste of resources.

However, both these public pleas have completely ignored the tremendous potential of such a Shivaji statue in the Arabian Sea in promoting international and domestic tourism on the one hand and at the same time its potential to function as the first line of defence and intelligence gathering centre at the same time. What comes io mind is the significant role played by Statue of liberty in promoting tourism in New York Though the statue was gifted by France to the US, when the US erected it, US was neither economically nor politically a major power. But statue of liberty helped diverse nationalities' in New York to unite. Yet, one could genuinely have their differences on priorities: Proving succor to hungry poor or promotion of tourism.

But what really changed my approach to it not its potential in promoting national and international tourism but the significance it can play in our security planning after 26/11 Mumbai terrorist attacks. This completely forced me to change my outlook towards the plan for a statue in the Arabian Sea. None could have anticipated in June 2008 when Ketkar wrote his piece that something like 26/11 could happen in Mumbai that is India! But 26/11 saw almost seventy hours of battle between Mumbai Police, Indian armed forces and units of National Security Guards on the one hand and ten highly motivated and determined Pakistani terrorists on a mission to do and die! In organizing this terrorist attack, planners in Lashkar-e-Taiba must have spent same amount of time, intelligence and resources as Al-Qaeda might have spent in planning and organizing 9/11. But neither Indian intelligence agencies, nor Navy or Coast Guard ever effectively had any clue on the impending attack, as the Americans had no clue on 9/11. Mumbai attackers came by sea route, a first in the history of terrorism as the use of civilian airplanes by Al-Qaeda terrorists in 9/11. This unique fact must change every right thinking Indians' approach to the proposal of erection of a statue in the Arabian Sea. We should now see it not only from a tourism angle but also from security angle as well. That idea is also there, incidentally in Mr. Ketkar's piece referred above when he concluded by saying "such a statue, standing in the middle of the sea, warning all terrorists to keep off Mumbai...." He might have said it mockingly, but it is truly an important function that can be performed by intelligence and security set up that should be set up at the basement of the Shivaji statue.

That is right; however, statue cannot warn but its location should be the first line of defence of Indian vast coastlines. India has a coastline of nearly 7600 km and over 2 million sq km of Exclusive Economic Zone (EEZ). Foreign poaching into Indian EEZ has been frequent and governments of the coastal states have often ignored such illegal fishing by foreign vessels. But having established their abilities to sail unnoticed into Indian shores Pakistani terrorists have shown what India's enemies can do. If they have done it once they can do it again. Hence, the tourist venue of Shivaji statue should be seen as a part of national reconnaissance and surveillance centre-a sort of first line of defence-in providing intelligence, rightly against modern use of terrorism as an instrument of foreign policy by states inimical to India. While tourists could watch the vast sea through telescopes, the basement of the statue could be used for more serious business of watching on the incoming unauthorized ships, vessels or fishing boats!

Not only we should welcome a Shivaji statue in Maharashtra, but I also suggest that every Indian state government blessed with a chunk of coastline and EEZ, should erect statues of regional historical figures with the help of federal government. Beginning from Gujarat on the West Coast and West Bengal on the East Coast, states should create a chain of statues to look like a necklace of pearls around India's vast coastal lines joining at the Kanya Kumari. Indian history is full of stories of valour of various rulers during the ancient times as well as those of first war of independence. The pendant in the necklace of statues could be an attractive statue of Jhansi ki Rani at the confluence of the Bay of Bengal, Arabian Sea and the Indian Ocean.

These pearls-like statue centres, apart from acting as the first line of defence will promote national tourism. It should also be possible for developing regional understanding through development of inter-regional tourism through ships. It would also help in promoting national unity through equal respect to major regional heroes.

The Free Press Journal, 24 February 2010

Is an Idea Man irrelevant for a man of action?

Kamal Nath, Minister for Highways, dismissed men in Planning Commission as a bunch of "armchair advisors". If he had said that the Planning Commission as an institution was irrelevant, I would have agreed and said that it's high time that India abolishes it. As a democracy we do not need a planning commission as a tool to conceptualise for India's economic growth as a whole. Planning Commission as an institution is just created by Pandit Nehru by an executive order, and is not a creation of the Lok Sabha by a law.

But Kamal Nath said it with reference to an individual member-Montek Singh Ahluwalia. Government needs individual advisers in various capacities. And no government, department really works without an idea man/or men. Take for instance, Ministry of External Affairs (MEA), which has a policy planning division, similar policy planning or revenue intelligence divisions would be there in ministries like Revenue or Finance.

Even Department of Highways under Kamal Nath would require a division to think in advance on feasibility of building certain highways or otherwise. A ministry/department cannot function effectively unless some one is tasked to think! Think and think! This is because, those who attend to implementation part of the job on day-to-day basis, cannot also do the job of thinking! Hence, the minister appointed to plan or to think cannot be described as an armchair advisor-unless in a derogatory manner. A newly appointed minister comes with certain new ideas but once he runs out of them or they wear him out. he looks for new ideas to resolve issues relating to his ministry or undertake new programmes. I can vouch this by my personal experience. Rajesh Pilot as a minister for Internal Security in the Narasimha Rao government, was an effective minister, but always had a running battle with his senior minister for Home Affairs-Shankar-rao Chavan. In response to certain suggestions made by this writer, Rajesh Pilot called him for consultation on implementation of my suggestions. Similarly, I wrote an article soon after Indian nuclear tests in Tribune (Chandigarh). George Fernandes as the then Minister for Defence called me on the same day evening to seek some more information!

Often, ministers acquire their attitude of irreverence to intellectuals from senior bureaucrats in the ministry. In India bureaucracy is so entrenched in administration it has a firm opinion that what works is what emerges from their work! It holds simply in contempt those who hold contrary views and sees to it that external challenge to its supremacy is simply destroyed. The best example I can give here is the so-called armchair effort to establish a National Security Council (NSC) in India during my lifetime. All efforts were countered, for instance, by former bureaucrats. Thus, a former foreign service official-D S Kamtekar in March 1990 asked: "Why moot the proposal for a totally new institution" when existing institutions work best?

Similarly, another former IAS official, Madhav Godbole in March 1996 argued against NSC on the ground that Cabinet Committee on Political Affairs does the work proposed to be assigned to the NSC!

Despite their opposition, task force led by K C Pant in April 1998 proposed the creation of NSC. I had appeared before the task force to plead for its creation. Though the BJP-led NDA established NSC in November 1998, it died before the NDA went out of office in May 2004. What was reluctantly created died because of non-use! But bureaucracy saw to it, before its death, the position of National Security Adviser (NSA) it created, is retained for the use of retired bureaucrats - J N Dixit was the first beneficiary followed by M K Narayanan and now Shiv Shankar Menon!

In India armchair adviser's work is rarely acknowledged, though they are always picked up to attribute failures. Another issue, I took up was: Parliament having Standing Committees on Defence, Foreign Affairs and the likes. I not only wrote articles in all available avenues and sent them through the help of late Madhu Dandavate, then MP to the Minister in Charge of Parliamentary Affairs at different times. I sent Madhu Dandavate's supporting letters to Speakers of the Lok Sabha of the times!

In 1991 then Lok Sabha Speaker, Shivraj Patil announced the creation of Standing Committees! Men of ideas whether they come from inside the government or outside, perform an important function of improving our socio-economic and political life. Men of ideas and men of enforcement are not antagonistic entities but two sides of the same coin!

The Free Press Journal, 15 July 2010

Nehru's foreign policy, flawed and all

President Pranab Mukherjee, in his annual lecture on Pandit Jawaharlal Nehru at the JNU, New Delhi on November 13, while showering all-round praise on him, said that "India is what it is today because of Nehru." There cannot be even an iota of doubt cast on the President's statement. The ongoing 125th birth anniversary celebrations have elicited reams of writing on Nehru's achievements. But not one has touched upon Nehruvian blunders. Can we ignore them?

John F Kennedy would say to his aides that a mistake in domestic affairs could cost a few lives. But a mistake in foreign affairs could destroy the entire nation. Kennedy was of course, reflecting on nuclear weapons. But the general tenor of his assertion is that wrong decisions in foreign affairs could cause irreparable damage.

So, if one were to apply the Kennedy yardstick, Nehru made certain major blunders in foreign affairs, though undoubtedly, he was the architect of Indian foreign policy A dispassionate analysis helps us realise that formulating foreign policy was far too challenging for Nehru rather than domestic affairs. That is because Indians did not have any experience in the foreign policy department until 1946. Till then war, peace and external relations were subjects handled by the Governor-General of British India.

As the Convener of the Congress Party Foreign Policy cell since 1927, Nehru was the one person who had most experience in this regard; he travelled abroad much more than many others. But after Independence, he had to conduct foreign policy with the help of ICS officers trained in domestic affairs. It thus, follows that much as we credit Nehru for some successful external affairs policies, blame must equally accrue to him for every policy failure in that area. Let us examine three of his decisions on major policy issues, widely perceived to be wrong. Today, these have become major irritants in Indian external affairs and a stumbling block in India's emerging as a major power in world politics.

The first test of Nehru's ability to successfully conduct foreign/national security policy came two months after Independence, when Pakistan attacked Kashmir. It became apparent that Nehru was more of an idealist, rather than a realist. It was his idealistic internationalism that made him order a ceasefire in 1948 and take the case to the UN.

Nehru ordering a ceasefire was resented even by the armed forces. He expected a favourable response from the UN because Pakistan was the aggressor, since Kashmir had acceded to India. Nehru had forgotten that the UN was a political body and not a court of law. In the prevalent Cold War scenario, the UN Security Council was not willing to see Pakistan, which was aligned with the US, as the ag-. gressor. Long after Nehru, Western powers used the Kashmir issue to constantly stir up security concerns in the Indian capital.

Second, as far as China was concerned, he never perceived it to be threat to national security. This policy approach has been called 'defence by friendship' approach by the British historian, Michael Edwards. Even the thought that China could crush friendship at the altar of its own national interest does not appear to have crossed Nehru's mind. Sardar Vallabhbhai Patel had clearly warned him not to trust China. There was such a contrast between our two countries - Nehru was committed to the Gandhian ideology of non-violence, peace and tolerance, while China was looking to transform itself from weak and underdeveloped to a strong, militarily powerful totalitarian state.

Chester Bowles, and an Indophile and US ambassador to India, has pointed out the parallels in the economic needs and political significance of India and China and their different approaches in meeting these problems: China, from the beginning, was determined to assert her influence as a radical, revolutionary nation willing to use militant power in international politics, while India chose the more constructive path of mediation, non-alignment and peaceful accommodation.

Finally, in the area of development of atomic energy and weapons, he laid the foundation for science and technology But his strong belief in peace and non-violence led him to embrace nuclear disarmament. He was willing to use the favourable international environment to advance national interests, even after his realisation in October 1962 that China was not a friend. But he never changed his mantra of nuclear disarmament. His successors followed his policy unquestioningly After China conducted nuclear tests in October 1964, had India too followed suit, it would have become a member of the NPT in 1968, rather than signing it as a non-nuclear weapons state. Journalist Seymour Hersh writes of the then US Secretary of State, Dean Rusk, recommending that India be encouraged to develop its own nuclear weapons, in response to the Chinese testing them. But Nehru's successors would not be shaken from their blind faith in his wisdom and his policy guidelines.

His policy of inclusiveness is highlighted by his supporters - they refer to his inclusion of Shyama Prasad Mukherjee and K C Neogy, for instance. But his soft approach toward Pakistan left several senior members, in the cabinet unhappy; Mukherjee and Neogy resigned in June 1950. They felt it was important that the nation not barter away "vital national interests." Dr B R Ambedkar was another cabinet member to resign, citing foreign policy failure as a reason. He said: "Anyone who has followed the course of our foreign policy could not fail to realise the sudden change that has taken place in their attitude towards us. On 15 August 1947, when we began our life as an independent country, there was no country which wished us ill. Every country in the world was our friend. Today, after four years, all our friends have deserted us. We have alienated ourselves." This confirms that Nehru was a human and to err is also human.

The Free Press Journal, 26 November 2014

8

US GOES TO WAR AGAINST IRAQ

America putting maximum pressure on UN to authorise use of force against Iraq

US President George Bush now a days does not speak of chasing Osama Bin Laden. He speaks of only of Saddam Hussain of Iraq. He has become Enemy number one. The American scholars and concerned citizens in the US and American watchers in India have a dilemma in understanding the rationale for a sudden switch in concerns in US foreign policy.

In the UN in his speech Bush had chided the member nations on their tolerance towards Saddam. Saddam Hussain has violated practically every resolution passed by them sixteen to be precise on Iraq after it was forced to retreat from Kuwait in 1991 .He forcefully, almost like a cowboy with whip in hand said, if you can do it, better; if you can't, we will do it alone. He has been giving rationale for going it alone. After all, the UN had in 1991 authorised the US to use force against Iraq. Then there is only a cease-fire, no peace yet. So it is a continuation of work half done for the US.

His great pal British Prime Minister, Tony Blair was building up global support for his buddy, Bush. Poor Tony! Who will tell him that American scholars dismiss him as of no consequence? American policy makers take him for granted. But he declared that policy of inaction is not the policy they are going to subscribe to. He has issued an intelligence dossier on Saddam's misdeeds. It is normally not British practice to divulge intelligence, but in this case he has done it to build up the case against Iraq.

The surprising development was that the US Congress passed a resolution authorising president to use unilaterally force to compel Iraq to destroy its weapons of mass destruction. The US Congress seems to have been bullied by the US president. A divided Congress Senate under the Democratic control while the House under the Republicans was in a hurry to go in recess to campaign for their re-elections 5th November.

A similar resolution, called the Gulf of Tonkin in 1964, passed during the Lyndon Johnson presidency authorising him to use force if necessary in the Vietnam War later led the then chairman of Senate Foreign Relations Committee, William Fulbright to rue his falling for the pressure from the President. Fulbright accused the Johnson administration of misleading the Congress and two fell out on the War related issues.

Be that as it may, how does one explain sudden change in the priorities of George Bush in his fight against terrorism? Who is a greater terrorist for him-Saddam or Bin Laden? some tentative explanations can be offered. First and the foremost seems to be that after the initial bravado on the global war against terrorism, Bush engine seems to have lost steam. As such there is a lack of direction on the war against terrorism. Michael Hirsh, former Foreign Editor of Newsweek writing in Foreign Affairs says that "a year later there is still very little clarity about the real direction of U. S. foreign policy and war on terror."

Second, and contributing to the first, there seems to be a jurisdictional conflict between the Central Intelligence Agency (CIA) and the Federal Bureau of Investigation (FBI). In an academic sense it indicates the current problem of inseparability of external security and internal security. But more concretely, the CIA resents increasing role played by the FBI in the war against terrorism. It has warned that if driven to wall, Saddam might not hesitate to use the weapons of mass destruction, which the US unilateral action is proposed to prevent in first instance!

Third, president Bush is advocating a dangerous doctrine in this year's National Security Strategy of unilateral "option of pre-emptive action to counter a sufficient threat to our national security...." In the past the US had pre-emptively intervened as in the case of Grenada in 1982. But past interventions have been limited to Latin America, which is its back yard. However, if the pre-emptive intervention is turned into a doctrine, it is more likely than ever of being misused. It will bring back ancient principle of Matsya Nyaya or big fish eating the small fish creating chaos in international relations.

Fourth, deep in the psyche of Bush family here is a desire to complete what senior Bush had promised his goal would be in the 1991 Gulf War-getting rid of Saddam Hussain out from Iraq. After all Saddam was bolstered up by Reagan (1981-891) and Bush senior (1989-93) by sharing intelligence information against Iran and providing weapons.

Then for the US Iran was a greater enemy than Iraq. But failure of senior Bush became a mocking point during 1992 election in which he was seeking a second term. Clinton defeated him. If son succeeds in doing what father promised and failed, it could be of a plus point in election campaign in 2004.

Finally, the just concluded mid-term elections on November 5 were extremely important to president Bush. History shows that Presidents' parties have generally lost some seats during the mid-term elections to Congress. Defection of one member-Jim Jeffords from Republican Party in June 2001-had shifted power in Senate to the hands of Democrats making Tom Dashcle the majority leader and putting a break in Republican agenda of appointing conservative judges to the Supreme Court. Sandra O'Connor, a Republican Judge in the Supreme Court (SC) had even postponed plans for retirement as Democrats were in majority enabling them to block appointment of a right-wing Republican nominee to the SC.

The last month election speeches every where had ended by Bush invariably mentioning his commitment to remove Saddam Hussain. That strategy has worked as in the mid term elections.

Republicans have not only retained their control over the lower house but also given them a one member majority in the Senate. Now he can claim that he can win power to Republicans. Bush was in search of an issue that can ensure him a second term President.

The importance of global war against terrorism thus has declined in its significance electoral perspective. Terrorism as an enemy is highly diffused and Bin Laden as enemy has been too illusive, unlike Afghanistan as an enemy in the initial months after September 11.

But not only demonised Iraq is a constant target but also its leader cannot move from cave to cave in Baghdad as Bin Laden did in Afghanistan and does in Pakistan today, despite the fact that he can creater many who look like Saddams.

Thus, Bush gamble seems to be one of talk tough to apply maximum pressure on the UN to resolve to authorise the use of force agaisnt Iraq to enable weapons inspectors to give a damning report, and if necessary retain the option of an attack in late 2003 Bush won his election by Republic controlled SC manoeuvrings in 2001. He wants to win a second term in 2004 by his own strength.

The Free Press Journal, 9 November 2002

Should India contribute to the stabilisation force in Iraq?

The American soldiers are being killed every day in Iraq. The US occupying forces have lost over 70 soldiers so far-more than men killed while they invaded Iraq. Whenever dead bodies arrive from battlefield Americans begin to question: Why are the US forces there in Iraq? Why are the Americans dying in the distant place? When these questions are raised widely in the nation, popularity chart of President shows a downward trend.

The US now wants India to send troops to Iraq as stabilisation forces. During L. K. Advani's visit to Washington, DC this was the number one priority for the US officials to discuss, while for Advani, cross-border terrorism promoted by Pakistan was the No 1 issue. One can understand American dilemma. Though the Bush administration caused destabilisation of Iraq, it wants others to contribute to the stabilisation.

Reason: Indian lives are much cheaper than those of the Americans. This is not surprising. The United Nations (UN) also gives compensation to the families of those killed in action at differential rates more to the Westerners than to those from Third World soldiers. The argument thc UN makes is that the pension they would have got in their own countries would have been different.

Should India contribute to the stabilisation force in Iraq? The case in favour of sending the troops lays in the fact that India-US relations are growing upward in all fronts and when a friend is in trouble another friend ought to help him. India sending troops to help Americans to stabilise. Iraq also implies that it would help the US to strengthen its support to India's war against cross-border terrorism. It will help India to win subcontracts to rebuild Iraq and even participate in oil exploration. But should India throw away all principles for narrow and limited economic gains?

A strong case can be made against not sending Indian troops. First, India was opposed to the US Iraqi war. The Prime Minister was advocating a 'middle Path' of Iraq complying with destruction of Weapons of Mass Destruction (WMD) and the US acting through the UN. The US on, the other hand was itching for a war against Iraq on the lines of Wolf and Lamb story. The wolf, in the story, was determined to eat the lamb, objects to its drinking water at down side of the stream by accusing it of polluting the upstream water! When lamb pleads that from lower level it cannot pollute the water at the upper level, wolf accuses lamb's grandfather polluting it and swallows the lamb anyway. The US inability to find the WMD despite all its technological sophistication only confirms the moral of the story though Iraqi dictator is not as innocent as the lamb in the real story.

Second, the Union Parliament had passed a resolution condemning (Ninda) the US war in Iraq. The grounds on which the US action was criticised have not changed and Parliament has not rescinded its resolution. Hence, the government sending the troops now when there is. no material change in the situation only make a mockery of parliamentary democracy. It is contempt of the people by the government as such the people's representatives could punish the government for their failing the people and can make it an issue in the next elections in 2004.

Third, the Prime Minister, has more than once said: "that the role of the United Nations was marginalized following America's war on Iraq." Our sending troops will not help in restoring the credibility of the UN. On the other hand, if the nations refuse to send troops until the US brings back the issue of reconstruction and stabilisation of Iraq to the UN, it could help the reasserting the role of the UN. Prime Minister had said that: "India would intensify efforts to redeem the role of the UN and to make the New World order fair and balanced."

Fourth, the Prime Minister had said that he would like to consult the countries around Iraq and take their opinion into decision-making. The press reports say that the immediate neighbours of Iraq like Saudi

Arabia, Turkey and Iran are not in 'favour of India lending a helping hand to the US which is perceived in the Islamic world as occupying force-despite the Americans claiming to be liberators! They too want the UN troops and not the Indian.

Fifth, Indian policy makers have to be sensitive to the concerns of the people in third world. Saddam Hussain was a secular leader in the islamic world. He was branded as a terrorist, which he was not. But he and his Baathist Party members now speak in terms of terrorism and Jehad. Ordinary people on the streets speak in terms of lighting the Americans to the last drop of their blood.

Sixth, Now Iraqis have begun to attark those Iraqis who collaborate with Americans such as those who join the Police force under the US occupation. They will not spare the Indian troops. India had sent troops to Sri Lanka in 1987 at the invitation of their government. Prior to 1987 we had cordial relations with Sri Lankan Tamils as well as the Sinhalese. But Indian Peace Keeping Force (IPKF) not only lost over one thousand soldiers but also earned the ill-will of Tamils and suspicion of Sinhalese. In Sri Lankan Tamil psyche IPKF stood for innocent people killing force!

What we together with international community really need to do is to encourage the US to hand over the crisis management to the UN, as it was done in the case of Afghanistan and earlier in Kosovo. The UN is the only appropriate agency to evolve a democratic constitution to Iraqi people to enable them to govern themselves. Without the involvement of the UN and Iraqi people, no stabilisation force can really provide peace and security to the people in Iraq and its neighbours.

The Free Press Journal, 8 July 2003

Iraq War: intelligence failure or intelligence cover?

President Bush was in such a great hurry to attack Iraq to get rid of Saddam Hussain, that he alleged that Iraqi dictator had continued his programme of weapons of mass destruction (WMD) even after he agreed in 1991 to destroy them. To prove the point he alleged that clandestinely Saddam was buying uranium from an African country, Niger. As though that was not enough, he linked him to Al-Qaeda terrorist organisation. Hence, a war against Saddam Hussain became the part of global war against terrorism in the eyes of George Bush.

The Iraqi dictator was toppled on April 20. After three months of search for WMD, appointing special squads, and expressing confidence of finding them the US was unable to find any evidence to prove that Saddam Hussain was in fact actively involved in developing WMD. Former weapons Inspector, Blix made a valid point. With Saddam out of power, in the changed environment in the absence of fear, Iraqis must have come forward to help in finding the WMD. This failure coupled with the daily arrival of body bags of soldiers killed in Iraq has lowered altogether credibility of the US claims that theirs was a preventive and pre-emptive war fought to see that Saddam Hussain did not terrorise the world with his WMD.

Then the White House for the first time came out with an admission that intelligence reports on which Bush relied were of dubious credibility. Then the Bush administration came out with the theory that the Central Intelligence Agency (CIA) misled the administration on the intelligence. As the US got involved in a domestic debate on the justification of the Iraqi war, an intense debate was already going on in Britain as to the credibility of intelligence.

Then George Tenet, CIA Director, owned up publicly responsibility for misinterpreting the information on the question of Iraq going for African uranium. If the CIA Director was responsible for Bush being misled, Bush should have fired the director. In 1961 during John F. Kennedy's administration, the President bungled in allowing anti-Castro invasion of Cuba, which became a major foreign policy embarrassment known as the Bay of Pigs crisis.

The US effort to topple the Fidel Castro regime then had led to his seeking the Soviet nuclear weapons, which in turn led to the Cuban Missile crisis. Be that as it may, in the Bay of Pigs fiasco, the previous administration of President Eisenhower had authorised secretly training and attack on Cuba by anti-Castro rebels who had come to Florida as refugees. When Kennedy became the President, it became a "disposal problem." If President did not give a go ahead to the Republican Party-promoted clandestine scheme to overthrow Fidel Castro, opposition would have made it an issue in the electoral politics. So Kennedy went ahead with it. But it turned out to be a great fiasco. Thousands of Cubans opposed to Castro who constituted the invasion force met with watery grave as Castro's armada sank invading boats. The CIA had expected a revolt to take place in Cuba as the invading forces would be landing in Cuba, which did not take place. Adlai Stevenson who then was the US ambassador in the UN was first led to deny the US involvement, which however soon became obvious. The US lost face in the UN as well in the world.

President Kennedy then called the Director, CIA, Allen Dulles and told him: If it were a parliamentary system, it would have been he who had to resign. But since it is a Presidential system with a fixed term, Dulles had to own up the responsibility. President fired Allen Dulles! In the present case nothing of the sort has happened so far. On the other hand, Republican Senators have expressed their confidence in George Tenet and President Bush will not fire him as apparently he has taken blame on himself for the misleading intelligence.

However, President, by all accounts would have known that he is using unverified intelligence, as it was convenient to justify his predetermined end. The Foreign Ministers of two allies-US and Britain, knew the fact that intelligence is of unreliable type. On June 5, when Powell poured out his information on clandestine activities of Saddam in the UN Security Council officially, privately, he and British Foreign Secretary, Jack Straw expressed their concern about the intelligence and claims being made by their "political bosses!" But Bush still maintains that he and Blair "based their decision on good, sound intelligence".

In Britain it is equally murky. Prime Minister Blair justified his decision to attack Saddam regime by a military invasion. He also has not expressed any regret. On the other hand, the person who is suspected to have blown the whistle, David Kelly, defence advisor, is dead under mysterious circumstances. Now it is known that he committed suicide under great stress. One can understand such a thing happening in a developing democracy in Afro-Asian region. But that it happened in the mother of parliamentary system is not only intriguing but also shocking.

Thus, it might not stop there. Hopefully, Parliamentary committee on defence certainly would further investigate the circumstance under which the death of defence official occurred. The chain of events, though at the moment it is only, a speculation, might lead to removal of Blair for brazen misuse of intelligence in justification of Iraqi war. In the parliamentary system it is not too difficult or unknown. What could be the fate of George Bush in November 2004 elections? Earlier all speculative calculations indicated that war on terrorism and Iraqi war would help him to win presidency for a second term. However, now his popularity polls are declining. Already Democratic hopefuls are raising, Bush use of intelligence as a cover to justify the war in Iraq as an issue in election campaign.

In the Congress there are also demands to investigate by appointing a bipartisan Select Intelligence Committee the entire episode of the US war in Iraq. The US Congressional approach in the issues like this is well known: The lawmakers will give President full freedom to pursue his policies on the theory "he knows it best'. However, once the policy begins to backfire, lawmakers begin to question. Now that Iraqi dissidents are killing daily a few American soldiers, body bags will hasten the process of investigation. Will George Bush, son of George Bush, Sr. President during the 1st Gulf War also go the father's way by losing his re-election efforts?

The Free Press Journal, 23 July 2003

French stand on Iraq misunderstood by US

In our country most of the newspapers cover their pages by reproducing articles from, foreign newspapers mainly New York Times, Financial Times, Sunday Times, Los Angeles Times etc. Some times these articles have a relevance to Indian readers as these reflect views of foreign countries with which India has close connections or the issues raised by the articles like the economic issues at WTO or the Cancun meeting. But sometimes a reproduced article's relevance is hard to decide. Recently one newspaper reproduced an article from Sunday Times describing how Mark Thatcher joins the club of the rich and expresses his desire for his mother Margaret Thatcher and former British Prime minister to live with him in Cape Town!

However, my focus here is on another such irrelevant article published on September 18 in New York Times under the caption of "Our War with France." I fail to see its relevance to Indian readers. Friedman addressed his article to "we Americans." He thinks that they need to come to terms with the fact that "France is becoming our enemy." I feel like defending France as one who knows American and also French foreign policy. Remember France is the one country that did not bandwagon with the US in 1998 to condemn Indian nuclear tests.

My friends may say we should : be thankful to Friedman, because, he is the one who suggested during the early days of US tug of war with Germany and France over Iraqi war that France be replaced by India in the UN Security Council as its permanent member. We Indians may feel happy that Friedman favoured India in his arguments.

Then Americans wanted to call French Fries as Freedom Fries! But the fact is: Friedman gets angry very fast and disproportionate to the case he makes.

It is not as though today under President Chirac that France is seeking to be independent of US policies while remaining in North Atlantic Treaty Organisation (NATO) and European Union (EU). Even in the 1960s, then French President De Gaulle was seeking a space for manoeuvrability for France. When President John F. Kennedy during the Cuban Missile Crisis of 1962 sent former Secretary of State Dean Acheson as his special envoy to De Gaulle to explain the Soviet Union's perfidy in placing nuclear capable missiles and inform him his decision to impose naval quarantine against Cuba, De Gaulle refused to see the pictures of location of missiles as the proof of the Soviet perfidy on the ground that if a decision has already been taken, there was no need for consultation.

And that has been the problem with the US policy makers that rarely they have taken their allies seriously. The US carries this attitude in a big way in their dealings with South American nations. It leads a regional organisation called Organisation of American States (OAS). The US has used it only to inform the vital decisions taken in relations to the member states rather than seriously consult them whether it is on Cuban crisis in the 1960s or the military intervention in the Dominican Republic in 1964 or the numerous issues affecting the region.

This approach is far more blatantly exhibited by the US now as there is no challenger to its supremacy in international relations. Thus, when France wants the US to listen to their point of view, Americans like Friedman, think that it has become an "annoying ally." When France says "listen if you go your way, we will not join you' France is considered a "jealous rival."

Friedman is of course not totally unawares of "arrogance" of President Bush and his Secretary of Defence Rumsfeld, as a factor in French insistence in the need to find a solution to Iraq war within the framework even now, of the United Nations. But Friedman thinks that the French proposal for passing on power to an Iraqi authority is against the interest of Iraq as "there is no coherent, legitimate Iraqi authority able to assume power...." Given the will, it should not be too difficult to get a coherent authority at least as coherent as in Afghanistan and allow Iraqis rule themselves.

Friedman says the US is fighting to prevent emergence of "Saddamists and Islamists" in West Asia. American he argues, are interested in promoting democracy in Iraq while "France has never been interested in promoting democracy in the modern Arab world." Now it is less said the better regarding the US support to democracy in the Arab world. Serious scholars in the US and elsewhere consider that much of financial support to Islamists and terrorists come from Saudi Arabia least democratic in the Arab world but closest ally of the US!,

Friedman is unfair to France when he says, "France is becoming our enemy." On the other hard as an independent ally of the US France is forewarning that even, now it is not too late, Longer the US stays in Iraq, it will make more Iraqis "Saddamists and Islamists:" more Iraqis will turn to be terrorists. Friedman is most" uncharitable when he says "France wants America to sink in a quagmire there in a crazy hope tthat a weakened United States (will pave the way for France to assume its 'rightful' place as 'America's equal, if not superior, in shaping world affairs."

France is only trying to see that the US does not fall in a Vietnam like quagmire once again. France is only trying to prevent the US from getting itself dug deep into a quagmire. That goal is better served if world moves to be a multipolar one. In that goal others like Russia, China, EU and India are with France. Longer the US faces irresolvable problems in Iraq, more of those who now keep quiet like Russia, for instance, come into open to tell that problems of the world are so numerous that we need a contingent of police men rather than one Friedman! World is too big to be shaped by the US single-handedly, however powerful it might be!

The Free Press Journal, 7 October 2003

Index

D

H

I

N

O

P

X

Y

Z